CONTENTS

KU-647-151

THE GOLF WORKSHOP

THE
GOLF
WORKSHOP

Keith Williams

Foreword by Ian Woosnam

The Crowood Press

First published in 1998 by
The Crowood Press Ltd
Ramsbury, Marlborough
Wiltshire SN8 2HR

© Keith Williams 1998

British Library Cataloguing-in-Publication Data
A catalogue record for this book is available from the British Library.

ISBN 1 86126 042 3 hardback
1 86126 175 6 paperback

Picture credits
Instruction photography by Phil Inglis.
Colour photography by Matthew Harris / The Golf Picture Library,
'Junior Golfers' by Steve Pope / The Golf Picture Library.

Line illustrations by Annette Findlay.

Photograph previous page: Greg Norman.

Acknowledgements
1) '*The Search for the Perfect Swing*' Alistair Cochran & John Stobbs
for The Golf Society of Great Britain

2) Governlock Golf Management Group, 6C Canaan Lane,
Canaan Court, Edinburgh EH10 4SY. *Tel* 0131 447 6590

Dedication
To my family.

Throughout this book the use of pronouns covers both males and females. All
technical information is directed towards right-handed golfers – apologies to
all left-handers!

Typeset and designed by
D & N Publishing
Membury Business Park, Lambourn Woodlands
Hungerford, Berkshire.

Printed and bound by Paramount Printing Ltd, Hong Kong.

FOREWORD

Although the game of golf itself is quite intense, I have found that golfers tend to make the game more difficult by allowing unnecessary or irrelevant aspects to complicate things. Understanding, knowledge and skill play an important role in helping players enjoy and get pleasure from the game. Allowing your natural ability to win through is the ultimate golfing experience.

I have known Keith Williams since we were junior golfers, playing together in the Shropshire & Herefordshire County Junior team. He has always been a competent golfer, having played the PGA European Tour, but he preferred the role of a coaching professional. He has a detailed knowledge of swing technique and the art of shotmaking. He appreciates the importance of allowing natural talent to win through and above all, the need for good communication to convey any technical information at a level to suit each individual player. He has successfully taught players of all levels from beginners, international amateurs through to Tour players and has built up a sound understanding of all aspects needed to enhance a player's game.

I feel sure *The Golf Workshop* will not only offer you a broad understanding of all aspects of the game, but will emphasize sound golfing principles together with some unique insights that allow a player or coach to appreciate additional ways of developing their skills and games.

Enjoy the book, there's something here for every golfer!

Ian Woosnam

PREFACE

It is the nature of golf that it requires a special commitment if you are to develop and improve your skills. The essential qualities for successful play are a combination of correct technical knowledge, appropriate physiological requirements and positive psychological virtues. Few players are blessed with more than an adequate supply of all three.

Professional and leading players use their ability to develop and enhance their skills. They are aware that knowledge and training must work hand in hand if they are to manage and employ their individual talents to maximum effect. Not only do they appreciate the importance of good planning and the need to structure their golfing life, they are also aware of the adverse effects of poor organisation and a lack of direction. The coach plays an important part in this grand plan; indeed, few golfers have achieved success without the help and direction of a coach at one time or another.

The important point is this. No matter how diverse their style or talent, the successful players are the ones who have brought these many aspects together to the greatest effect. Positive results will always follow.

The Golf Workshop aims to cover all those factors that will help lead the player towards reaching his or her personal goal or goals. Throughout the book you will notice that certain instructions are repeated. I make no apologies for this: golfers need constant reminding of the key elements that lead to successful play. An effective swing motion is, after all, all about repetition. The ultimate aim of any player is to learn to make his best swing as often as possible, particularly under pressure.

Most golfers play the game for enjoyment and pleasure, and the rewards that come with achieving an acceptable or even above average level of success are immeasurable. Each golfer has their own personal mountain to climb and flag to fly.

I therefore wish you the best of luck and – most importantly – the best of golfing times!

PART 1
INTRODUCTION

1
THE GOLF COURSE

Origins

There have been, and still are a number of opinions as to the origins of the game of golf. The Chinese claim its origination as far back as the fourteenth century, the Dutch from the fifteenth century and the Scots from around the 1550s. Whichever one is accepted there is no doubt as to the ancient history of this game. One of the most famous and renowned courses as well as now one of the bastions of the game of golf is the Royal and Ancient Golf Club of St Andrews. The Old Course at St Andrews began its legendary existence in the nineteenth century, and throughout the following decades has influenced the game on a regular basis.

Most courses were built near to the sea, aptly named 'Links' courses and did not originally have nine or eighteen holes, but were far more basic in concept with each hole having an approximate starting point and being completed by 'holing out' at a distant point which varied greatly in length, and did not necessarily follow a set route – the fairways utilized the flatter expanses of ground and the bunkers were basic holes in the ground filled with the natural sand found under the turf. Eventually teeing grounds became more cultivated, fairways and greens were laid out to a higher standard and the number of holes and course layout were set out to be played in an organized regular fashion.

Golf clubs sprang into being, increasingly at inland locations and most built near railway lines for easy access and convenience. In 1902 there were estimated to be 751 clubs in England and 606 in Scotland. Some of these clubs actually shared golf courses, and so there were more clubs than there were actual courses. The United Kingdom total in that year was 1,503 clubs, but with only 1,060 golf courses. Equipment was fairly basic in the earlier days, with balls originally made of feathers and progressing through the gutta-percha era on to the more modern Haskell ball which was the first three-piece ball with a central core and a wound rubber thread and was patented in 1899. Now the more modern golf ball is made of a far superior construction from the most advanced man-made materials available.

Golf clubs were originally of a wooden shafted construction with basic metal or wooden heads. A piece of leather was wrapped around the top of the shaft to form a handle and to help the golfer maintain a better hold on the club. There were no major manufacturers of equipment, and each club was initially hand-made by either the local craftsman or soon after by one of the original golf professionals who earned their living by club- and ball-making, teaching, golf course maintenance or playing exhibition matches.

Layout

Most golf courses are made up of nine or eighteen holes, although some actually have an unusual number such as eleven, twelve or thirteen holes, with certain of those holes played twice to make up a full eighteen hole compilation. The length of each hole varies usually between 100 and 600 yd, with variations for lady golfers, juniors or tournament play.

Holes are either par 3, 4 or 5 with the par being based on a simple length status that varies for men and women – see tables in Chapter 2. The total length of a bona fide R & A or LGU golf course varies from location to location, but generally men will play a course with a total measurement of somewhere between 5,600 and 7,000 yd and women a course measuring between 4,500 and 6,000 yd. The total length of a golf course forms the basis of an evaluation which is known as Standard Scratch Score (SSS) which is in effect the total difficulty assessment for that particular course.

Fig 1 A typical scene from earlier days illustrates the difficulties of golf course construction.

Design

Today, once a suitable piece of land has been found and finance arranged, a developer will generally enlist the services of a 'Course Architect' to put together an acceptable design and concept for a golf course. Finance is an important aspect, which dictates the type of course that can be built. Some courses have been built on a low budget figure, but generally a full eighteen-hole course will require a minimum of £750,000 with a full championship course perhaps designed by an architect of Jack Nicklaus's standing, which could cost up to £6,000,000 plus to build, not necessarily including the cost of the original piece of land itself.

The architect will quickly have a basic concept for a course layout, and in wanting to use the available land most effectively, will take into account such matters as topography, wind direction, natural drainage, local features – such as mature trees, ponds, ditches, hedgerows and so on, and the overall boundaries of the golf course. Some holes will be flat, others sloping, some will play fairly straight, others will have a deliberate dogleg design – that is, they will bend from left to

right or vice versa. The holes will be of differing lengths, some greens will be larger than others, sand bunkers, dips, hollows, water hazards, the rough and semi-rough will all play a part in the hole and course design. It is the architect's role to make the course as interesting, challenging and varied as possible given the terms and conditions he has to work with.

Most courses in the UK are now built inland, and have a parkland feel to them. It is rare for a links course to be built, for example, like St Andrews in Scotland due to a lack of available land near to the sea.

Modern course design is far less in harmony with natural surroundings than in past generations, and so courses are built with a high number of man-made features such as mounds, large bunkers or lakes, the latter making course irrigation a much more independent factor and more cost-effective for the owner. There have been some very ingenious course designs over the last decade or so, and golfers who have visited the United States of America in particular will have been mesmerized by the ingenuity and innovative ideas that they are sometimes faced with.

11

2
THE GAME

The Handicap System

The handicap system has evolved over many years and in its basic concept allows golfers of all levels of ability to compete against each other on a relatively equal basis. In the UK handicaps commence at twenty-eight for men and thirty-six for ladies, and as the individual golfer improves his or her quality of play and produces lower scores for a round of golf, so the individual handicap reduces by virtue of the organized handicap system which is administered by the player's own golf club. A player's handicap can continue to reduce right down to zero, or scratch, as it is referred to. In exceptional cases some players achieve a plus handicap, which in effect means that they have to add shots onto their gross score rather than deduct their handicap.

Whenever players play a competitive round of golf, at whatever venue, they have the potential to lower their handicap. Conversely a poor score can lead to a readjustment which will increase the player's handicap. It is the player's responsibility to 'hand in' the relevant score card, and to accept the adjustment as per the system. It is possible that an individual golf club might lower a player's handicap outside the accepted system if the player shows evidence of improved standards, but may possibly be failing to produce the lower scores in recognized handicap counting competitions. This reduction of handicap is based on a 'known play' system, and is generally a fairly rare occurrence.

There are certain anomalies within the men's and ladies' schemes, but in general terms the systems are relatively compatible.

Scoring in Competition

Recording a score – is basically a simple process of recording your score at each individual hole and then adding up the total to correlate a player's total gross score for the round. In Medal round golf a player deducts his or her handicap from the Gross score to achieve a Nett score for the round. The player with the lowest nett score would win a nominated Stroke Play competition unless it was based on a gross score only stipulation. In professional golf there are no handicaps and so the player with the best gross score usually over four rounds of golf, that is, seventy-two holes will be the winner.

There are variations of competitive golf based around the Medal golf systems such as Stableford points, Bogey Score, but these do not need to be dealt with here.

Match Play golf is a straightforward process whereby players can compete against one another or in pairs on a hole-by-hole basis. Once a player has won sufficient holes with a lesser number of holes remaining to play then the match is effectively over. For example, three holes up with only two remaining to play and the match would be won by a score of 3 and 2. If a game went to the eighteenth hole with both players equal – All Square – a Sudden Death play-off over extra holes would follow whereby the first player to win a hole outright would be the match winner.

Golfing Terms	
Par	The stipulated score for a hole.
Birdie	One under/lower than par.
Eagle	Two under/lower than par.
Albatross	Three under/lower than par.
Bogey	One over/more than par.
Par for the course	The par total of all individual holes added together.

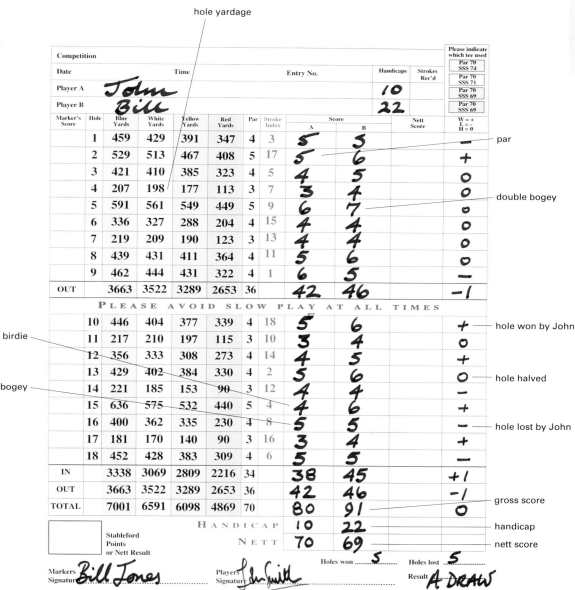

Fig 2 In match play the result would be a halved match. Under the handicap system, Bill would receive 12 shots from John – one at each of the holes with a stroke index numbered 1–12 on the card. In Medal play, Bill's nett score is actually one lower than John's.

Forms of Play

There are a number of other forms of formats of play as well as straightforward Medal or Match-play. These include:

Singles   Medal or Matchplay. A player plays his own ball throughout.

| Fourball | Two players team up to play either Medal or Matchplay golf. Each plays his own ball, with the lowest score for the hole counting for the team. |
| Foursomes | Two pairs play against each other with only one ball used by each side. The players hit alternate tee shots, and then play alternate shots thereafter until the ball is holed out. |

There are a number of alternatives, but these are in the main regular formats.

Standard Scratch Score

Each hole is evaluated on its length and difficulty and given a stroke index between 1–18, with factors such as length, topography, local wind direction and hole design being taken into account in this assessment. Hence the most difficult hole would be given the number one assessment and the least difficult hole number 18. This individual stroke index from one to eighteen is used for competitive purposes and allows the game to be played on a fair basis both in Stroke Play and Match Play events.

HOLE AND COURSE MANAGEMENT STATUS

	Men		Ladies
Hole length (yd)	0–250	Par 3	0–200
	220–500	Par 4	201–400
	440+	Par 5	400+

Par for each hole is set by the golf club in relation to the length and playing difficulty of each hole and is fixed within the above ranges, e.g.: if a hole is 450yd it may be allotted Par 4 or 5 depending upon its average playing difficulty.

STANDARD SCRATCH SCORE

MENS

Yards	Par
7,001 to 7,200	74
6,801 to 7,000	73
6,601 to 6,800	72
6,401 to 6,600	71
6,201 to 6,400	70
5,951 to 6,200	69
5,701 to 5,950	68

CALCULATION OF SCRATCH SCORE – LADIES

The Scratch Score is compiled from the sum of the Ratings of individual holes (*see* following Rating Table), with adjustments for (a) the amount of run and (b) course difficulties.

Course Rating
Allot each hole a Rating by applying its measurement to the following table and then add the Ratings to arrive at the Course Rating.

LADIES RATING TABLE

Yards	Rating	Metres
up to 100	2.7	up to 91
101 to 112	2.8	92 to 102
113 to 124	2.9	103 to 113
125 to 140	3.0	114 to 128
141 to 160	3.1	129 to 146
161 to 180	3.2	147 to 165
181 to 200	3.3	166 to 183
201 to 218	3.4	184 to 199
219 to 236	3.5	200 to 216
237 to 254	3.6	217 to 232
255 to 272	3.7	233 to 249
273 to 290	3.8	250 to 265
291 to 308	3.9	266 to 282
309 to 326	4.0	283 to 298
327 to 344	4.1	299 to 314
345 to 362	4.2	315 to 331
363 to 380	4.3	332 to 347
381 to 398	4.4	348 to 364
399 to 416	4.5	365 to 380
417 to 432	4.6	381 to 395
433 to 448	4.7	396 to 410
449 to 464	4.8	411 to 424
465 to 480	4.9	425 to 439
481 to 496	5.0	440 to 453
497 to 512	5.1	454 to 468
513 to 528	5.2	469 to 483
529 to 544	5.3	484 to 497
545 to 560	5.4	498 to 512
561 & over	5.5	513 & over

Fig 3 How par and the Standard Scratch Score for a course are compiled based on measurement details.

The course itself is also given an overall assessment of numerical difficulty based on similar factors to those when assessing each individual hole. This total factor referred to as Standard Scratch Score for the course, can vary between 66–74 and does not always agree with the par total for the course. As most courses have at least two different total length measurements for men plus ladies and sometimes senior and junior golfers, this total Standard Scratch Score can vary dependent on which course measurement is used.

Rules and Etiquette

The Rules of Golf are often thought by many to be overly detailed and confusing. It is true that there are a great many different rules and that sometimes players are unable to decide which one is applicable to a situation, but generally most of the day-to-day situations that golfers experience on the course are covered in a straightforward way.

The rules themselves are governed by the Royal and Ancient Golf Club of St Andrews (R & A) and the United States Golf Association (USGA). They cover all aspects of the game and are reviewed every four years to keep them updated. It is not only the rules of play that are monitored and controlled by these authorities, but a vast array of other related matters. Throughout the years, golfers, clubs, committees, tournament organizers and PGAs from all around the world are all in consultation with the R & A and the USGA. A great number of books and videos are available covering aspects of the rules, tournament administration and decisions based on the rules of golf.

Fig 4 There is only one official rule book, but plenty of other sources of information for players.

It is not necessary to have a full knowledge of the rules to play and enjoy golf, but it is certainly important to understand and appreciate the more basic ones; for example, when, where and for what reasons to take a penalty or free drop, plus how to drop the ball itself. Clearly some knowledge is essential from the beginning, but most is learnt as players develop their ability to play the game and gain experience on the course.

Summary of Aspects Covered by the Rules of Golf

1. Definitions of the game, e.g 'Ground Under Repair'.
2. The game – 'playing a ball from the teeing ground into the hole by a stroke or successive strokes in accordance with the Rules'.
3. Match play, stroke play and other forms of play.
4. Golf equipment – clubs and balls including the specifications for design and performance.
5. The player's responsibilities, such as marking a card correctly and speed of play.
6. Order of play – for match play and stroke play, playing out of turn.
7. The teeing ground – tee markers, ball falling off tee, playing from correct teeing area.
8. Playing the ball – searching for the ball, identifying the ball, playing the wrong ball.
9. The putting green – touching the line of the putt, testing the green surface, ball overhanging the hole, the flagstick.
10. A ball moved, deflected or stopped – by the player, partner, outside agency, equipment.
11. Relief situations and procedures – dropping procedures, placing ball, cleaning ball, loose impediments, obstructions, hazards, lost ball, out of bounds, unplayable lie.
12. Disputes and decisions – penalties, referees' decisions, disqualifications.
13. The Golf Club Committee – waiving rules, handicap control, the course, competitions.
14. Local Club Rules – everything appertaining to an individual golf course.
15. Handicaps – controlled by the national unions – for example the English Golf Union.
16. Rules of Amateur Status – professionalism, prize money, expenses, scholarships, and reinstatement as an amateur.

Some Thoughts on Etiquette

Golf is a game of honour, courtesy and sportsmanship. Among the courtesies expected on the golf course are:

Be ready to play when it is your turn and to do so without delay.

Do not talk, stand close or move about when a player is analysing the shot, taking a practice swing or playing the stroke.

The player with the lowest score on the most recent hole that was not tied, tees off first – this is called having the honour.

Once off the tee the ball furthest from the hole should, when practical, be played first.

If you or your group are delaying players behind you and there is an open hole in front of your group, step aside and signal the following group to play through. This is crucial to maintaining the pace of play for all players on the course, as well as their enjoyment. One slow, inconsiderate group can ruin everybody's day.

Repair damage or irregularities to the golf course as you play. This includes raking or smoothing footprints or other marks made in a sand bunker, replacing divots that you dislodge from the tee or fairway and repairing any ball marks your ball makes when landing on the green.

When on the green, avoid walking between the hole and any of the balls to be putted. Avoid standing near to the hole or in the periphery of vision of anyone who is putting.

Leave the green as soon as your group has finished putting. Mark your scores on the next tee, and remember – play without delay.

In Summary

Play the course as you find it, play the ball as it lies, and if you cannot do this, do what is fair.

3
THE PLAYERS

There were very few competitions or tournaments originally, and those that were played were open to amateurs and professionals alike – the former very often proving the most successful.

As the popularity of the game increased, so did the quality and availability of equipment. The cost was still extremely prohibitive and so the game remained a rich man's sport. The working caddies very often played in their spare time borrowing equipment from club members, and as their standards improved and their skills increased they became professional golfers to enhance their living standards and their futures from the game. Famous players from the late nineteenth century and early twentieth century included such names as Old Tom Morris, Young Tom Morris, James Braid, J. H. Taylor and Harry Vardon.

Fig 5 Vardon, Braid, Taylor and Sandy Herd – some great players from the early part of the twentieth century.

Fig 6 Bobby Jones.

Once the Professional Golfers Association of Great Britain was formed in 1901 the dominance of amateur players in tournaments began to decline, although an exception was Bobby Jones in the 1920s. Today golf tournaments are played world-wide and major events are watched on television by millions of golfing enthusiasts. International superstars now dominate the game and the names of Tiger Woods, Ian Woosnam, Seve Ballesteros, Nick Faldo, Fred Couples, Jack Nicklaus, Arnold Palmer, and Greg Norman are renowned throughout the sporting world.

The nature of golf means that individual player profiles vary considerably. There are so many aspects of the game that have to be taken into consideration that to formulate a small number of specific profiles in some senses is fairly unrealistic. Before listing some, however, it is important to understand what variables or characteristics make up the individual golfer – Physical attributes such

as overall physique, strength, flexibility and balance; mental skills such as desire, determination, concentration, attitude, visualization and competitiveness; kinesthetic qualities such as feel, rhythm, and co-ordination. All sports require a certain combination of these attributes, but golf clearly identifies the preferences of the individual, which become evident in their style of play. Players have certain skill factors that are common to them and as they develop their playing capabilities, they come to rely upon and play to their strengths more and more. Most players also realize the need to strengthen and develop the weaker elements in their overall game and so it is not unusual to see players slightly change their style, but not necessary their profile, although it is rare for any player to change dramatically.

The Natural Player

It has been stated that there is no such thing as a natural golfer, and it would be fair to say that the likelihood of a human being picking up a golf club, learning the rudimentaries of the game and developing his skills to a high standard without some form of outside influence or without developing any technical faults, would seem very unlikely indeed. In reality there are plenty of natural golfers around playing at a wide variety of levels. In sport there are many examples of players who have natural and instinctive hand – eye co-ordination. This is a major component in golf and allows many unorthodox golfers to swing with technically incorrect styles but still be able to play golf very successfully. Examples of this are evident even among the very top professional players such as US Ryder Cup golfers Fred Couples and Ray Floyd or top European player Colin Montgomerie, who have techniques that are quite individual to them and would not generally be coached to other developing players. Yet these three, and many other tournament professionals are not hindered by their individualistic styles, preferring to play the game with technical movements that suit them best, whether these are synonymous with the textbook methods or not.

Within this natural golfing profile there are a number of sub-divisions such as players who always appear superior when driving off the tee, those who have great talent around the green or

The Mechanical Player

I doubt if anyone believes that it is possible to play golf totally mechanically, but there are those who appear to be more dominated by the technical aspects of swing movement and adhere to the philosophy that the only way to be consistently successful is to swing the golf club in the most perfect manner possible, so that the movement repeats itself time after time on a regular basis. Desire to swing so perfectly is not just unique to the professional players. Many ordinary club players have been seized with the desire to emulate their heroes and set out on a path of learning through books, videos and professional coaching with the sole priority that knowledge and its correct application will undoubtedly lead towards the golfer's 'golden rainbow'. Sadly their goals are rarely achievable. The ability to change swing movements and to use any technical improvements consistently eludes many avid and enthusiastic technicians. It is one thing to swing the club in a perfect style, but totally another to take this movement onto a golf course under normal playing circumstances and competitive situations.

The development of coaching schemes at all levels and the intensity of the media coverage of successful players has in some cases proved quite detrimental to young aspiring golfers, who should without doubt concern themselves more with good basic swing fundamentals and leave the intense technical aspects to those professional coaches whom they have entrusted to help them climb their golfing ladder to success.

There have been undoubted examples of golfers who have achieved tremendous success through adhering rigidly to a more mechanical philosophy – Ben Hogan was possibly the first and perhaps the most successful of all time. His whole golfing lifestyle was built around the discipline concept that it was possible to control all aspects of the swing movement and with dedicated practice to co-ordinate and repeat these and his individual movements on a regular daily basis. More recently Nick Faldo almost revolutionized interest in swing mechanics and its potential to help players progress to greater heights through a structured swing programme. Although already a player of great ability and achievement, he successfully restructured his swing movement and went on to win professional tournaments at the very highest

Fig 7 Tiger Woods, one of the most gifted natural players ever.

those who have something special when it comes to putting out once on the green. Greg Norman and Laura Davies have for many years been renowned for their accuracy and length off the tee, John Daly and Tiger Woods for their length particularly, Gary Player and Seve Ballesteros are famed for their incredible short game skills, Ben Crenshaw and Phil Michelson appear to hole more putts on a regular basis than almost any other top tournament professionals.

The list of natural golfers is endless, particularly if one has witnessed the likes of Ian Woosnam, Sandy Lyle, Jumbo Osaki and Tiger Woods at their best.

19

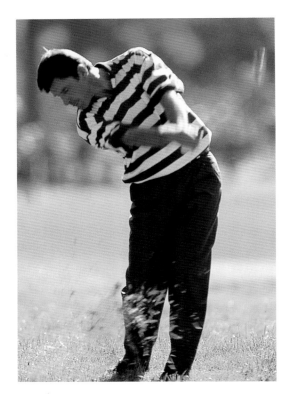

Fig 8 Nick Faldo – a player who has always sought perfection from his game.

avoids taking unnecessary risks, and that might lead to dropping valuable shots to par. This style of player rarely becomes complacent or gives up trying during the round, and will invariably have the ability to make a reasonable score even when not playing particularly well. Powers of concentration and determination are strong aspects of these players, who invariably make the most of their capabilities on a regular basis.

Perhaps the greatest golfer of all time, Jack Nicklaus would be the ultimate thinking golfer. His physical qualities as a player were enhanced if not superseded by his amazing mental ability. Superb preparation, intelligent course management and first-class self-control were further heightened by great powers of concentration and a tremendous desire to win. Add to this the rare capacity to be able to raise the standard of his game prior to a major tournament, which gave Jack Nicklaus more than just a slight edge over almost all other players.

of levels on a regular basis. Mechanical swingers are few and far between, although perhaps there are many golfers who adhere to some form of mechanical fundamentals within one or two departments of their game.

The Thoughtful Player

It is hard to say exactly what constitutes an intelligent golfer, or perhaps better phrased a thinking golfer – it might be suggested that he or she is one whose style of play maximizes their strengths and constantly minimizes the potential damage of their weaker elements. An intelligent golfer tends to be one who is very aware of what is going on around and the advantages to be gained from good personal and course management. They will be fully aware of the dangers that the golf course might throw at them, but are constantly disciplined to play in a manner that

Fig 9 Jack Nicklaus – the ultimate thinking golfer.

20

Bernhard Langer is an outstanding example in this group of players and although I have listed Nick Faldo under the mechanical golfer heading, there is no doubt that one of his greatest assets is his intelligent, self-disciplined play. In the 1990s he has been the ultimate thinking and playing machine in golfing terms.

The Stylish Player

This is the golfer who not only has the correct swing mechanics, but carries out the movement with a flair and stylishness that arouses envy in those other golfers who find the game far harder work. In earlier years American Sam Snead was the man who had all the right ingredients to be the ultimate successful player – a long smooth, elegant golf swing, wonderful rhythm, superb ball-striking skill, plenty of power and usually an excellent on-course temperament.

His potential was occasionally let down with some poor play perhaps caused by a lack of concentration or the odd spell of indifferent putting. Latterly there is no one more stylish than Payne Stewart who combines a rhythmical flowing swing and strong competitive attitude with wonderful sartorial elegance.

Often stylish players seem to underachieve despite the ease and elegance with which they appear to play the game. Possibly their natural swing ability is not matched by the necessary standards of short game, putting or mental skills.

Fig 10 Sam Snead – one of the most elegant and gifted players from the 1940s and 1950s.

The Shot Maker

Shot makers are always some of the more exciting types of golfer. Generally their play is less orthodox than that of many others, but they have a wonderful ability to create golf shots, particularly when in some of the very difficult situations that golfers find themselves in on the golf course. Most of the players who could be categorized under this profile are relatively self-taught and in their learning years have developed increased skills through practising and playing interesting and challenging shots, perfected through the feel and control of their swing movements, ball control and natural visualization rather than the particularly correct technical fundamentals taught and learnt repetitively on the practice ground. It could be said that they often enhance or replace pure golf shots with ones that achieve the same results, but possibly in a less orthodox, yet more stylish and creative fashion.

This type of player is fairly easily identified by the variety of different shots he plays both in practice and on the course. He will enjoy playing different types of course and difficult holes due to the challenge of the shots required and the stimulation of experiencing a successful execution of these shots. Adverse weather conditions, particularly wind, can enhance this type of player's chances of success and there rarely seems to be a

21

situation that does not have a potential 'way out' in keeping a score together. Seve Ballesteros and Lee Trevino would be obvious choices for top awards in this profile category. Over these last few decades they have both extricated themselves from some extremely difficult positions under the greatest of pressures.

Perhaps it would be fair to say that Ballesteros's qualities are more often displayed in troublesome situations, whereas Trevino is more of a ball shaper and shot maker from more straightforward positions, but both always succeed in exciting the golfing public by creative play and breathtaking ball control.

The Unorthodox Player

The unorthodox golfer is probably the profile group that contains the greatest number of participants. The game of golf has so many facets that for most of us some form of unorthodoxy must apply. Unorthodox golfers are not failures by any means and one only has to look at the world's best amateurs and professionals to realize that even at the highest levels there is a large percentage in this group or category. Perhaps here would be a good point to clarify unorthodox – the set-up and swing movements might not perform to pure technical correctness – for example, a strong grip, a flat backswing, but it is noticeable throughout the highest level of play that all golfers return the clubhead correctly and consistently to the ball, and strike it in a similar way so that the distance the ball is hit is relatively similar and the short game control is of an equally high standard. Even the best putters in the world rarely have similar orthodox styles. For the handicap golfer an unorthodox technique often holds back a player and limits their potential for ongoing development. Of course there will always be exceptions, some achieve an acceptable standard of play, some become representative players and others world-beaters – there is no golden rule! Most unorthodox players improve their potential by encapsulating some form of other asset or assets referred to in the earlier player profiles. I have mentioned earlier Lee Trevino for his amazing shot-making skills – he was a very unorthodox swinger of the golf club, and perhaps the success of John Daly

Fig 11 Seve Ballesteros – one of the most exciting recovery players of all time.

with his huge backswing might surprise some. It takes all sorts and there is no one way to swing the club or to play golf. Good drivers of the ball will rely on this department; good putters will often accept their shortcomings as power players or ball strikers. It is the end result that really matters for as all golfers know it is not how, but how many!

4
THE EQUIPMENT

Over the many years that golf has been played there have been numerous advances in the design and development of equipment, particularly during the last two decades of the twentieth century when technology gave the club manufacturers great opportunities to be innovative and to create products that have without doubt made the game easier to play. Golf is probably the one sport where technological improvement does influence the nature of the game more than most. Yet although advanced design of equipment has meant that top professionals hit the ball further and straighter than ever, it is the average amateur golfers who have really been able to enjoy the benefits of developments such as metal/wood technology, cavity back irons, graphite shafts, two-piece ball construction, light-weight golf bags, more comfortable and effective waterproof clothing and even cushion-soled golf shoes. The changes have in effect been quite phenomenal and have allowed the average golfer to derive greater satisfaction, pleasure and potential from the game. Equipment has not been the only factor in this catalytic situation, the improvement of playing conditions in golf courses themselves, the

exposure and influence of top golf professionals, greater coverage of golf in all areas of the media, the increased availability of people's time and the importance of sport in people's lives, plus the increased opportunities to travel and play on more courses, with a wide variety of playing conditions have all influenced golfers and helped their development through greater exposure and increased experiences in the golfing world.

Evolution of Club Design

As the game itself has evolved so has the need to improve and develop the appropriate equipment. Originally a set of clubs was made up of all woods including a wooden putter, although somewhere around the mid-nineteenth century a small selection of irons was introduced to a typical set adding greater versatility and improved playing potential. Shafts were originally made from thick and heavy branches of hazel wood, later with ash and still later with hickory – a tough hard wood originating from North America. Heads were shaped from apple or beechwood although neither proved as

Fig 12 The clubs of yesteryear bear little resemblance to some of today's modern equipment.

strong as the persimmon which replaced them. Persimmon is of tropical origin and provided the necessary resilience and feel to deal with the parallel development of the golf ball.

The first crafted clubs had the shafts spliced to the heads, which were long-nosed with shallow club faces. The shafts were particularly whippy and so the playing characteristics made it difficult to combine both clubhead speed and accuracy. All shots tended to be swept cleanly off ground which necessitated the introduction of some thin-bladed iron clubs so that a ball lying poorly or in a hole or wheel mark could be hit with a downward blow with much greater ease and reliability.

These hand-forged irons had no grooves on the face, but still proved adequate in allowing the golfer to get the ball airborne with an acceptable amount of control. Eventually these were replaced by the next generation of drop-forged irons. Grooves were added to the club face to increase spin and improve ball flight characteristics.

For many years there was little change in club design – irons remained forged and were of a blade characteristic with few additional features except of a purely aesthetic nature. Woods became more bulbous and deep-faced with the addition of hard inserts in the centre of the face to improve the strength and life-span of the club. Solid wood heads were joined by another version made from laminated wood – layers glued together for additional strength and durability. Brass or steel sole plates fitted to the underside of the head improved weight distribution by providing a lower centre of gravity, which led to a higher flight of the ball. It also minimized damage to the underside of the club itself.

In the 1960s an engineer name Karsten Solheim designed the first cavity back irons and putters using a method called investment casting to produce the heads. The cavity back concept developed under the Ping brand name offered improved playing characteristics by moving the weight nearer to the perimeter of the head. This in effect expanded the sweet spot of the club face and increased the margin for error considerably, particularly for less skilful players. From this point onward the manufacturers improved the design and playability of iron clubs by developing this cavity back concept. Bladed irons although providing more feel and feedback about impact have become far less popular even with the regular tournament professional. The modern cast iron may be made of harder steel and provide less of the vital feel required by top players, but the manufacturers can now offer greater consistency of product quality and a wider variation of clubhead design to suit all types of golfer. Some irons even have face or cavity inserts that are said to offer improved feel, greater distance and most importantly control characteristics.

The development of woods has been somewhat more dynamic since the introduction of the stainless steel/metal wood head early in the 1980s. The original concept was not so much to provide improved playing characteristics, but to offer greater durability for golfers who prefer to use the modern two-piece ball which is extremely hard and has a tendency to damage the natural wooden-headed clubs. These metal heads were hollow and often filled with a polystyrene type material to help reduce the noise made at impact. Although resembling wooden heads in shape and feature, thereafter the similarity differed considerably. The hollow, cavity design widened the club sweet spot and proved very effective in offering more consistent ball control. It was far easier to get the ball airborne off the fairway and to play a driver with less loft on the club face from the tee. The design also reduced the sideways spin characteristics of a wooden club, so golfers found their slices and hooks less exaggerated, leading to noticeable improvements in this department of their games. Manufacturers experimented with various materials and concepts including graphite and plastics, but found that titanium provided the ideal opportunity to take wood head design still further forward. In an effort to improve the playing characteristics of the stainless steel metal woods, perimeter weighting technology endeavoured to use a thinner material on the club face so that the weight could be moved more towards the edges of the club. Although stainless steel had a limit, titanium offers fewer restrictions due to its lower mass (lighter) makeup. Heads can be made far larger with titanium – irons also – improving the size of the sweet spot and offering yet more playability. Combining these characteristics with the modern golf shaft, has led to some dramatic and dynamic improvements within the golf club industry, all fortunately to the benefit of the golfer who wishes to improve his own playing standards.

The Shaft

Perhaps more than any other equipment aspect the golf shaft is the one component offering each and every player the individual opportunity to hit the ball longer and straighter. There are now innumerable options and shaft choice for a player. Choosing which one is most suited to that individual's game is not always an easy task, but with the advent of computer-aided club analysis equipment and improved manufacturers specifications, much of the guesswork is now almost a thing of the past.

The Role of the Shaft

Very simply the shaft has two roles:

1. To transfer the power generated by the swing to the clubhead.
2. To transmit the feel back to the hands.

Every different shaft will produce a different feel, transfer of power and shot trajectory. Making sure the shaft is correct for the individual player is very important.

During the 1920s one of the greatest innovations in the development of golf equipment occurred – the introduction of the steel shaft. The USGA

Types of Golf Shaft

Wooden	Hazel, Ash, but most successfully Hickory. Cane has also been used to a limited extent.
Steel	Introduced in the 1890s but made legal from 1925 by the USGA and in 1931 by the R & A. In 1913 Accles & Pollock patented the seamless tapered shaft. In 1927 the True Temper Sports Company patented the step-down method of manufacture. Late 1970s the Frequency Matching System was developed by the FM Precision Golf Corporation.
Fibreglass	Tried, but not popular in the 1960s
Aluminium	Some success in the late 1960s, but short-term only.
Titanium	Quite popular during the mid-1970s, but did not offer enough playing characteristics when fitted to wooden clubs or irons. More popular in metal heads during the 1980s onwards.
Composite	Generally graphite, but often with the addition of various materials. Most successful of all modern shafts offering improved playing characteristics for all players in woods and for less strong players in irons also.

legalized steel shafts in 1925 and the Royal & Ancient in 1931. The step forward to steel was a relatively natural process. With the development of the golf ball, the inconsistency of the wooden shaft and the growing shortage of available hickory, the manufacturers of the day were looking for progress. The properties of the steel shaft were improved flex control and less torque, which meant a player could swing faster and harder, and not lose control of the club face. Not all players of the day liked the new shaft, many preferred to stick with their hickory-shafted clubs, but it soon became evident that by using steel shafts the gains far outweighed the disadvantages.

The shafts enabled the players to improve their swing technique to a more modern style and one that influenced the technique of today's players. Not only were players able to develop sounder

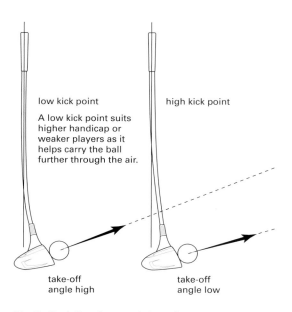

low kick point

A low kick point suits higher handicap or weaker players as it helps carry the ball further through the air.

high kick point

take-off angle high

take-off angle low

Fig 13 Shaft flex characteristics – flex point.

25

and more versatile swing techniques, there was a general development in the range of golf clubs that were available to players. Matched sets of woods and irons could be truly offered for the first time – the steel shaft offering a consistency of feel and playability, unavailable in wooden shafted clubs. The numbers of irons in a set increased as did the manufacturers' potential in offering golfers a variety of clubs specifically designed for each type of shot required on the golf course. This progress invariably offered players such an improvement in playing potential that the courses on which they played were found to be less of a challenge, and reduced in the effective playing length, so ultimately the development of the golf shaft has, to an extent, played a major role in the regeneration of golf courses themselves.

Without doubt the latest innovation in the composite graphite shaft has revolutionized the playability of modern golf clubs. The lightness of the shafts allows manufacturers to make clubs of a lighter total weight, yet increase the overall length and swing weight of each individual club. Players at all levels from tour professional to novice can benefit from the potential advantages offered, particularly in the woods where the combination of longer shafts and increased clubhead weight can create considerable improvement in

clubhead speed. In irons graphite shafts particularly benefit the less strong players such as seniors, ladies and juniors where the same characteristics, although more limited than in the woods, can be of greater benefit.

A Few Facts about Shafts

Flex. The flex of a golf shaft can be described as the bending characteristics, flexible to stiff. They can be categorized as follows:

L = Ladies
A = For seniors, strong ladies and some juniors.
R = For most average men or accomplished
    lady players.
S = Stiff for low handicap players and
    professionals.
X = Very strong players and professionals.

There is a considerable amount of bend in a shaft during the golf swing, particularly approaching impact. The following information will prove useful to all golfers:-

Torque The torque of a shaft can best be described as the twist created by the weight of the clubhead in conjunction with the speed of the golfer's

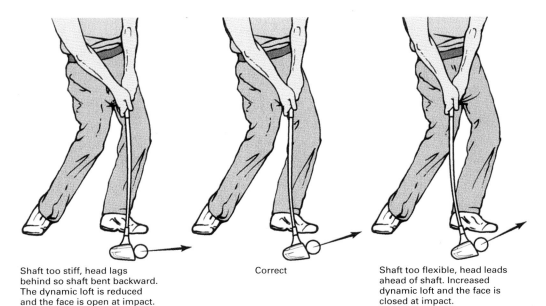

Shaft too stiff, head lags behind so shaft bent backward. The dynamic loft is reduced and the face is open at impact.

Correct

Shaft too flexible, head leads ahead of shaft. Increased dynamic loft and the face is closed at impact.

Fig 14 The effect of shaft flex with swing speed.

swing. Torsion movement within the shaft will have an effect upon clubhead alignment at impact. Generally the playing characteristics of graphite shafts are more affected by torque than that of steel shafts.

Stiff v. Flexible It is not an easy task to match a golfer with the correct shaft specification for his or her swing action. There are so many variations of shaft available, many with similar playing characteristics and as most golfers including professionals have swings that vary to some extent from day to day, it is unlikely that any one particular shaft is the correct one, or the only one that will suit a player anyway. Golfers should always favour shafts that are more flexible rather than too stiff for their swing characteristics.

Too Stiff Loss of distance. Loss of height (trajectory) of shot. Loss of clubhead feel, particularly at impact. Gain to accuracy.

Too Flexible Increase in distance. Increase in height. More feel of the clubhead, particularly at impact. Potential decrease in accuracy.

The Clubhead

Loft can be defined as the angle between the club face and the shaft, and is the main factor in ball trajectory. The more lofted the club the higher the trajectory and shorter the distance the ball travels. The shorter shaft of most lofted clubs will accentuate this principle. The less lofted clubhead will cause the ball to fly on a lower, more powerful trajectory in relation to the distance the ball travels through the air. A ball travelling lower on a more powerful trajectory will obviously run more on landing, than one of a high trajectory that is landing on a more vertical descent.

The loft differential of irons tends to have a 3–5 degree difference between each club, the length increases by around ½in per club the lower the number of iron.

No:	2	3	4	5	6	7	8	9	PW	SW	Lob W
Loft:	18	21	24	28	32	36	40	45	50	55	60
(degrees)											

These specifications often vary with different manufacturers and so can only be used as a guideline.

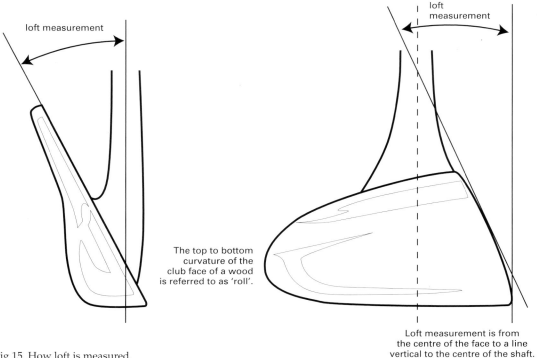

loft measurement

The top to bottom curvature of the club face of a wood is referred to as 'roll'.

loft measurement

Loft measurement is from the centre of the face to a line vertical to the centre of the shaft.

Fig 15 How loft is measured.

Wood clubs again have no set loft ratio, but fall into this sort of pattern.

Loft: (degrees)	Driver/ No 1 Wood	Fairway Driver	3W	4W	5W	7W
	7–11	12–13	14–15	18	21	25

The carry distance for each club varies from golfer to golfer, but generally with irons 4 degrees of loft differential will increase or decrease the carry of the ball by about 10yd. The angle at which the ball commences its flight (launch angle) will be more vertical, due to the increased loft of the higher numbered iron, plus that extra loft factor increases the amount of backspin applied to the ball. This also means that the speed at which the ball comes off the club face will decrease as the loft increases.

With wooden clubs the parameters are slightly different. Increased loft will produce a higher flight, for example, an 11 degree driver as opposed to a 7 degree one, but the launch angle and loss of ball speed off the club face are less pronounced than with an iron. The backspin increases by approximately the same amount as an iron, but with only a 2 degree increase or decrease in the loft specification. One extra factor that affects the performance of a wood, particularly a driver, is the position of the Centre of Gravity. Should this be positioned towards the back of the head and low down, then the ball will tend to fly on a higher trajectory even if the loft of the club is the same as one with the centre of gravity positioned more forward and higher, which will cause the ball trajectory to be one of a lower more penetrating flight.

How Clubs are Weighed

All clubs have a dead weight and what is called a swing weight measurement. Dead weight is the actual total weight of the club and will be measured in grams or ounces. There may be quite a variation between the lightest club, usually the driver and the heaviest, the sand iron. There is a gradual progression or weight from the longer clubs towards the shorter ones. The dead weight of clubs may vary enormously, but a graphite shafted wood would be approximately 325–375 g with the irons being slightly heavier.

Swing weight is the actual balance weight of the club – the weight relationship between the shaft, grip and head – and is measured from a fixed fulcrum point set nearest to the grip end of the club. It is the swing weight that offers a golfer the measurement of feel when swinging the club. Each club should have a similar swing weight to enable a player to gain a consistency of feel. The exceptions to this will be the putter, which is generally not measured in swing weight terms, and the sand iron which is the heaviest club and has the highest swing weight due to the large sole of the clubhead. The swing weight scale ranges from AO the lightest to G0 the heaviest, with most women's clubs falling between C0–C9 and men's C9–D8.

It is popular for golfers particularly those playing off single figure handicaps to adjust their clubs from time to time, which may have an adverse effect on both the overall weight and swing weight. Increasing dead weight has the effect of slowing down the clubhead in most instances, so contrary to popular belief it is worth remembering that lighter clubs can offer the potential to gain clubhead speed. An increase of 2g of weight on the clubhead will increase the swing weight by one point, whilst 4g of the grip end will be needed to decrease it by one.

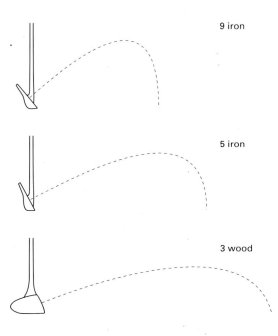

9 iron

5 iron

3 wood

Fig 16 The 9 iron has a higher and less penetrating flight than the less lofted and longer shafted 5 iron and 3 wood.

Why Woods Have Curved Faces

In early times the original woods were long and slender with relatively flat faces – the driver was fairly straight; the lofted woods were often concave to help ball flight and control. As heavier and harder balls were developed and became popular these woods were not only poorly designed to control the ball, but were also subject to damage and destruction far more easily.

The design of woods changed to a more bulbous, rounded shape for durability and improved playing characteristics. The flat-faced concept was found to make ball control far more difficult with the deeper-faced woods, but by using a convex shape on the club face, ball control was improved particularly with off-centre golf hits.

As woods developed in design, manufacturers found that by curving the face both top to bottom referred to as roll, and from toe to heel referred to as bulge, the control of golf shots could be improved considerably. The bulge and roll factors enable a player to reduce the damaging effect of side spin or backspin on the ball, caused by an incorrect impact position.

There is quite a science to the curvature of a club face, which has to be combined with an understanding of the centre of gravity of each particular club. It is not a point that the average golfer needs to understand to any great extent, but one that will prove relevant in playability terms

Bulge or curvature of a wood help a player to keep the ball on target even when hit towards the toe or heel side of the face

toe shot

centre shot

heel shot

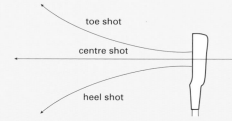

An iron has less helpful characteristics with its straighter face.

toe shot

centre shot

heel shot

Fig 17 Off-centre hits.

when choosing a wood or set of woods. Invariably if a player can hit the ball consistently from the centre of the club face, in or near the sweet spot, then there is little thought needed for such detail.

Lengthening the club will increase both dead weight and swing weight, as will heavier heads. Heavier grips will increase the overall weight, but reduce the swing weight. Fitting new shafts that are of a different specification may affect both weight factors if the shafts are lighter or heavier than the original shafts of the club. This is particularly relevant should golfers wish to have lighter graphite shafts fitted. In general terms golfers should choose the lightest specification of clubs that they could personally swing well with as this offers the best opportunity to enjoy both distance and accuracy.

How Equipment Has an Effect on Tee-shots

It has always been the golfer's obsession to hit the ball as far as possible off the tee – hence the reason why most golf shops have a vast array of specialist drivers for sale to satisfy that need. Golfers often find consistency and reliability difficult, and yet it is the only shot in golf where we are able to choose our lie and position. Often it is a player's incorrect club selection that cause the errors rather than the swing execution. An important point of which most golfers are unaware, is that in terms of carry distance through the air, the vast majority of players do not hit the ball significantly further with a driver as opposed to a 3 wood – on average less than 10yd – and so it is the roll or run after landing that provides the extra distance with the driver off the tee. For some players the driver actually flies less distance in the air – a significant disadvantage! The loft of a 3 wood or 12 degree driver may be noticeably advantageous for many players and for on-course situations that demand height on the shot in hand.

Remember:

• The stronger the loft of the club face the longer it is possible to hit the ball. A strong loft may mean a lower flight, but an increase in the distance that

the ball rolls on landing. A strong loft does affect accuracy, so this must be taken into account.
• Weaker players may benefit by using a 3 or 5 wood off the tee, as a low clubhead speed will not provide sufficient power to gain any benefit from a driver with a more powerful loft on the club face.
• If carry should be the main priority, it may be better to drive with a 3 or 5 wood. The extra loft will also help a player to strike the ball more consistently and reliably.
• Use a driver when the ground is hard for maximum roll and distance, a 3 wood if the ground is soft and there is little roll.
• More skilful players and longer hitters should take note of the tour professional's club management from the tee – a driver for maximum distance, a 3 wood for maximum carry and accuracy, a long iron for accuracy.
• Do not forget to try a more lofted driver.

Custom-fit Clubs

Golf is possibly one of the most difficult sports for which to choose the correct equipment. A full set will contain fourteen individual clubs, usually three woods, ten irons and a putter, each one having a different specification, yet from the player's point of view almost all needing to feel and play as similar as possible, so that some form of consistency can be established. The value of this individual requirement can often be experienced when players try out fellow golfers' equipment – rarely will they be able to just pick up a 'foreign' club, and feel as settled with it as with their own established model. When they do, it is often a reason to make

a change on a more permanent basis from the ones that they are already using.

Advances in design, greater knowledge and understanding of personal requirements, a wider selection of equipment and the publicized exacting demands by tour professionals regarding their clubs, have all played a part in encouraging golfers to seek out equipment that is far more correctly suited to their skill levels and playing needs. Not all golfers demand this form of custom-fit requirement, and many are content to purchase clubs straight off the shelf, but in most instances, particularly for the more established players there will be a considerable amount of trial and error before a final choice is made.

It would be unwise and unfair to say that no golfer should regularly use any type of equipment unless they have taken considerable time and energy to ensure it suits them best, as some players possess the talent or skill to play with a wide variety of clubs. Yet it is fair to say that the higher the standard of player, the more diligent they are in choosing their equipment. There is no real need to leave anything to chance. Although, the choices are immense, access to good technical advice is not difficult to seek out through any golf professional, club maker, manufacturer or knowledgeable retailer.

The following details will clarify some of the mysteries of personalized or custom-fit clubs, and although the task of guaranteeing the correct choice may seem a high risk initially, following simple procedures minimizes most of this, if not eliminating it altogether.

The variables that must be taken into account are:

• Club design
• Lie angle
• Loft angle
• Club length
• Face angle (woods only)
• Club weight
• Shaft choice
• Grip choice
• Make-up of set.

Club Design

The appearance and design of the club are the two key elements. Appearance is very much an

The specification for juniors will vary dependent upon the age and height of the individual. The following example is for a typical 10–12 year old.

Clubs:	3 wood,	5,	7 &	9 irons,	putter
Lengths:	36in	31in	30in	29in	29in
Lofts:	20in	32in	40in	48in	3–4in
Lie:	To suit individual				
Shafts:	Length to suit individual – Junior Flex				
Grips:	Junior Size				
Heads:	Junior specification				

Fig 18 Custom-fit for juniors.

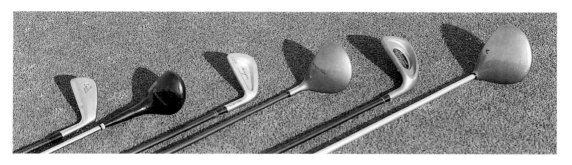

Fig 19 A small selection of the current equipment available. Note how much larger the clubheads are on the titanium iron and woods.

aesthetic matter, but an important one. The player must feel confident to hit a good shot, and so looking down at a club that increases confidence is very important.

Iron heads can be either made of forged or cast steel and although many golfers believe that using a forged clubhead increases the feel of impact, the truth is that few players can differentiate between forged and cast heads. Cast heads often offer increased playing characteristics through the potential to improve the results of off-centre hits due to the weight of the head being situated more towards its perimeter – a design feature that has certain limitations with forged clubs. Large soled heads will certainly help novice players to get the ball airborne with greater consistency.

Woods come in many shapes, sizes and materials, but so far no one factor has made a significant difference except perhaps that metal woods, due to their perimeter weighted design concept, once again offer improved characteristics for off-centre hits. The larger the head size, the more potential for minimizing errors, but ultimately if the ball is struck from the centre or sweet spot, all clubs have exactly the same potential.

Lie Angle

The lie angle is measured from the centre line of the shaft to the sole of the club in its normal playing position. The lie of a club plays a key role in providing accuracy for golf shots, and so it is an important factor that all golfers need to check on a regular basis. Fortunately most cast-iron heads and all woods heads maintain the same lie angle throughout the whole of their playing lives. For woods and irons the toe must be raised slightly off the ground at the address position. This is to compensate for the fact that the shaft will bend downward by 1–2 degrees during the swing movement.

A club that has too flat a lie angle at impact will cause the ball to go to the right, as the face will be tilted slightly in that direction. One that has too upright a lie will have the face tilted to the left, and so the ball will follow in that direction.

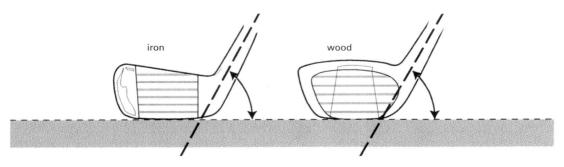

Fig 20 Lie angle.

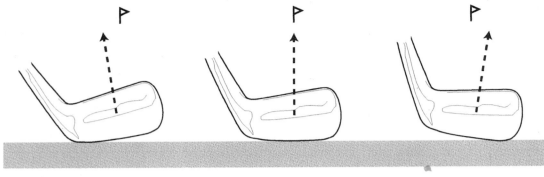

lie too upright – ball flies left of target　　lie correct – straight ball flight　　lie too flat – ball flies right of target

Fig 21 Effect of incorrect lie angle.

The length of the club will affect the lie angle – longer clubs need flatter lies, shorter clubs more upright ones. Also, the more lofted an iron the more off-line the result of the shot in relation to its overall carry length if the lie is incorrect. It should be

remembered that not all tall players need upright lie angle clubs, nor do shorter golfers necessarily need flatter ones. The lie of the club at impact is a key element, much more so than the one at address.

Finally, it should be noted that cast heads cannot be adjusted to any great extent, and so a player should endeavour to ensure that the lie angle is correct from day one. Forged irons are far more versatile, but will need more constant checking, as more regular play will cause the lie to alter. Woods cannot be adjusted, but almost all have a curved sole design so that they are satisfactory for all specifications of the golfer.

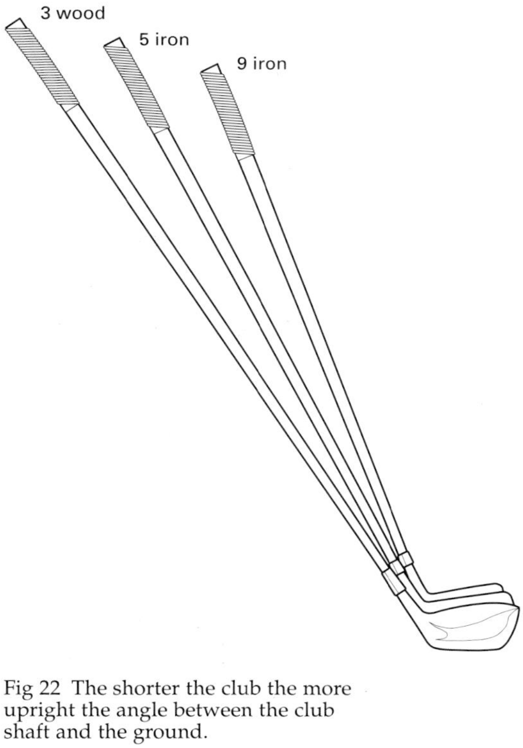

Loft

The loft of any club is the key element in ball flight and distance. It is measured from the centre line of the club face to the centreline of the hosel (or neck) of an iron or a point perpendicular to the sole of a wood.

Club Length

Length is another factor in determining how far a ball is hit. In general terms the longer the club the further the ball will go, although there is bound to be an optimum point at which a player is unable to maintain sufficient control to warrant the increased length. Control is an important consideration where length is concerned. Irons are rarely advantageous to any player once the length is extended by more than an inch or two

Fig 22 The shorter the club the more upright the angle between the club shaft and the ground.

3 wood

5 iron

9 iron

beyond standard. Woods are generally easier to control with extended shafts, due to the natural sweeping motion of the swing action, but the potential advantages of gaining extra clubhead speed must be tempered with the requirement for control and consistency. A few tour players have drivers that are as much as 5–7in longer than normal, but most will use ones of fairly standard length, preferring reliability rather than playing to the odds. Clubs should only be shortened if a player has exceptional physical requirements or would benefit by the increased clubhead control shorter clubs can offer, without being affected detrimentally by the potential reduction in clubhead speed.

Face Angle (Woods Only)

Face angle effects the direction of shots and can have an influence on the trajectory of the shot also. In simple terms it can be described as the direction the club face is aiming in relation to the shaft and the target.

If the direction of the face is towards the left of target the face angle is closed. If it is to the right, the face angle is open. Golfers tend to assume that a wood is always manufactured with a square club face. This is not actually correct. As most golfers suffer with a slice, manufacturers favour designing woods with a slightly closed club face angle. This not only benefits a player by helping reduce the amount of slice spin on the ball, but offers the obvious potential of more distance from the straighter hit shots. Although the face angle can influence shots that go to the left or to the right, it is not a cure to a player's swing error, which will need a more practical application to improve.

Face angle does have an effect upon the loft of a club, for example, an 11 degree driver that was slightly open at address, say 2 degrees - would require squaring up at impact, therefore the player would have to close the face by 2 degrees, thus reducing the address loft so that the effective loft of the face at impact would be 9 degrees.

Accomplished players will be more aware of the advantages and disadvantages of face angle, but whatever the standard of player, it is an aspect to be appreciated rather than studied in great depth, and one to which most golfers should turn for expert advice in relation to their personal needs. Often trial and error is the best route to finding the ideal face angle.

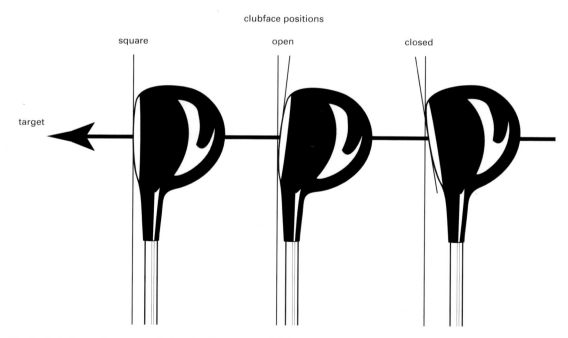

Fig 23 Not all woods are manufactured with a square club face.

Club Weight

Club weight has been covered earlier in this chapter, but it is worth repeating that all players should ensure that they select the correct dead and swing weights.

Shaft Choice

This is probably the most difficult variable of all as there are so many choices and specifications open to the player. The choices are for steel, titanium, composite or graphite at this time, and the range of each within the given field is immense. It may be that when a golfer chooses a more popular publicized model the manufacturer will limit any choice believing that the selected shaft characteristics and weight are the most suitable for the design and features of that particular model. When choosing a less publicized custom-fit model of club, there is often the wider choice of shafts from the club maker, golf professional or manufacturer. This offers greater variety and more personal choice, but ultimately means that professional advice is more relevant and important to the player.

Specifications for shaft and the performance of each for the individual golfer are determined by a combination including flex, torque, kick point, bend point, balance point, deflection and frequency. Although most relevant points were covered under the section *A Few Facts About Shafts*, it should be recognized that the shaft plays the vital part in making each club perform efficiently. The speed of the swing and the centrifugal force work to make the club shaft bend and twist during all golfers' swing movements, which makes it critical that the shaft matches the player's swing characteristics effectively. Most shafts will be matched to a player by measuring the speed of the golf swing in the first instance and then correlating other factors such as ball flight characteristics, physical strength and personal feel.

Composite and graphite shafts being of a lighter weight offer the golfer greater potential for increasing the swing speed. It is once again a matter of choosing the lightest appropriate shaft to help maximize the potential for the individual golfer.

Grip Choice

It is not so much the type of grip that is relevant for a golfer, as it is the size of it. For an exact fit the middle two fingers of the top hand should wrap around the grip so that the tips can just touch the base or heel of the palm. A gap between the tip and the palm indicates that the grip size is too thick, whereas if the tips dig into the palm, the grip size is too small. The player's right hand will tend to wrap around the narrow end of the tapered grip more easily, but because the right-hand hold is more fingers dominated than that of the left hand (a combination of palm and finger hold) it is not usually a detrimental factor.

Grips that are too small encourage a player to use more hand and wrist action, whereas those that are overly large may cause the hands and wrist to be limited. Both factors will affect feel and accuracy for a golfer, but for example can be used to advantage for some players when a thinner grip encourages more active hand action to help square up the club face for a slicer, or a thicker grip limits it to help reduce the effects of a pull or hook shot caused by a closed club face. The style, type or materials used in grip construction are of a personal preference, and if of a standard specification it should not affect other factors such as swing weight and so on.

Makeup of Set

This is really a matter of individual choice, as most golfers would prefer a particular breakdown in the club selection he or she chooses to play with. Most will favour three or four woods – 1, 3, 5 plus possibly a 7 wood, and nine irons – 3 through to a sand wedge. It may be that a golfer does not have great success with the longer, more difficult numbered irons, and would prefer a wider choice of woods. In this case the player might choose the addition of a 4 wood and/or possibly a 6, 7 or 9 wood. There are in fact many golfers who play with almost a complete set of woods, and just a few irons to use for the higher shots or short pitches, chips and bunker shots near to the green.

Stronger players may choose to use only a 1 and 3 wood, but have irons numbered 1 to sand wedge, or choose a utility or lob wedge rather than the 1 or 2 irons. It is all a matter of choice and the ability to use that choice effectively. It is logical to choose the most appropriate set makeup to suit the type of golf course played most regularly, and also the odd utility club or customized specification may prove useful such as a lofted driver for tree-lined courses or a lofted, high bounce sand iron for deep sand bunkers.

Most golfers prefer to match the irons, although this is not a necessity, whereas with woods there tends to be a more variable choice, with the driver rarely matching any of the other woods.

A little trial and error and some analysis of a player's strengths and weaknesses can make choosing the correct set makeup fairly straightforward, and offer an important improvement to any player's game. Ultimately, it is about achieving an acceptable level of accuracy and general consistency in playing terms.

Equipment Summary

In the UK alone golfers spend millions of pounds each year on new equipment. This not only covers the clubs and balls themselves, but all the other ancillary items that go into making up a golfer's complete outfit – bags, trolleys, waterproofs, shoes, gloves, tee pegs and much more. It is always worth investing a little time and energy in seeking the right professional advice and making the correct choice. Take a look into any tour professional's bag. It may be a surprise to find a varied array of clubs on view, but you can be sure that many years of experience, time and effort have gone into actually selecting the most appropriate choice.

The Golf Ball

The modern golf ball has to conform to the rules laid down by the Royal & Ancient Golf Club of St Andrews and the United States Golf Association. Most of these rules are intended to act as constraints in limiting the distance performance, not so much the playing characteristics as backspin or ball control – although any design having a significant effect on accuracy will also have to meet the guidelines set out.

The earliest reference to golf balls is found in 1554, and it is thought that golfers played with wooden balls and then one with a leather cover and probably stuffed with animal hair. The most successful balls however, were stuffed with wet goose

Haskell
circa 1900

Moulded Gutta
circa 1876

Gutta-Percha
circa 1850

Feathery
circa 1760

Wooden Ball
circa 1590

Fig 24 The development of the golf balls has come a long way over the years.

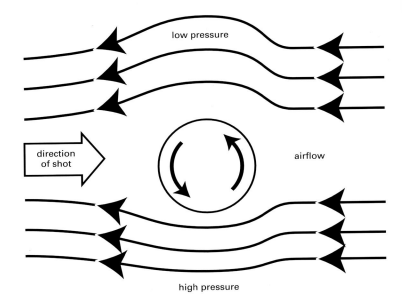

low pressure

direction of shot

airflow

high pressure

Fig 25 Dimples help produce backspin, which affects the air pressure – low above and high below – causing the ball to rise.

Summary of Rules Relating to Golf Ball Manufacture and Conformity
(Royal & Ancient Golf Club of St Andrews)

1. *Size*   1.68in minimum. There is no maximum.

2. *Weight*   1.62oz maximum. There is no minimum.

3. *Velocity*   The ball must not travel at more than 255ft per second.

4. *Distance*   The ball must not travel more than 296yd under strict test conditions.

5. *Symmetry*   Test conditions measure the flight time and directional orientation within given parameters.

to manufacture, wooden clubs themselves became less effective in terms of ball strike and control. The solid Gutta ball was moulded rather than hand-made and caused far more vibration on impact due to its harder characteristics, which led to makers of clubs using wooden golf shafts of a more durable and less twisting nature. The flight characteristics of this ball were low and running. Towards the end of the nineteenth century the development of the golf ball accelerated quickly, when the smooth covered surface was replaced by the first generation of dimpled ball.

The dimpled patterns were fairly basic, some in fact had convex bumps rather than concave dimples. Also around the turn of the century, manufacturers discovered that they could improve the feel and control by winding rubber thread around a solid rubber core and then adding a solid Gutta-Percha cover.

feathers that expanded on drying, and were hand made by specialist ball makers. These feathery balls were very expensive due to the time taken to make them. They were not particularly hard wearing and became misshapen relatively quickly. The feathery ball was perfect for the long-nosed wooden clubs in use due to their softer construction, but when they were superseded around 1850 by the Gutta-Percha ball, that was harder and more lively and cheaper

Ball Type	Spin Rate (rpm)		
	No 1 Wood	5 Iron	PW
Wound balata	3,800	6,300	9,100
Wound surlyn	3,800	6,300	4,900
2-Piece	3,400	5,900	4,100
N.B. details approximate			

The Haskell ball patented in 1899 revolutionized the game, and it not only offered improved ball flight and playing characteristics, but went up to 30yd further than the 'Guttie' ball.

Not too long afterwards it was discovered that balata, a natural material found in South America, improved the feel of the club face still further, so it replaced gutta-percha as a cover material.

In Britain and certain countries around the world, a ball of 1.62in diameter was used up until the 1980s. This anomaly was made illegal for tournament professionals in the 1970s and for amateurs by the end of the 1980s. The 1.68in diameter ball became the worldwide accepted norm.

In more recent years three-piece wound balls with balata covers have proved far less popular due to the cost in manufacturing and the ever-increasing popularity of the more durable two- or three-piece construction ball. Natural balata has been replaced by more man-made materials such as surlyn that offer greater consistency and durability. Even top class tour professionals find that the latest two- or three-piece balls can provide adequate feel and control, and although the synthetic balata three-piece balls are still the most popular with these players, more and more of them are changing to the two-piece solid core versions.

Today's golf balls fall into three main performance categories – distance/durability; distance/feel/spin; high spin/feel. It is very much up to each golfer to find their own preference, but needless to say golfers who are of lesser ability or lack sufficient distance will go for the distance and durability advantages, whereas accomplished or more powerful players will seek the additional advantages of high spin and feel.

There is so much development taking place in golf ball design that golfers are faced with an ever-changing supply of information regarding the benefits of each ball. New dimple types and patterns offer improved flight, greater stability and control. Improved feel is offered, whilst at the same time distance can be maintained or increased by aerodynamic development. One fact is for sure, no golfer has ever found the perfect ball, or has ever used just one type for a particularly long period of his career.

Golfers should try all available options until they are satisfied with the ball type they intend to use on a regular basis.

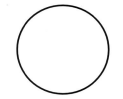

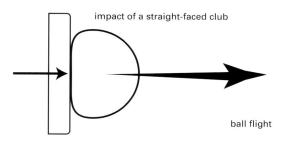

impact of a straight-faced club

ball flight

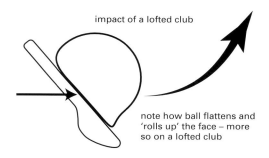

impact of a lofted club

note how ball flattens and 'rolls up' the face – more so on a lofted club

Fig 26 The effects of impact on a golf ball.

Choosing the Right Ball

With so many choices available it is almost impossible to state that one type of ball will suit a particular player, the following points are worthy of reference in making the appropriate choice:

• Balls are usually made with a two- or three-piece construction, although the latest technology has helped bring about the introduction of a four-piece construction ball.

• A two-piece ball will be made up of a large central core and thickish cover, a three-piece of a smaller central core, a middle layer and a thinner cover. The four-piece ball is one with an additional layer or double cover.

• In general terms the larger the inner core or thicker the cover, the less feel and control are available. A smaller core, additional middle layer and thin cover offer increased backspin properties enhancing both feel and control. A softer cover will offer improved feel but less control the thicker the specification.

• The core is generally made of a solid construction. The latest innovation includes such additions as Titanium in the core material.

• The cover is usually made of either a thin synthetic balata or thicker surlyn material. The balata cover has always been thought to offer the greatest feel and control properties, but is less hard-wearing than surlyn.

• Dimples on the cover provide the flight characteristics by helping improve distance and aerodynamics whilst offering a certain amount of aesthetic value. The dimples may be set out in many types of different patterns such as octahedron, dodecahedron and icosahedron dependent on manufacturers' research into performance benefits. The shapes of the dimples themselves are varied in depth and design. The number of dimples varies immensely – the lowest being 302, the highest 552.

• Balls used to be of three different compressions, 80, 90 and 100, but generally only 90 and 100 compressions remain today in wound construction balls. Additionally, there has been an introduction recently of balls specifically made for lady golfers. These are obviously of a lower compression and would be compatible with the now defunct 80 compression balls of past times.

• If distance and durability are a golfer's requirement then the more solid two- or three-piece distance balls will provide the appropriate benefits.

• If control and feel are the main virtues sought by the player rather than distance, then the high-spin, thin-covered, 2-, 3- or 4-piece construction balls are the correct choice. A balata cover may be preferential due to the increased feel available.

• Balls of a two- or three-piece construction with a surlyn cover offer a compromise by providing reliable distance and durability, plus acceptable feel and control.

• Less powerful golfers with slower swing speeds, including ladies or seniors should seek a ball that does not have too hard a cover, but one that has a softer feel with ball flight characteristics that have a high trajectory for increased carry and distance. The softer feel will help to improve approach shots and those on and around the green.

The Ball – Temperatures
Temperatures affect the performance of a golf ball – the warmer the climate the further it travels.

Distance Through the Air (yd)	Temperature (°C)
227	43
223	32
220	25
215	15
210	10
200	5

The above distances are approximate and are based on a drive of 220yd at 25°C

• It may be beneficial in windy or adverse weather conditions to use a different type of ball – one that has lower flight characteristics will not be affected so much by the wind, and has obvious ball control advantages. Should the ground conditions be very wet and not offer the advantage of roll on the ball, then a ball that carries further through the air is the best choice.

Summary

There are certain common requirements that golfers are looking for in choosing a ball to play – they will need to consider the distance factors, both carry and roll; the ball flight, not only the trajectory of the ball, but also the potential to control the ball from left to right or right to left; durability in general wear and tear terms either from poorly struck shots such as thins or tops, the action of sharp club face grooves hitting down onto the ball or abrasion from bunker shots; colour and consistency of each ball. The one obvious preference for all players is to choose the ball that goes the furthest for them. Golf balls do now have superior performance characteristics over those of past decades due mainly to the advances in design and development, but all must conform to the USGA and R & A rules which at least keep the distance, direction and control factors still very much reliant on the golfer's skill.

PART 2
THE WORKSHOP

5
FUNDAMENTAL SKILLS

The fundamentals of executing a golf shot can be broken down into two parts – the pre-shot actions and the swing itself.

The Pre-shot Actions: The Grip

The importance of placing the hands into the correct position on the golf club cannot be overexaggerated. In holding the club correctly the player is in effect dictating not only the control of the position of the club face during the swing, but the way in which the whole swing itself works. It is often said 'You never see a good player with a poor grip, or a poor player with a good grip', but there are exceptions to every rule and it may be better to understand at this point that there is no such thing as one perfect grip for all players. The correct grip is the one that best suits the individual player, and allows that player to be able to repeat the consistency and quality of their shots on a regular basis. There are, however, certain factors that help players to hold the club in the most orthodox and acceptable position, and that have proved to be successful for the majority of players.

As the arms hang down naturally from the shoulders so the palms face inwards and towards one another. This forms the basic position for the two hands when gripping the club. Taking hold of the club in the left hand initially, the handle should rest across the centre of the forefinger (index finger) and along the middle of the palm, so that the fleshy pad at the heel of the palm rests slightly on top of the handle of the club. As the fingers close around the handle, the last three fingers of the left hand hold the club firmly against the heel pad of the palm. This position allows the thumb to sit slightly to the right of the top of the handle whilst the V formed by the thumb and lower section of the forefinger will point between the chin and right shoulder, allowing two or three knuckles to be visible to the player. The left palm will be facing slightly downward and looking back towards the right knee.

Whereas the left hand is referred to as the palm grip the right hand has the handle positioned into the base of the fingers. As the right hand closes so the palm wraps comfortably around and over the left thumb. The right thumb will sit slightly to the left side of the handle with the V formed between the thumb and forefinger, pointing between the chin and right shoulder. The knuckle of the right forefinger will generally be the only one visible to the player. The right palm faces towards the target and the sensation of gripping the club should be felt in the central three fingers of the hand. There are three accepted options in uniting the hands whilst taking the correct hold of the club.

1. **The overlapping or Vardon grip** (Fig 27) This grip position was used and recommended by Harry Vardon, one of the great players from the early part of the twentieth century. Basically, the left hand holds the club as suggested earlier and as the right hand is positioned, the little finger overlaps the knuckle of the left forefinger. This grip tends to suit players with relatively medium to large size strongish hands, otherwise the overlapping little finger may feel ill-positioned and uncomfortable.

2. **The interlocking grip** (Fig 28) is one that suits players with smaller hands or weaker grip strength and as such is an excellent beginner's grip, or one to recommend for ladies or juniors. To effect this grip the player interlocks the left forefinger with the little finger of the right hand. This should be done in a comfortable fashion so that the correct position of the hands is not affected in any detrimental way. A player who has successfully used the interlocking grip throughout his career is the great Jack Nicklaus who, although being relatively big and strong, has fairly small hands.

3. **The baseball or ten finger grip** (Fig 29) is perhaps the most natural and comfortable for most beginners, although it does have some merit for ladies, juniors and golfers with poor hand actions. The hands are not actually 'joined together' in any physical way when using this grip, so it is important to ensure that the outsides of the left forefinger and right little finger sit as closely together as possible, ensuring that the hands work as one unit throughout the swing action.

Grip options (1).

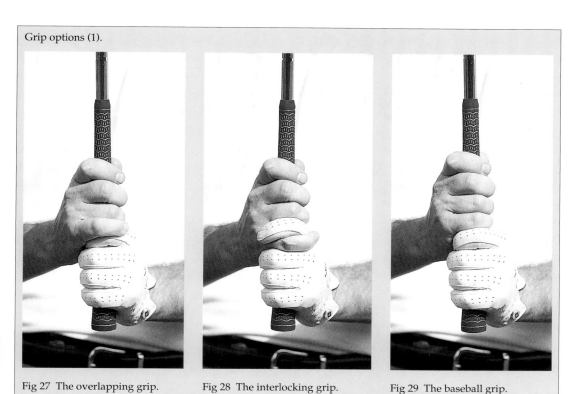

Fig 27 The overlapping grip.

Fig 28 The interlocking grip.

Fig 29 The baseball grip.

This grip position allows a player more right-hand domination and, as such, is generally not popular with more accomplished players who fear that too much right-hand action during the swing will lead to dangerous or inconsistent shots. For some this may not be so critical and does offer certain advantages for higher handicap or weaker players, as this extra right-hand domination can help increase clubhead speed and power.

Choosing the Correct Grip Option

When we look at the speed at which a golfer is attempting to swing the club, and the amount of club face control required to hit a straight shot, we can appreciate the importance of at least holding the club correctly.

Most right-handed golfers have more natural strength in the right side of their bodies, and although this can be used to great effect if the swing is controlled, it can also lead to very detrimental effects if the right side or right hand prove overly dominant. The overlapping and interlocking grips allow the golfer to have only three fingers of the right hand on the handle, so can be seen as a positive step in helping minimize any right-hand dominance. The baseball grip however allows a rather more liberal contact of the right hand on the handle of the club. Golfers should be aware of this right-hand or right-side factor as it makes their choice of grip a very important one. A balance has to be achieved, as golf is a game neither dominated by excessive right- nor left-side control. When both sides of the body are

co-ordinated and in harmony with one another, timing, power and control come naturally to the golfer.

Unfortunately, an incorrect grip position is the catalyst for further errors within the swing movement. It is sometimes difficult for a golfer to recognize this fact, and often they spend many hours endeavouring to change their swing movements or correct certain errors, without appreciating that a simple correction of their grip will more often than not lead to an improvement in their swing action.

There will always be exceptions to every rule, and over the decades there have been top players who have used unorthodox grips such as José Maria Olazabal with a weak grip, and Paul Azinger and Bernhard Langer with strong left-hand

41

grips. These three and many others, prove that it is possible to play golf to a very successful standard whilst using an unorthodox grip. As visible as the incorrect grip position might be, what is not so obvious is the ability of these players to incorporate some form of swing compensation to allow them to maintain consistent club face control on a regular basis.

The Effects of a Poor Grip Position

When a golfer positions the hands too much to the right-hand side of the handle it is referred to as strong grip. Too much to the left-hand side of the handle is referred to as a weak grip.

A strong grip position is evident when a golfer shows more than three knuckles of the left hand, the V formed between the thumb and forefinger point to or just outside the right shoulder and the palm faces downward towards the ground. The right hand is then encouraged to move round and under the handle, so that the V formed between the thumb and finger also points to or outside the right shoulder. This grip position encourages the player to close or hood the club face at impact, which reduces the loft of the club face making it far stronger so that the 5 iron has the effective loft of a 4 or 3 iron. It can also affect the swing path and the angle of approach factors of the swing. The swing path is encouraged to travel too much from the inside and the angle of approach to become too shallow. The subsequent impact position will generally impart a strong

right to left side spin on the ball which has the potential of providing a more powerful flight and adding increased distance for some players. It can also lead to a lack of control and extreme inconsistency in ball striking terms.

A weaker grip position is usually evident when a player's hands are positioned so that only one knuckle of the left hand and two or three of the right hand are visible at address. The V formed by the thumb and forefingers points between the chin and left shoulder and the left palm faces to backward or even slightly upward. This grip position leads to the club being returned to the ball in an open or weak position. In effect there is an addition of loft to the club face so that a 5 iron only has the potential to hit the ball a 6 or 7

Grip options (2).

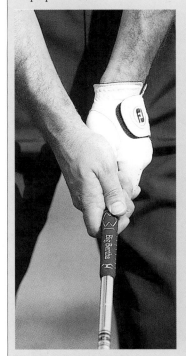  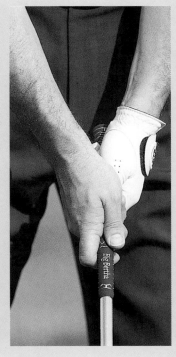

Fig 30 An orthodox grip.

Fig 31 A strong grip.

Fig 32 A weak grip.

iron distance with a far higher and weaker trajectory to the shot. A weak grip is not one that encourages correct wrist cock or an active hand rotation prior to impact and consequently it can also have some detrimental effects on the swing path and angle of approach factors. Players using this type of grip tend to swing the club on an out to in swing path, which causes the clubhead to approach the ball at too steep an angle. These swing characteristics lead to a player imparting a left to right side spin on the ball and create the typical slice shot that most average golfers experience at some time during their playing lives. The more lofted clubs will not be affected quite so dramatically in directional terms, but will certainly lack a more powerful forward trajectory. The ball flight characteristics experienced by most players using a weak grip may not be particularly powerful but do allow a player to play with some form of control and consistency, and so in many cases golfers are content to settle with this particular option.

Other Facts about the Grip

There are several other important facts that are very relevant to obtaining and making an effective grip position. The tightness or pressure a player applies when holding the club is one of the major factors that limits many players with regards to swinging in a successful and consistent fashion. It is difficult to describe how firmly the player should hold the club – it will vary from individual to individual dependent upon physical strength and emotional confidence. However, it is neither beneficial to hold it too tightly or too loosely. A grip pressure that is too tight is the one that is clearly evident in most golfers.

Beginners and novices invariably fear letting go of the club during the swing action and as a consequence grip much too tightly until, that is, they have enough confidence to appreciate the correct grip pressure required. All players are affected by tension and nervousness and will instinctively hold onto the club more tightly, limiting their natural or normal feel and restricting the hand and wrist action during the swing itself. No matter how difficult the shot, particularly the delicate high pitch over a bunker to a tight pin placement, or the state of a player's score during a game, it is important to check the grip pressure so that there is no danger of 'strangling' the action of the club through an unnecessary tightening of the grip pressure.

Grip pressure will vary depending upon which shot a golfer has to play, for example a player will generally hold the club in a more relaxed fashion when making a putting stroke as opposed to hitting a driver off the tee. The need for additional power often has a detrimental effect on the golfer, whereas, ironically, if they maintained a comfortable and relaxed grip position they would invariably be able to produce extra clubhead speed and improved timing, which would enhance both distance and control. A player's grip pressure increases and becomes stronger as the swing progresses and the speed of the clubhead quickens, so that at impact the grip is at its most firm and effective. Should a player grip too tightly at address it is highly likely that their grip pressure will actually loosen during the swing itself, causing the clubhead to twist in the player's hand at impact which will be clearly evident at the completion of the swing. Some experts have advised players to imagine holding an egg or small

bird in their hands, others a tube of toothpaste that is squeezed more tightly as the swing approaches impact. Whichever mental image best suits a player it is important that the initial grip pressure is relaxed but firm. The pressure points of the grip should be in the last three fingers of the left hand, the middle two fingers of the right hand and the right palm applying a gentle pressure to the top of the left thumb which itself applies a gentle pressure onto the top of the handle. Some players enjoy feeling a little pressure between the right thumb and forefinger as they squeeze the club gently in the right hand.

All golfers should be aware of the positive relationship between a good grip position using the correct grip pressure and the effectiveness of their golf swings. An effective wrist-set during the backswing creates the leverage required in the downswing to play powerful and consistent golf shots. The clubhead must be able to travel at great speeds and in doing so centrifugal force will create great energy in the downswing – the golfer must control this through the grip.

No position at address or movement during the swing seems as difficult to change as that of the grip. Adopting the correct grip position right from the early days of learning the game is an important factor and one that will invariably help the golfer to develop his or her swing in a more effective manner. For those golfers who are able to play to a pleasurable and acceptable standard with an incorrect grip position, then change may not be advisable, but for those who are dissatisfied with the standards of their game and are aware of the detrimental effects that their grip position is causing, there can be no excuse for not setting about a change of grip to a more orthodox position.

The Set-up

Once again the relevance of achieving the correct set-up fundamentals cannot be underestimated. Aim, ball position, posture and weight distribution are all key elements in helping a player to hit the ball successfully and consistently towards the target. These fundamentals ensure that a golfer is able to return the club on the correct path, from the correct angle of approach and with the club face square at impact.

Aim – The Square Set-up

To achieve an orthodox square alignment at address a player must first line up the leading edge of the club face square or at right angles to the target and then place their feet, knees, hips and shoulders parallel to this square club face alignment. As simple as it sounds it is the one major aspect of the pre-swing preparation that all players should constantly check out. In fact it is the first key aspect that all successful players will examine carefully when they are not playing well.

Whilst square alignment is one to be highly recommended to all players there are those who have achieved success by aiming to the left or the right of the target at address. If a player aims to the left of the target there are basically two alternatives in propelling the ball correctly to that target – the first is to allow the ball to start left of the target in the direction that the body is aiming and to impart a left to right side spin on the ball so that the ball moves back towards the target during its flight, the second is for the swing path to move to the right of the body alignment, but on line to the target so that in effect the player is swinging from an in to out direction in relation to the body position. This process is simply reversed if a player aims to the right of the target at address, so that the swing path propels the ball to the right of the target, and a right to left side spin on the ball allows it to move back towards the target during its flight or, alternatively, the player must swing the club across their body line and pull the ball towards the target by using what is an out to in swing path in relation to the body, but one that is down the ball to target line. Many players do achieve considerable success and consistency by purposely playing for a fade or draw shot, but it would not be recommended for any player to align themselves incorrectly and to adjust the swing path so that it was across the body line to any great extent.

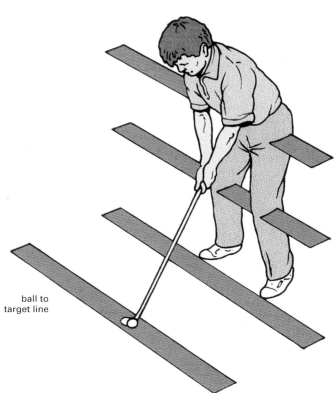

ball to target line

Fig 33 A square alignment at address.

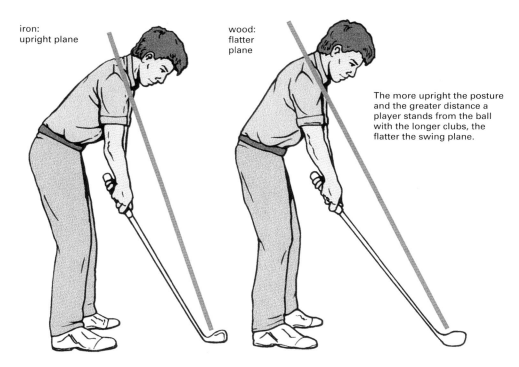

upright plane

wood:
flatter
plane

The more upright the posture
and the greater distance a
player stands from the ball
with the longer clubs, the
flatter the swing plane.

Fig 34 Correct posture and swing plane.

_Address – Posture and
Weight Distribution_

To appreciate the qualities of a good set-up all golfers should be aware of the involvement of the body with regard to posture and weight distribution. If these two elements are of an acceptable standard then the player has every chance of repeating a consistent swing movement. The posture and position of the body must be athletic and free of tension. The flex of the knees, the forward bend from the hips or pelvic area, the straightish angle of the back or spine and the natural hanging forward of the hands and arms should all take place in a comfortable, relaxed but controlled fashion. The head should be positioned as if it is an extension of the back, so that as the player looks down at the ball there is no sign that the chin is being tucked into the upper chest area. There will be a variation in the position of a player's posture, depending upon which club they are playing. Shorter shafted clubs dictate that a player must bend over more to accommodate the correct address position, whereas when playing wooden clubs a player will stand much taller with the back angle far straighter and on a more vertical angle. There will also be a variation dependent upon the individual height of the player where, in most cases, the shorter golfer will tend to stand as upright as possible and the taller one to bend over more to accommodate the length of the golf club.

The actual distance a player stands from the ball at address ultimately dictates the posture. If the ball is too far away from the body the player will need to lean over towards the ball, causing the upper body to tilt forward and downward to some extent. The opposite is true when a player is positioned too near to the ball, so that the back has to assume a more upright angle and it is likely that the knees will be far more flexed. Either of these extremes will have a significant effect on the player's swing movements, so it is important that a player achieves a consistent routine enabling the ball to be positioned the correct distance from the feet at address.

A simple routine is illustrated overleaf and may prove useful in helping a player to gain consistency both in posture and the distance they stand from the ball.

Balance and weight distribution are key elements in any sport. For a golfer to be able to make the correct rotational swing action they have to have good balance control both in a sideways – left to right – and a front to back capacity. A player will be confronted with swing difficulties if the weight remains too much on the left side during

FUNDAMENTAL SKILLS

45

Fig 35 Posture and ball distance routine.

(a) Stand fairly upright with your arms extended away from your body.

(b) Lower your arms in towards your chest, keeping the clubhead about 18in above the ground.

(c) Flex your knees slightly maintaining good balance.

(d) Lower your upper body forward from the hips until the club settles behind the ball.

the swing action, as will happen if the weight moves too much onto the right side. Problems will also arise should a player move the weight back towards the heels during the swing, or forward towards the balls of the feet.

At address, the weight distribution should be between the balls of the feet and the heels. As a player's posture tends to lean over more for shorter irons, there is a tendency for the shoulders to be positioned slightly more forward with the weight pushed more towards the balls of the feet, with the player sensing more pressure on the upper muscles at the front of the legs. The opposite can be said to be true for the longer clubs where the more upright back angle tends to push the shoulders back slightly and allow the weight to sit more towards the heels.

Many players question whether their weight should favour either the right or left side at address – this question can be answered simply by looking at which club they are about to use, that is, if a player is using a pitching wedge the stance will be relatively narrow, the ball will be positioned more centrally between the feet, and consequently the player's weight distribution will be more evenly distributed or will even favour the left side. With a driver the ball is positioned more forward opposite the left heel, a wider stance is used and the player will feel that the body is more behind the ball with the weight favouring the right side at address. In neither case should the player purposely overemphasize a right- or left-sided weight distribution. It is not only natural for the weight to feel more on the right side when using longer clubs, but also a necessity with regards to the swing action which will be much more of a sweeping movement the longer the club used.

Stance and Ball Position

The width of the stance may vary depending upon the player's personal preference, the club selected for use and the type of shot to be played. From middle irons most players prefer to position the feet about shoulder width apart which they will adapt to a slightly wider position with a longer iron. The less physical nature of the swing for a shorter iron dictates that the player will normally choose to use a slightly narrower stance with the feet approximately the width of the chest apart. Conversely, for wood play particularly off the tee, a player may wish to widen the stance further to allow for greater control and stability during the swing action.

The overall width of a player's stance is an important factor when one looks at the type of shot to be played. Because of the power required in wood play a wider stance not only provides a more solid base for the swing, but also helps the player to lower their centre of gravity and to enhance the potential width of the swing arc, whereas for short shots such as chipping or pitching which necessitates the good use of the hands and arms and a free swing motion, it is far more applicable to use a narrow stance, perhaps one that favours the feet being aligned slightly to the left or

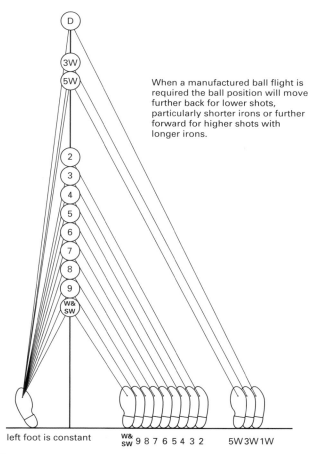

When a manufactured ball flight is required the ball position will move further back for lower shots, particularly shorter irons or further forward for higher shots with longer irons.

left foot is constant   W& SW 9 8 7 6 5 4 3 2   5W 3W 1W

Fig 36 Ball position constant.

open to the target. A wider stance will limit the player's mobility and freedom to swing, whereas a narrow stance will allow the player to swing freely and the hands and arms to dominate. It may be worth a player considering these factors when choosing a stance that suits their personal swing characteristics.

Ball position is of far greater importance than many golfers appreciate, as the ball must be positioned so that a player contacts it at the optimum point in the swing arc. If the position is too far forward or too far backward in the stance then the chances of a consistent ball strike and of control are greatly reduced. There is no one position that will suit all players, as some prefer to vary the position of the ball with each club, generally moving it further back towards the middle of the stance the shorter the iron, whereas others are content to keep the ball in one constant position in relation to their left heel. It is probably simpler to develop a technique that settles on one fairly constant ball position, with the width of the stance varying as the right foot is positioned slightly wider the longer the club in use. As a guideline it is acceptable for irons to be played about 2in or 3in inside the left heel whereas woods will be more effective by being positioned either opposite or just inside the left heel.

It may be necessary to adjust the ball position depending on the lie of the ball; for example, if the ball was sitting on a bare lie it would be advisable to move it more towards the centre of the stance ensuring a crisp downward contact on the ball. This would also be the case if the ball was resting in deep rough or was positioned on a down slope when effective ball contact is very important. On the other hand, if the ball was sitting up particularly well on the ground or if a high-flighted shot was

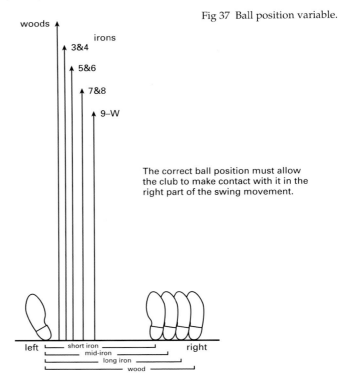

Fig 37 Ball position variable.

The correct ball position must allow the club to make contact with it in the right part of the swing movement.

required, then the player would position the ball forward and more opposite the left heel. In all cases the golfer must be fully aware of the way that the swing works so that in understanding that irons need to be struck with a more downward blow than woods they can appreciate the importance of ball position.

It is now fairly obvious that the importance of a correct grip and set-up fundamentals cannot be overstressed. Without these being achieved proficiently, the chances of any golfer playing controlled and consistent golf are likely to be severely limited. There are always exceptions, and it is not appropriate to say that golf cannot be played successfully, or, more importantly, enjoyed if these fundamentals are not a part of a player's golfing disciplines. They are, however, important enough for the best players in the

world to continually check out, as their first line of defence should their play deteriorate. Also golf coaches will emphasize these points to all golfers from the mere beginner to the most accomplished player.

Players should dedicate a large amount of their practice time to establishing routines that make integrating these fundamentals into their personal games an easy task. Only by repetition will the correct aspects become more natural – achieve this and the golf swing becomes a far more simple, effective and reliable action.

The Swing

A successful swing movement can be summed up as one that works both consistently and effectively and allows a player to maintain a standard of play that satisfies their own

Fig 38 The swing.

(a) A square alignment and good posture, set up the swing.

(b) The takeaway is on an inside path, with the club shaft parallel to the ball to target line.

(c) The swing is on plane at the top of the back swing.

(d) At impact, the angles of the body are maintained, but the hips have cleared to the left.

ambitions. Golfers throughout the world are continually seeking to improve their golfing proficiency whether it be through professional coaching, reading books, watching videos, observing the world's top players on television or just grasping a tip at the local clubhouse bar before their next round of golf.

If we accept that there is no perfect golf swing that will suit everybody, how does a player go about finding or developing one that suits him or her personally? Each golfer has a style that is best suited to their individual characteristics – physique, mental strengths and natural co-ordination. If a player can develop a swing that takes most advantage of these natural attributes and can be kept simple and effective, then there is the greatest chance of achieving success as a golfer.

Let us look at what are accepted swing fundamentals and how players must adapt these to best suit their individual needs.

Swing Plane

Many golfing philosophers believe that if golf was simply a matter of swinging the clubhead straight back and up and then returning it on a straight down and through path, it would be a relatively simple matter to contact the ball in a manner that would send the ball directly to the target. That is not, however, how the swing action works. A golfer stands sideways onto the ball, and at a given distance from the ball dependent upon the length of the shaft of the club being used. This means that the swing action moves on an inclined angle or plane. This swing plane has two facets – direction of the swing and angle of approach to the ball. Direction is the most important for without control of this factor the game of golf is almost impossible to play well. The angle at which the club approaches the ball does not so much affect accuracy, but does have a fairly profound effect upon the distance the ball travels, as the trajectory of the ball flight is fairly well dominated by it. It is an accepted fact that most successful swing movements incorporate a swing path that travels on a slightly inside to square to inside swing path as illustrated below.

The swing plane can be referred to as flat if it travels around and behind the body at

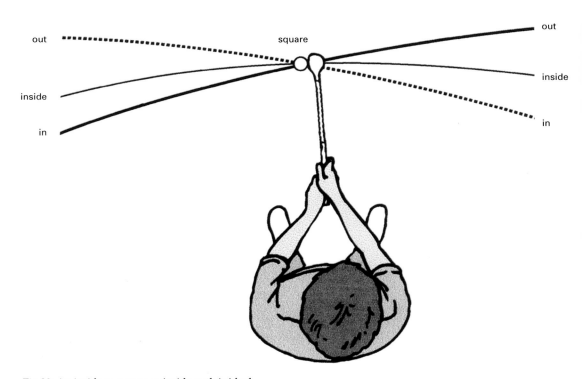

Fig 39 An inside to square to inside path is ideal.

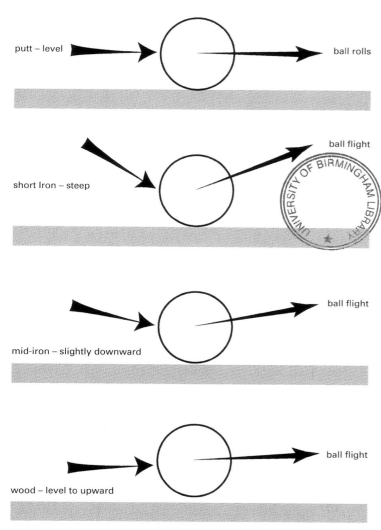

putt – level ▶ ← ball rolls

short Iron – steep ▶ ← ball flight

mid-iron – slightly downward ▶ ← ball flight

wood – level to upward ▶ ← ball flight

Fig 40 The angle of approach of the clubhead varies for each club.

criterion for a successful and accurate golf shot – the downswing movement dictates the direction and angle of approach to the ball. No matter in which position the backswing is completed – flat or upright – it is the following downward movement that really matters. So many golfers strive for a perfect backswing position only to miss out on the fact that unless they can return the clubhead to the impact position correctly from the top of the swing, their efforts are, to all intents and purposes, relatively wasted. Developing an efficient downswing movement is far more effective for the player than making a pretty looking backswing. This is illustrated by many top class professionals who appear to have rather unorthodox movements during their backswing, but are able to re-route the swing path of the clubhead during the downswing, and gain very effective results indeed. As a player uses the longer clubs and the length of each shaft increases, it will be necessary to stand further from the ball at address, and the posture to become far more upright, hence the swing plane will become flatter naturally without the player having to make any swing adjustments.

The angle of approach of the clubhead to the ball is affected by the player's posture and swing plane fundamentals (see Fig 41). Too steep an angle of approach can make the swing arc lose much of its width, and there is a consequential loss of power, whereas too shallow an angle of approach will tend to cause the clubhead to contact the ball incorrectly so that control and ball striking qualities are diminished.

It is clear how closely related the swing plane, swing path and angle of approach are, and how they can affect the factors that influence the flight of the ball. A

too shallow an angle. An upright swing plane is one where the club moves upward at a more vertical angle with the club being positioned above the neck or back of the head at the top of the backswing. Basic geometry would indicate that the flatter movement should make achieving an inside downswing path more easily than the upright swing plane, which works nearer to the vertical axis and could, in

instances, lead to the downswing movement being on a more outward rather than inward path.

A flatter, more inside swing plane will deliver the clubhead to the ball on a shallower angle of approach, whereas the upright version will certainly create a steeper angle of attack into the ball. It is worth noting at this point that many golfers misunderstand the essential

51

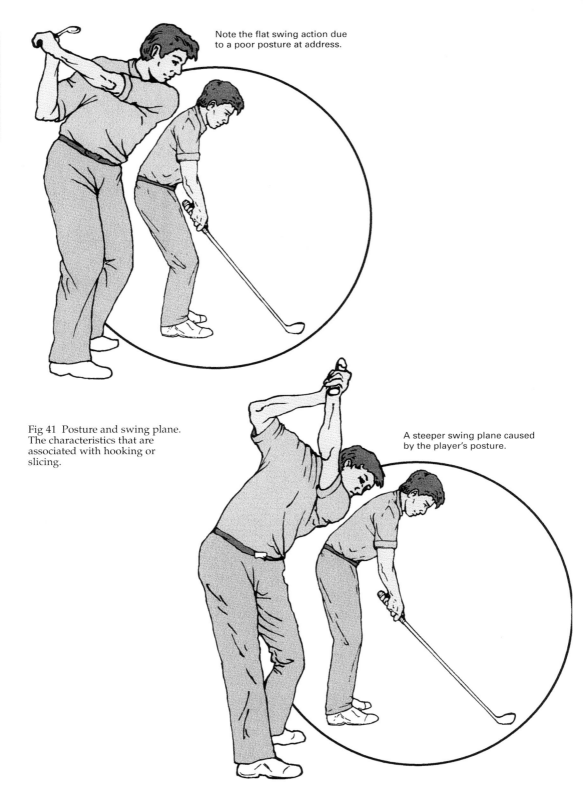

Note the flat swing action due to a poor posture at address.

Fig 41 Posture and swing plane. The characteristics that are associated with hooking or slicing.

A steeper swing plane caused by the player's posture.

flatter plane results in the ball flying on a lower trajectory, with more opportunity for a player to draw the ball and consequently increase the potential distance that the ball travels with each shot, whereas an upright plane will tend to flight the ball with a higher trajectory with increased back spin and although offering greater accuracy, may limit the potential distance the ball travels.

The Movement Golf Swing

So far we have looked at the set-up fundamentals, and how they influence factors such as swing plane. Given that a player is able to understand the importance of these fundamentals it is far easier to appreciate the movements that make up a correct and efficient golf swing.

The swing can be described as a backward and upward movement of the clubhead, pulling the hands and arms behind and around the body, and encouraging the shoulders to turn with a powerful rotational movement away from the target. This leads to a rotation of the hips which, in turn, pulls the left knee slightly forward and inward, with the left heel rising slightly for some players. As this rotation or coil is taking place there should be a natural weight shift towards and into the right side of the body whilst at the same time, the wrists cock upwards setting the club shaft at an approximate 90 degree angle in relation to the left forearm. This movement of the hands, arms and club form the player's swing plane, which at the top of the backswing should have the club shaft positioned more or less over the right shoulder. The downswing commences with a forward weight shift initiated by the lower body, and the hips and upper body unwind to the left as the right side turns through and towards the target. As the weight

shift moves onto the left side the wrist angle formed during the backswing straightens or releases, and there is a natural rotation of the hands and forearms, creating clubhead speed and the timing of the golf swing. Just before and at impact there is a cohesion of all the movements, allowing the swing path, club face and power factors to all connect together to create what should be the perfect golf shot. The turn to the left continues with the right side moving fully through, so that at the completion of the swing the majority of the player's weight is on the left foot, and the upper body is perfectly balanced over the hips and legs. The arms have swung around and over the left shoulder, and the player is facing the target.

The basic swing movements of each golfer will vary from player to player depending upon natural ability, but all successful ones will integrate good balance, co-ordination and timing. Most golfers should be careful not to make their swings too mechanical as endeavouring to achieve exact pre-defined swing positions can hinder rather than help their golf. Hand and eye co-ordination and good feel are important factors for all golfers. The more a player appreciates the qualities of their own individual swing movement, and works to minimize the effect of their weaknesses the greater the opportunity for improvement in technical terms.

The Dynamics of the Swing

Having outlined the individual movements within the swing action it is worth considering the actual way in which they interact with one another – the dynamics of the golf swing. The swing itself is all about the capabilities of the golfer to build up sufficient speed of the clubhead to propel

the acceptable distance towards a given target.

Movement and energy are very important in a player's swing and therefore, weight transfer, leverage and release sum up the dynamic movement of the golf swing. Even at address the golfer should never be stationary, but should be priming the dynamic nature of the swing by either waggling the club, possibly flexing the knees, glancing to the target or any other effective movement that allows a golfer to commence the backswing in a powerful and rotational fashion. It can perhaps be compared to a tennis player waiting to return a serve – always moving and ready to react that little bit more quickly and efficiently. So the dynamic nature of the golf swing is evident relatively early on, even before the actual swing itself commences. Once the clubhead movement really gets under way there is a build-up of energy and power. Although the backward movement of the clubhead is initiated by the hands, there is almost simultaneously a slight lateral movement of the body toward and into the right side. This combines with a rotation of the shoulders, hips and knees which in essence creates a coiling effect as the upper body turns relatively freely ahead and against a slower moving lower body. The shoulders should turn to a full 90 degree position, the hips to about 45 degrees and knees slightly less again. The club shaft should point parallel to the ball to target line. The point at which each golfer commences the downswing varies quite considerably dependent upon swing style, but in almost all cases there is no deliberate pause at the top of the backswing. Once the forward movement is initiated by the lower body shifting laterally towards the target, the dynamic nature of the golf swing becomes

Fig 42 A dynamic swing movement.

(a) At address the player prepares for the dynamic nature of the swing.

(b) The clubhead leads the hands into the backswing movement and the body begins to turn.

(c) The wrists are set and the upper body winds up against the lower body.

(d) At the top of the backswing the player's shoulders are fully turned and the weight is correctly behind the ball.

Fig 42 A dynamic swing movement *(continued).*

(e) The lower body provides the power and leverage in the downswing.

(f) At impact, the hands, arms and body return to a dynamic position.

(g) The momentum of the swing pulls the player's body through.

(h) The full unwinding of the body is evident with the weight positioned solidly onto the left side.

Fig 43 There is no more dynamic a player than Tiger Woods.

clearly evident. The lower body is working ahead of the upper body with the clubhead following behind. The weight shift leads to a re-rotation and unwinding of the body back towards the target and then to the left. This combined with the arms catching up with the upper body, and the correct uncocking of the 90 degree wrist and club shaft angle, provides the release of the golf swing when the clubhead is meant to be moving at its fastest and most effective speed. At impact the club, hands, arms and body are all in perfect alignment, and the ball is struck sweetly from the centre of the club face. The momentum and speed of the movement cause the golfer to continue the follow through so that the hands finish high and over the left shoulder, with the weight solidly onto the left side of the body. The whole movement is dominated by the correct balance and co-ordination of all the combined elements of the swing. Should any one part overpower the others the chances of maximum effectiveness are reduced. The hips and legs provide the real drive and power of the swing, the hands and arms, the potential to convert the acceleration and release.

Kinetic Movement

Whilst looking at the dynamics of the golf swing it may be useful to briefly describe the motions within the movement that are referred to as the kinetic elements. What actually creates the drive and force within the golf swing is the interaction between the powerful coil of the body, and the transmission of energy through the arms and hands along the club shaft to the clubhead itself. Many scientific studies have revealed detailed information regarding the search for power within the golf swing – none more detailed than *The*

Search for the Perfect Golf Swing by Cochran and Stobbs. Most agree that the swing is basically a double pendulum, with the arms and club shaft making up two levers, and the wrist, the hinge in the middle. The whole swing works around a swing centre or pivot point, this being the player's spine. The rotation and coil of the body, the slight lateral movement towards the right side and the cocking of the wrists combine to help the player create a wide swing arc with maximum power potential. The player has created resistance from ground upwards, and this resistance once released, will work back down towards the ground, so bear in mind the importance of a stable, solid stance and good footwork throughout the swing. The downswing reversal of weight transfer and the uncoiling of the body to the left, combined with the correctly timed uncocking of the wrists whilst the club remains on a correct swing plane and path, make up the 'secret' elements of power golf. The hands do not provide the power; they transfer the potential energy through the club shaft to the clubhead. All this must occur whilst the golfer maintains control of the club face and the ability to consistently repeat the swing movement.

Distance and Directional Factors

All golfers are driven by the desire to hit the ball as far as they are able. The major question is what is that distance capability? There is really no exact way of being sure, although the swing movement itself has to incorporate five important elements if any player is to capitalize on their full potential. This distance factor is also closely allied with direction as no player gains greatly if long hitting is combined with poor accuracy.

The five factors are:

• Speed of clubhead.
• Path of swing.
• Position of club face.
• Contact of the ball on the club face.
• Angle of the downswing approach.

Speed of the Clubhead

The speed that a player is able to generate through the clubhead is determined by certain human factors – strength and flexibility, swing technique and co-ordination of the swing movements. Non-human factors are the length of the club shaft, loft of the club face and the physical makeup of the golf club itself such as graphite shafts, metal heads, swing weight. The latter of these two elements is touched upon in the equipment section.

Strength is a very important factor in golf but is not as vital as it may appear. To use two examples that might illustrate this point. Firstly, many men imagine that their strength will ensure the potential for long hitting. Not so, for sheer physical strength counts for very little if the person has poor flexibility, muscular co-ordination or a poor swing technique. Without flexibility or muscular co-ordination the whole swing movement will be disjointed and maximum speed may well be at the wrong point in the swing, either before or even after impact. Even with strength and co-ordination, but with poor swing technique the control and consistency will not be possible. Secondly, lady golfers and juniors have less physical strength than most men, but with sufficient strength, good muscular co-ordination and acceptable technique even a slightly built player can generate effective clubhead speed and hit the ball long distances.

So strength and flexibility have to be adequate to allow a player to utilize the other factors that play such an important role in the overall swing action. Swing technique would appear to be obvious, but does not mean to suggest that everything has to be of a textbook style. Good repetitive fundamentals will give a player a major opportunity to strike the ball hard and effectively. Co-ordination is a vital element and enhances the dynamics of the swing movement. Good co-ordination is not just a muscular action, it is a combination of both mental and physical attributes. Many golfers are natural hand and eye co-ordinated people, but for those who find ball games far more unnatural, golf is a game that will require greater perseverance and effort to produce the effective results that they desire.

Overly mechanical movements rarely produce consistent clubhead speed or ball-striking qualities.

Swing Path and Position of Club Face

It is important to look at these two factors together as they are so closely related that it would be impossible to deal with one

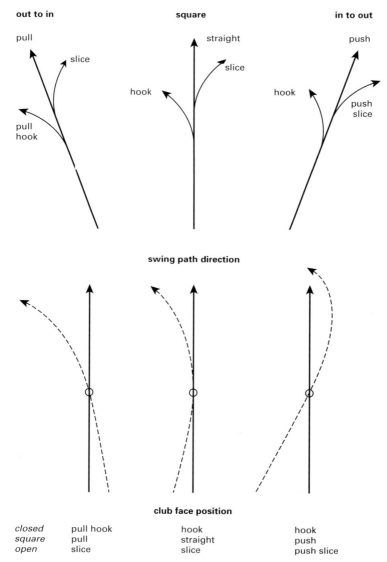

Fig 44 Swing path, clubhead and ball flight characteristics.

58

without really referring to the other. The swing path, club face and ball flight information illustrated will, hopefully, clarify how the path of the swing and position of the club face in relation to that path are clearly related to the direction in which the ball travels. It is important to appreciate that the ball will not travel in a straight direction all that often. In most cases the ball is spinning either to the left or to the right, and as such this spin will cause the ball to deviate during its flight – in the direction of the spin, so that it is possible for a ball to commence its journey to the left of the target, and yet the left to right spin, produced by the player's clubhead contact on the ball at impact, is strong enough to make the ball move on a curved flight so that it finally finishes its journey to the right of the target. In this instance the player would have sliced their golf shot.

Both the swing path and club face position have an influence on the direction that the ball starts in, but all golfers should be aware that it is the club face that is the dominant factor. If for example, two players had the same swing path and let us use an out to in one for this illustration, and player A's club face was only slightly open to the swing path, whereas player B's was far more open, then A's ball would travel leftward for a longer period of time and distance than player B's before the left to right spin imparted at impact made the ball move its direction to the right of its original path. Player B's ball would not only move to the right sooner than A's because the left to right spin was more excessive due to the more open club face at impact, but it would continue to travel further right for the rest of its journey, with a relatively high loss of forward momentum, due to that spin.

If we now take player (A) and add the clubhead speed factor we can further illustrate an important, yet relatively simple golfing fact. If (A) makes two identical golf swings except that the first swing creates a greater clubhead speed than the second, the ball on the first shot will start out nearer to the path of the swing than will that of the second shot. This is simply because the greater velocity of the clubhead on the first shot will cause the ball to be slightly more influenced by the swing path than that of the second where the clubhead speed being less will allow the open face to have more of an effect at the impact position. To summarize, the greater the clubhead speed the more the ball will be influenced by the path of the clubhead, the lesser the clubhead speed the more the direction of the club face affects the starting direction of the ball. This is often not understood by golfers who, if they were aware of these facts, might appreciate why the more powerful clubs like a number 1 wood or 3 iron are generally more difficult to control in terms of direction than the lofted irons such as a 9 iron or pitching wedge. Longer shafts help create more clubhead speed potential, but at the same time create more difficulty with regard to swing path and club face control, whereas the shorter irons are easier to swing on a correct path, and the slower clubhead speed helps the average player gain far greater club face control.

All golfers should at least have a sufficient understanding of the influence of the swing path and ball flight factors to allow them to evaluate the quality of their shots. This offers them the opportunity to seek to rectify or minimize any problems before the next shot, or to repeat or attempt to repeat the movements that created the previous good shot.

Ball Contact

All golfers have experienced the pleasure of hitting the ball right out of the centre or sweet spot of the club face, and all have endured the frustration of a mishit shot. Many do not appreciate that a well-timed, centred shot will travel quite a bit further than an off-centred one.

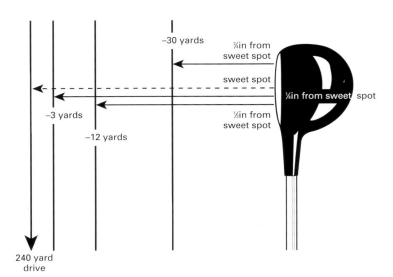

Fig 45 Off-centre hits. Should the club face not be square, then a more glancing blow will further reduce the distance the ball travels.

59

The illustration on the previous page was taken from a study carried out many years ago and published in a book called *The Search for the Perfect Swing* by Cochran and Stobbs, and shows the loss of distance on a shot when the ball is not hit from the sweet spot of the club face. This loss will vary from player to player and will depend upon the club used, but it does serve as a useful guide.

Angle of Approach

This has already been fairly extensively covered under swingplane, but suffice it to say the correct angle of approach allows for a maximum potential of clubhead speed to be delivered onto the ball at impact.

There are other factors that influence the distance and direction that the player hits the ball, but these are generally not ones within their control, such as weather – wind and rain, ground conditions on the course – dry or wet, equipment, altitude and possibly others. Most importantly, a golfer must concentrate on the five main factors whatever the circumstances.

Ball Control

Ball control has to be the prime factor in playing golf whether it is when striking a perfect long drive off the tee or tapping in a relatively simple 3ft putt. Ball control can be described as the ability of a golfer to hit the ball to a given target, and then ultimately into the hole. It matters not whether the golfer plays their shots high or low, slice, fade, draw or hook. What counts is where it finishes. If this can be achieved in a controlled, consistent manner and in a regular way, then the golfer is a match for anyone.

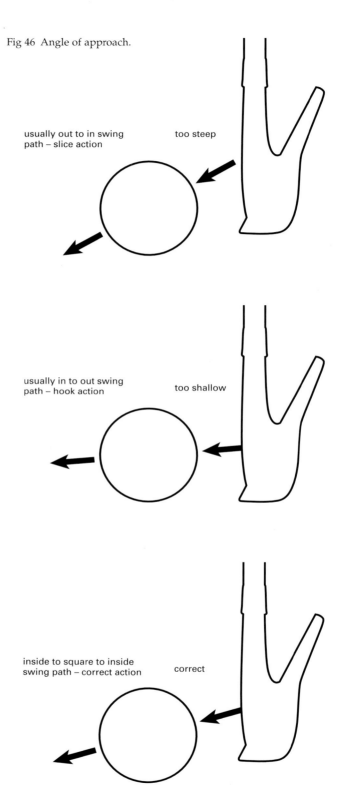

Fig 46 Angle of approach.

usually out to in swing path – slice action

too steep

usually in to out swing path – hook action

too shallow

inside to square to inside swing path – correct action

correct

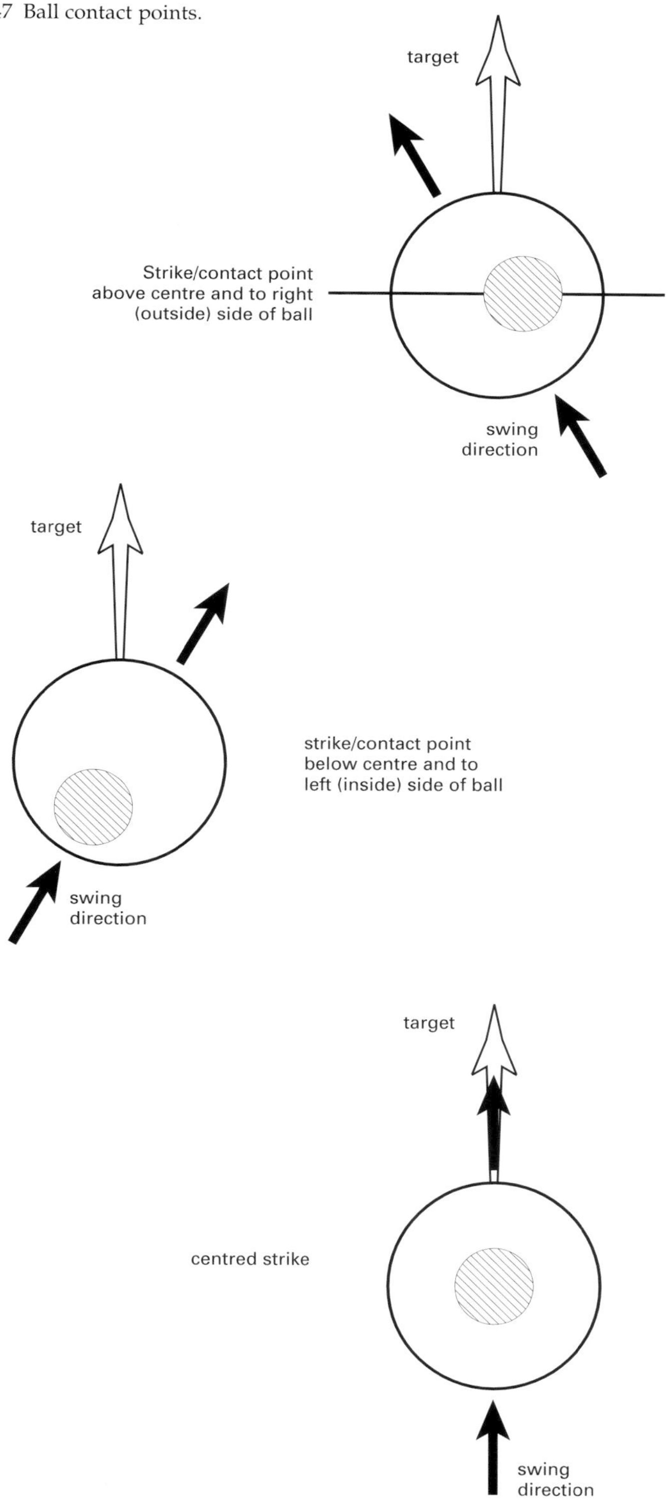

Fig 47 Ball contact points.

target

Strike/contact point
above centre and to right
(outside) side of ball

swing
direction

target

strike/contact point
below centre and to
left (inside) side of ball

swing
direction

target

centred strike

swing
direction

The more superior a player's ball-striking ability the wider the range of shots playable in a greater variety of circumstances. Low handicap amateurs and professionals possess these skills because their techniques and practice routines all help them develop greater depth within their golf games. Without good ball control they would not be the players they are, with it they are capable of achieving very low scores indeed.

The essence of ball control is to combine control of the swing path with that of the club face, plus the angle of approach of the clubhead. The ball can only fly in three directions – straight, to the right, or to the left, but there are many variations on how it travels to its destination. Many decades ago the famous South African golfer Bobby Locke hit all his full shots with a hook. In more recent years the American Lee Trevino played very successfully with a pronounced fade, almost a slice, Jack Nicklaus with a fade, Seve Ballesteros with a draw, and John Daly hits it straight. All very different, yet they all have the one great quality of superb ball control.

All golfers should work to improve their weaker elements, but they should not forget that all their efforts are likely to have limited success if they are unable to develop and improve their ball control skills. Observe golfers on a driving range – mostly the ball flies in such a variety of directions and at different heights, that a player has little chance of controlling it well enough to make a decent score on the golf course. Good swing technique should not only enable the golfer to contact the ball correctly at impact, but should offer them the opportunity to hit the ball with the shape of shot they desire and towards the given target. Practice helps to develop this ball control, and should be put into effective use on the golf course itself.

61

Simplicity and Routines

Whichever way we go about playing the game of golf there appears to be many bumps or hollows to knock us off our path. Nothing about the game is consistently easy. Each game brings about a new challenge, sometimes we can hit our tee shots just perfectly, yet putting lets us down, on another occasion the long irons seem simple to play, yet a straightforward chip fails us. This is golf! It is not a simple game, but it is important to keep it as simple as possible. The sensible golfer uses a coach to do most of the thinking and then uses his time to make practice and play as effective as possible. Observe today's golfing heroes, Tiger Woods, Nick Faldo and Ian Woosnam – it always appears so easy to them. Follow their example, keep it effective, keep it simple!

When delving into the technical aspects of the golf swing a golfer is usually liable to take on board too much information in too short a period of time. This is where much confusion and misunderstanding arises. All players, at whatever level, should be fully aware of their personal capabilities and in setting out on a game or swing development phase they should plan how they intend to go about it, and organize a structure involving, coaching, practice and course play. The availability of time or lack of it will determine how the plan is put together. The player's enjoyment of practice and ability to maintain efficient concentration will influence the way the plan is structured. Players need to be honest with themselves and to accept their limitations whether these are personal, financial, or have to do with the availability of coaching, practice facilities or perhaps commitment to competitive golf or on-course play. These aspects are covered in more detail later in the book.

Golf, like many other things in life, is most effective when players establish a routine. A good pre-shot routine, from focusing on the target, taking hold of the golf club, right through to the clubhead waggle or look towards the target are all important factors in contributing to a successful shot. Routine means what it says – usual, regular, repetitive – this is a vital point that golfers fail to appreciate. It has been stated that a human being requires 1,000 repetitions of a new movement before it becomes an instinctive one. Assuming that any golfer is capable of repeating the same swing movement 1,000 times –

which in most cases would be over a number of days, then we begin to appreciate the difficulty of changing and making effective swing movements. On a lighter note, most golfers, given that they understand the necessity to keep swing change relatively simple, are quite capable of an affective and productive change if they set themselves a realistic time schedule. It is not uncommon for players to actually find that the swing change becomes increasingly effective and rewarding as they have felt more comfortable and confident, usually after a period of time that has allowed them to relax from the more intense technical details and slip into a more subconscious and more natural mode.

Change is often very difficult and golfers must accept this. The game requires a great deal of rhythm, feel and repetition. They are all closely related – one will not be as effective as it might be without the support of the others. Good golfing routines help build consistency through rhythm, feel and repetition. Watch the top players – every shot has a routine pattern whether it is the pre-shot build-up or the actual time taken to swing the golf club. Learn from these fine players – change will be easier, more enjoyable and ultimately, more effective.

6
DEPARTMENTS OF THE GAME

The actual act of striking a golf ball can be broken down into two main departments – the full swing including driving, fairway woods, long and middle iron play and the short game including pitching, chipping, bunker play and putting.

Full Swing Shots

Swing technique has already been covered, but it can only be of benefit to expand on how this is applied to all full shots and how particular departments of the long game need certain technical adaptations. The essence of a good long game is to allow a player to hit off the tee successfully, onto the fairway and then to hit the approach shot onto the green as close to the flagstick as possible. The more regularly a golfer achieves this function the easier the game is to play and the greater the potential for lower scores.

Wood Play

The Tee Shot

Technology has taken the basic wooden golf club and offered an array of options all made of materials that bear no resemblance to wood itself. There is no doubting the playing advantages of most of these high-tech options, but whichever of these the golfer chooses, the task in hand remains the same – basically it is the golfer who must play the shot itself.

The tee shot should in reality be the easiest full shot to play.

The teeing ground is level, the grass cut short. The ball can be positioned anywhere between the two tee markers and the player is allowed to tee the ball up on a peg. What more could a player ask for! Yet most golfers will comment that their driving from a tee is the most erratic and frustrating part of their game. Much of this is due to a simple lack of understanding as to how the drive differs from other full swing shots. The drive is the only golf shot where the player is actually swinging the clubhead in an upward direction. In other words the golfer's swing has passed the lowest point of the swing arc and has commenced its journey up into the follow-through position.

Two factors need to be appreciated by the golfer. Firstly, assuming that a tee shot is being played with a number 1 wood – the driver, the club's loft, that is, the elevation of the club face and the reason why the ball gets into the air, is usually between 9 and 11 degrees. This is a fairly limited amount of loft and is only going to help the golfer get the correct flight and trajectory if the ball is struck by the club face at the correct point in the swing. With this limited amount of loft it would be very difficult for any golfer to hit consistently successful drives if the ball was struck on the downswing, that is, a descending blow.

Secondly, the fact that the ball is teed up means that the clubhead must strike the ball just as the upswing commences. A golfer must adapt the set-up position to suit the tee shot.

• The driver has the longest golf shaft of any club and so a player stands at his furthest from the ball at address. This shaft length creates a more upright body posture for a golfer, which together with the distance the player stands away from the ball creates a natural, shallow swing plane and wide arc. This is ideal for sweeping the ball off the tee peg at impact.
• The ball should be teed up opposite the left heel or instep. The stance will be slightly wider than with any other club to help the player maintain good balance, particularly as successful tee shots should always incorporate maximum body rotation and coil to produce the required powerful wide swing arc.
• The weight should be distributed to favour the right foot – approximately 60 per cent right side, 40 per cent left side.
• The hands may appear a little behind the ball at address – this is not uncommon even when observing some top professionals. The forward ball position creates this idiosyncrasy.

The swing movement should incorporate:

• A smooth, low takeaway of the clubhead.
• A good rotation of the shoulders with the weight moving comfortably into the right side.
• The club should be in a controlled position at the top of the backswing.
• The downswing should commence with a smooth

Fig 48 The tee shot.

(a)

(b)

(c)

(a) The address position sets the angle of the spine on a slight tilt – this is maintained throughout the swing movement until after impact.

(b) The ball is positioned opposite the left heel, the hands appear a little behind the ball.

(c) A full turn and controlled position at the top set up the downswing.

transition from the top of the backswing – do not attempt to hit too aggressively from the top otherwise control and power will be lost.
• Allow the clubhead to swing freely, building up speed at it approaches the impact position.
• Sweep the ball off the tee peg.
• Turn the body towards the target as the weight is transferred fully onto the left side during the follow-through.
• Maintain balance and good rhythm throughout the swing movement.

Not all golfers have the ability to use a number 1 wood consistently, and so many use what is termed a fairway driver or number 2 wood. Some, due to swing weaknesses use a 3, 4 or even 5 wood off the tee. These woods are designed with more loft on the club face – 12 to 21 degrees – so that they prove far easier for players to hit consistently well. Whether it is due to a lack of technical skill or because the golfer wishes to play for position off the tee, for example, a dogleg hole or a par 3, the additional loft of these woods usually means that a couple of adjustments should be made by the golfer:

• Firstly, tee the ball lower – the clubhead on lofted woods is shallower and has a lower centre of gravity to help get the ball more airborne.
• Secondly, the ball is struck at the bottom of the swing arc as to strike it on the upswing would only exaggerate the club's effective loft, sending the ball too high in most instances.

A point worth remembering is that the golfer is seeking to drive the ball forward with a powerful trajectory off the tee. The ball must carry its maximum potential through the air with additional roll on landing adding to the overall distance the ball is driven. This roll is important for the amateur player as every extra yard is often critical, whereas the tournament professional generally prefers to fly the ball higher and longer through the air gaining the advantage of greater ball control overall.

Lofted/Fairway Woods

Fairway woods can be played similarly to the way a player sets up to execute the lofted wood from off a tee peg. Once again the important factor is that the ball is

best struck at the lowest point in the swing arc and not on either the downswing or upswing. Key factors are:

1. The ball is positioned either opposite or just inside the left heel.
2. The hands will be level with the ball at address and should not be pushed forward or appear behind the ball.
3. The stance is slightly narrower than for a tee shot.
4. The weight is distributed approximately 55 per cent right foot, 45 per cent left foot.
5. Make a full flowing swing and sweep the ball away – do not try to help the ball into the air. Maintain a wide effective swing arc.
6. Complete a smooth balanced follow-through.

Lofted woods are particularly useful for amateur golfers when playing shots from the semi-rough. Given that the ball is sitting in a suitable lie the design of the lofted wood will help get the ball airborne quickly. The wider more rounded head of a lofted wood slides over and through the semi-rough more easily than a long iron and is far less susceptible to getting tangled

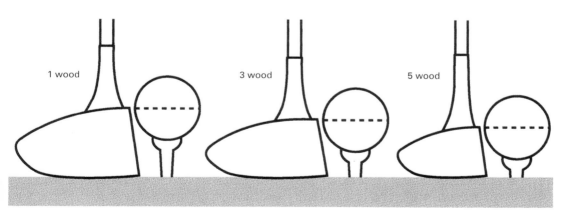

Fig 49 The centre of the ball is teed-up level with the top of each wood head. The deeper the clubface the higher the ball is teed-up.

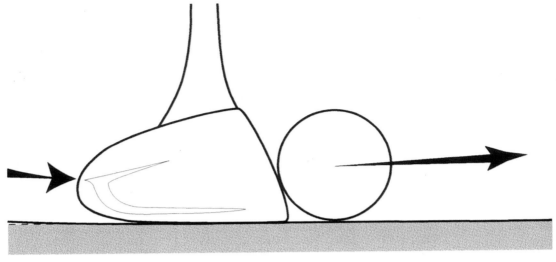

ball swept off turf due to low,
wide angle of approach

Fig 50 Impact for woods.

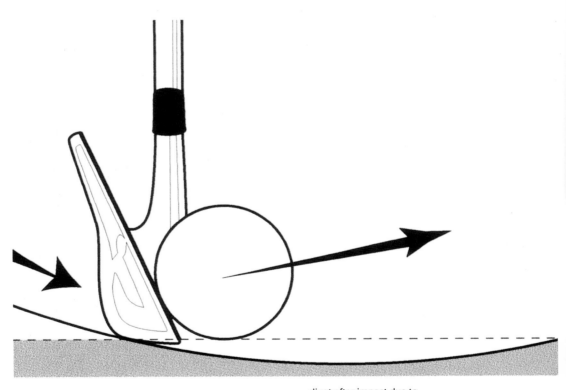

divot after impact due to
downward angle of approach

Fig 51 Impact for irons.

up in the grass. This can be a tremendous benefit in course management terms and will offer far more consistency and length of shots for most golfers.

Lofted wood can be a great ally to the amateur golfer, particularly those with a high handicap, ladies, seniors or junior players. Make good use of them and don't be frightened to try even a 6 or 7 wood option as these utility woods are designed to make the game far easier and more enjoyable for the players with poor long iron ability.

Iron Play

Long Irons

Long irons prove to be the weakest area for most average golfers. Many would in fact score better during a round of golf if they ignored their longer irons and settled for either a lofted fairway wood or positional play with a mid iron. Yet with the correct understanding of how to play the longer irons and a reasonable amount of practice and confidence building, all golfers could at least improve or develop their current abilities with these clubs.

Key features to long irons are:

1. The ball will be positioned just inside the left heel – it benefits some players to position it exactly as if they were playing a lofted wood shot.
2. The hands will be level or slightly in front of the ball at address.
3. The stance is at least shoulder width apart, possibly slightly wider.
4. The weight distribution should be approximately 55 per cent right foot 45 per cent left foot.
5. The posture will be fairly tall or upright due to the longer shaft of the irons.
6. Make a smooth, low takeaway movement and concentrate on turning the shoulders to a full position. The weight should favour the right side of the body; the swing arc should be as wide as possible.
7. The transition of movement into the downswing should be smooth and unhurried.
8. As the clubhead speed builds during the downswing the player should allow the body to turn leftwards, the weight to move towards and onto the left side and there should be a feeling of sweeping the ball off the top of the turf.

Good long iron players will contact the ball whilst on their downswing movement, thus creating a long, shallow divot, but high handicapped players, seniors, ladies and juniors may well benefit by keeping the execution of this shot identical to that of a lofted wood.
9. A full, balanced follow-through position with the weight transferred smoothly onto the left foot will encourage a good impact position.

Players must resist the temptation to hit too aggressively at the ball with their longer irons. Many seem to feel that the longer shafted, less lofted irons must be hit harder than the short or mid irons but this is not true, and in fact good swing speed and rhythm will invariably be of greater benefit than a forced effort. Also golfers seem to feel that they must help the ball to get into the air by endeavouring to scoop or lift it upward with the club face at impact. This is perhaps the major error of the average player, for as they add this extra effort during their downswing movement they are, in effect, forcing the clubhead past the hands far too early, which can only lead to the hands being positioned behind the clubhead at impact. In effect this means that the ball is being struck at the commencement of the upstroke and, in most instances, the bottom edge of the club face will make contact with the ball causing it to be topped or hit low with no real distance or control. Some shots may well be hit fat or heavy as the clubhead contacts the ground before it reaches the ball, this causes the golfer to take a divot prior to impact which leads to a complete mishit or scuffed shot that runs feebly along the ground.

The player must have the hands at least level with the ball or preferably slightly in front at impact, and as such must have the confidence to swing in a way that allows the clubhead to return to the impact position whereby the loft elevates the ball correctly into the air.

The Mid- and Short Irons

Generally most golfers have enough technical ability to hit the short irons (8–SW) and mid irons (5–7) reasonably consistently. These irons have relatively lofted club faces and the shaft length is short enough for a player to feel well in control.

The position of the ball in relation to the left heel is one of personal preference. One school of thought is to keep the ball position a consistent distance inside the left heel, and depending on the club selected, to vary the width of the stance by moving the right foot further outward. The other is to keep the feet a relatively consistent distance apart and to move the ball position progressively nearer to the centre of the stance as the irons becomes shorter and more lofted. There is no one particular way – each golfer should experiment until a satisfactory preference is settled on.

Key features in short and mid iron play are:

1. The shorter shafted irons make it necessary for the player to stand closer to the ball and with a

Fig 52 Long- and mid-iron play.

(a) The ball is positioned inside the left heel.

(b) The body turns behind the ball, the weight is on the inside of the right foot.

(c) At impact the weight shifts onto the left side, the ball is squeezed forward.

(d) A full follow-through with the body facing the target.

more 'tilted over' posture at set-up.

2. The hands are level or just in front of the ball at set-up.

3. The stance is about shoulder width – possibly slightly narrower with the shorter irons – the weight distribution approximately 50 per cent on both feet.

4. This set-up position and length of golf shaft ensures that the swing plane is more upright and that the arc of the swing is narrower than with the longer clubs.

5. The steeper backswing and downswing allow the player to hit downward into the back of the ball, creating increased backspin, improved ball control and accuracy. A divot should be taken after the clubhead strikes the ball, so in effect the clubhead does not contact the ground until the ball has already been struck.

6. At impact the hands will be slightly ahead of the ball – hence the ball first/divot to follow equation.

7. Good balance and rhythm will help to give consistent results – these clubs are referred to as the 'scoring clubs' in golf and it is imperative that the player not only hits the target with them, but better still gets the ball close to the hole.

Most golfers would improve their short- and mid-iron play by using them more often in practice. They are the ideal clubs to develop a good swing action and allow the golfer to build up a high level of swing feel and mental confidence, which they must then transfer to other areas of the game and onto the golf course itself.

The Short Game

Before looking more deeply into the different aspects of the short game it is a benefit to look at the role of the short game itself. No matter how good a driver of the ball a player is, or how well they play their approach shots to the green, all golfers miss the target on a regular basis. The top professionals average hitting twelve to fourteen greens in regulation, but may only hit eight or nine on a poor day. This means that to play to par they must be able to get their ball up and down in only two more shots. This, as most of us would have witnessed, they do with great regularity, and is the reason why they are able to play full-time golf successfully, and make a good living whilst doing so. Amateur golfers will hit between two to nine greens a round on average, depending upon their handicap level and their ability. This means that they will have far more opportunity and need to play short game recovery shots, and will have to rely on these skills far more often to help save their scores. Unfortunately few regular golfers seem to appreciate the need to practise their short game at all, let alone a sufficient amount to allow them some form of up and down average. The short game including putting can be up to 60–65 per cent of the score during a round of golf, yet most golfers prefer to spend the majority of their time practising their tee shots or long iron play, which may only really add up to about 25 per cent of the round. A golfer with a good short game is never out of a match, and no matter what standard of play experienced in the long game department, the player still retains the potential to score to an acceptable and satisfying level.

Chipping and Pitching

Let us first distinguish the difference between a chip and a pitch shot so that there is no confusion between the two different styles. The height at which the ball travels – the trajectory of the shot – dictates which term the shot falls into. A pitch has a relatively high flight, a chip has a low one. To expand a little more – the pitch shot will generally fly further through the air than it will roll along the ground, whereas a chip shot will roll further along the ground than the distance it travels through the air.

The choice of shot is very often at the discretion of the individual player, although there are some obvious instances where only one type of shot will be correct, for example, a 30yd shot over a sand bunker with pin position past that bunker. In this instance, only a pitch shot will allow the player to safely elevate the ball over the bunker and land the ball with enough control for it to roll only a limited amount of distance.

In most instances it is advisable for the average golfer to remember to always try to play a shot that rolls the ball whenever possible rather than lofts it, as a rolling shot is far easier to execute and far more reliable. In many cases the player should even consider putting from off the green's surface and ignore the chip or pitch shot altogether.

There are several other factors that influence the choice of shot for a player and these include the lie of the ball, the slope of the green, the position of the flag, the firmness and/or speed of the green, the wind and although not a physical factor, the confidence of the player in his own ability to execute the particular shot – some players prefer to play their favourite style of shot, one that is reliable and consistent in its results.

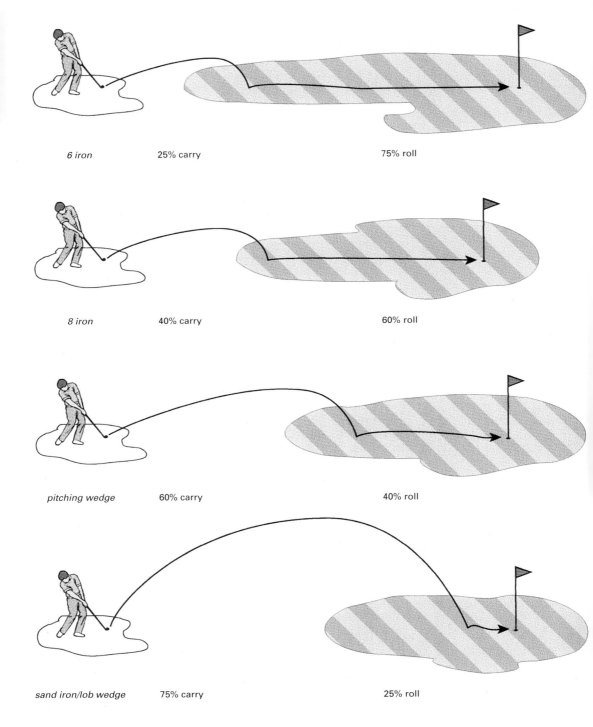

6 iron   25% carry   75% roll

8 iron   40% carry   60% roll

pitching wedge   60% carry   40% roll

sand iron/lob wedge   75% carry   25% roll

Fig 53 Typical pitch and chip – trajectory and ball carry distance.

Fig 54 The variations of club loft required to play pitch or chip shots.

The Chip Shot Fig 55

This should be the easiest of the two shots and one that all players should be able to play consistently and effectively. Unfortunately, many misunderstand the basic simplicity of its execution. Key features for chipping:-

The Set-up

• The width of the stance is narrower than usual – perhaps half to three-quarters the width of the shoulders.
• The left foot is pulled back slightly so that if a line were drawn across the toes of both feet, it would point slightly to the left of the target.
• The shoulders are square or parallel to the ball to target line.
• The ball is generally positioned in the centre of the stance.
• The weight distribution is favouring the left foot, perhaps 65 per cent left foot – 35 per cent right foot.
• The hands are forward of the ball at set-up – opposite the inside of the left leg.
• The centre of the chest is positioned either over or forward of the ball.
• Hold the club slightly down the handle for more control.

The Swing

• The swing movement is mainly from the arms and shoulders –
the wrists are relatively passive, the weight remains on the left side.
• The clubhead moves back on a slightly inside path, but has a relatively upright movement of the clubhead due to the weight being on the left side on address.
• The length of the backswing is relatively short – the clubhead rarely reaches even waist high.
• At impact the hands return to a position just in front of the ball, which, together with the weight remaining on the left side, allows the clubhead to make contact from a slightly descending angle of approach, so that the ball is in effect 'squeezed' against the turf by the club face.
• It is not necessary to take a divot with this shot, although the turf will be brushed after the ball

71

Fig 55 The chip shot.

(a)

(b)

(c)

(a) The ball is positioned well back in the stance, the weight is on the left side.

(b) The backswing is relatively short with minimal wrist action.

(c) The follow-through mirrors the backswing.

Fig 56 The pitch shot.

(a)

(b)

(a) The ball is inside the left heel and the weight slightly favours the left side.

(b) The open stance and wrist action set the club into position during the backswing.

(c) The follow-through finishes at about shoulder height.

(c)

has been contacted by the club face.

• The rhythm of the shot should be smooth, the balance remains on the left side and the head stays still until after impact.

• The follow through should be of about equal length to that of the backswing.

• On completion of the swing, the club face should not have passed the left hand, so that the left wrist remains relatively flat or straight. The club face should face the target.

A player should always endeavour to land the ball onto the green before it commences its roll, as this will at least offer a reliable landing area and give some guarantee of a consistent bounce on landing. It also helps a player's club selection and to get the mental picture and feel for the shot in hand. Although personal, club selection is best kept between the 6 iron to pitching wedge, with most players favouring a 7 or 8 iron for this type of shot. The club must elevate the ball just enough to land it onto the green's surface and then allow for the correct amount of roll up to the hole.

The Pitch Shot Fig 56

The pitch shot often causes golfers greater difficulty to play than the relatively simpler chip shot version. This is possibly because a longer swing is required which involves greater use of the hands and wrists, together with good co-ordination of the swing movements and the ability to elevate the ball more precisely over a limited distance.

The choice of clubs is more limited than with a chip shot with preference being placed on the pitching wedge, sand iron or lob wedge. The choice is dependent on the amount of height and control required for the shot in hand.

The Set-up

• The stance is narrower than usual and the left foot is pulled back slightly as with the chip shot.

• The shoulders are square or parallel to the ball to target line.

• The ball is positioned somewhere between the inside of the left heel and centre of the stance depending upon the type of trajectory required. The more forward the position of the ball the higher the flight of the shot.

• The weight distribution is about 55 per cent left side and 45 per cent right side depending upon the ball position and the trajectory of the shot required. For higher shots it may be beneficial to have the weight distributed on a 50/50 basis between the left and right foot.

• The centre of the chest and the hands are more or less opposite the ball.

• The club should be held a little down the handle for control and accuracy.

The Swing

• The swing movement incorporates more use of the wrists, which will set or cock upward during the backswing.

• On standard pitch shots the path of the clubhead is still slightly inside during the backswing. For more elevation an out to in swing path will add to the height of the shot.

• The hands will usually travel to about waist height during the backswing, but the wrist break will mean that the clubhead travels higher and on a steeper arc.

• The clubhead will return to the ball on a fairly steep angle of approach, with impact being just before the lowest point of the swing arc. The hands will be level or slightly forward of the ball at impact. Once again the player should feel as if the ball is

being 'squeezed' between the turf and the club face.

• The tuft will be brushed or a shallow divot taken just after impact.

• The rhythm must remain smooth; the weight favours the left side of the body and the head remains still until after impact.

• The follow-through should not incorporate any use of the wrist and as such will generally be of a slightly shorter length than the backswing. It is important that the left wrist does not bend or fold and that the left hand and forearm lead the clubhead.

• Upon completion of the swing the player's body and club face should look towards the target. If the club face rolls into a slightly closed position, not only could accuracy be sacrificed, but also the trajectory will be lower and the ball will roll more on landing.

Summing up Chip and Pitch Shots

More aspects of these two shots will be covered under the Specialist Skills section, but in the context of straightforward chip and pitch shots it is obvious that there are many similar principles. The shots do not vary as greatly in technique as some golfers imagine – it is mainly the weight distribution and wrist action that differentiates the two. The ball flight provides the obvious difference.

Good judgement will be improved by constructive practice, but this in itself is not enough. The player has to have a good visualization of the shot and the correct mental image plays a vital role in helping the player to choose which shot to play. By taking into account the lie, the location of the flagstick, the wind and the ground conditions, the player is building a picture of which shot will best suit the situation and which club must be selected to execute the shot correctly.

Fig 57 This practice drill allows the player to pitch over or to chip under the club shaft.

players use a stiffer, more mechanical style of technique, whilst others prefer a free-wristed flowing action. Some players prefer to use only one regular club for pitching and one for chipping, and to vary their style of shot as required, whilst others use one swing technique for each shot, but use a wide variety of clubs to vary the trajectory and control.

The clubhead must be accelerating through the impact position and the player must never try to help the ball into the air. These are two golden rules! Maintaining good rhythm and balance right through to the completion of the swing go a long way to creating a consistent, reliable style of play.

Bunker Play

Bunker play seems to be one department of the short game that frightens the average golfer, and yet when we watch tournament players they appear to find it one of the easiest shots to play well. Ironically it is the only shot in golf where the player does not actually have to hit the ball itself. A lack of understanding, poor technical skills and a low level of confidence all combine to limit a golfer's chance of success.

Before explaining the technical aspects of the swing it is important that all golfers understand the subtle advantages that bunker equipment can offer a player. A sand iron is designed with a bounce sole on the underside of the club so that it will not dig deeply into the sand – this is a unique feature, as the other irons in a set are designed so that the leading edge of the club face can dig into the ground, allowing the player to execute the correct and efficient shot through a downward angle of approach into the impact

Before playing the shot the player must create the necessary feel and so practice swings work in close harmony with these mental images. There are many individual interpretations of the short game technique. There is not a perfect ball position, or exact amount of wrist set that suits every player. Certain position. The sole or flange of the sand iron is inverted – the rear edge is lower than the leading edge, so that at impact with the sand, the back edge is creating this 'bounce' effect. The club slides through the sand creating a relatively long, shallow divot under the ball. The sand wedge is heavier than the other clubs, which also helps stabilize the club face on impact with the sand. Most sand irons will have 56 degrees of loft, although some players prefer to use one with up to 60 degrees of loft, so getting the ball into the air is not really a difficult task.

Standard or Splash Shot Fig 59

As this is a relatively easy shot to play then it would be advisable to keep the explanation simple and effective.

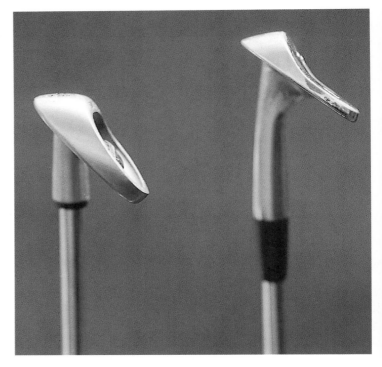

Fig 58 The sand wedge has a bounce sole or flange to prevent it digging into the sand too deeply.

The Set-up

• Set up with the feet and shoulders aiming to the left of the flagstick.
• A firm footing should be created by 'wriggling' the feet into the sand.
• The club face should be aimed towards the flagstick or even a little right of it. The face is 'open' to the body alignment and not only controls the direction of the shot, but also adds effective loft to the club for increased ball trajectory.
• The club should be gripped after set-up and club face are in position.
• In relation to the ball to target line the ball will appear well forward opposite the left instep, although in relationship to the alignment of the body the body is actually positioned inside the left heel.
• The weight should favour the left foot slightly.

• The hands should be positioned opposite the inside of the left leg and level with the ball.
• The body should be fairly relaxed with the clubhead positioned about 2in behind the ball, but above the sand so as not to incur a penalty shot under the Rules of Golf.

The Swing

• The length of the swing may vary from half-way back to almost a full swing position depending on how far away the flagstick is positioned.
• The swing is a relatively free movement, but the feet and legs are fairly inactive with the weight remaining on the left foot.
• The open stance will create an outward and upward backswing in relation to the target and a

steep angle of approach on the downswing.
• The club should strike the sand about 2in behind the ball so that it can 'cut' or slide across and under the ball, sending the ball out of the bunker on a divot of sand.
• The clubhead must continue to accelerate through the sand to the finish position.
• The club face must not close down as it enters the sand – the heel of the clubhead should feel that it is leading the toe side until after impact.
• The follow-through should finish with the weight solidly on the left foot, the body turned towards the target and the clubhead slightly outside the hands and in a fairly full position.
• The ball will pop out on a high trajectory and land softly with very little roll on the ball.

Fig 59 The splash shot.

(a) The ball is opposite the left heel, the feet shuffled into the sand, the stance solid (left).

(b) The club face aims to the flagstick, the player's alignment is to the left (below).

(c) The open stance and wrist action set the club steeply during the backswing. The shaft points parallel to the body alignment.

(d) The ball comes out on a divot of sand.

The height of the bunker face will affect the way the player approaches the shot, but generally to add extra elevation to the shot the player must open the stance more, position the ball more forward and open the club face a little further, so that the swing becomes increasingly more of a 'cutting' action. This will create a higher trajectory, but will also decrease the distance the ball travels so the player must ensure that the swing is longer and possibly more aggressive to compensate.

The Explosion Shot Fig 60

When the ball is buried under the top level of the sand it requires an adjustment to the standard bunker shot technique. This 'explosion' shot is rather like it sounds; the club must explode the ball out or rather 'splash' it out on a divot of sand. The

buried lie means that the club has to dig more deeply into the sand to ensure that it gets underneath the bottom of the ball.

The Set-up

• The ball must be positioned further back in the stance.
• The stance changes so that the feet can remain slightly open if preferred, but the hips and shoulders move into a more square or parallel position in relation to the ball to target line.
• The weight remains on the left foot.
• The hands are positioned forward of the ball.
• The club face is square to the target; with extremely poor lies the club should be 'toed in' slightly so that the digging action of the club is accentuated.

The Swing

• The clubhead must move upwards steeply so that the

hands and arms feel as if they dominate the backswing movement. The lower body should remain passive, otherwise too much body rotation may occur causing the swing plane to become too rounded or flat and leading to the swing arc being too shallow as it approaches the ball.
• Drive the clubhead down into the sand hitting at least 2in behind the ball, bearing in mind that the clubhead must be able to dig down and under the ball. The steep angle of approach will help the ball up and out of the sand, but will limit the amount of follow-through the player makes. The trajectory of the ball will be quite low and it will roll quite excessively on.

A buried lie limits the amount of options a player has. The technique used will create a lower ball flight, so that when playing the shot in a steep-faced bunker it may be necessary for a player, particularly one of average skill, to play in the safest

Fig 60 An illustration of how the ball position and club face are different for the splash and explosion shots.

direction rather than directly at the flagstick. Should the lie be very bad then the golfer should consider using a 9 iron or pitching wedge as the sharp leading edge of the club face on these irons will dig more efficiently into the sand. Unfortunately the stronger loft of these clubs has implications with regard to a lower ball flight. One necessity has to be balanced out with the other.

Summing up Bunker Play

Most golfers are guilty of making bunker play far more difficult than it really is. As with the chip and pitch shots the player must be able to assess the situation they are in – the lie of the ball, the type and depth of the sand, the height of the bunker face, the amount and firmness of the green between the ball and flagstick. They must be able to visualize what is required and to 'feel' the swing movement prior to the actual execution of the shot.

Good bunker play cannot be achieved consistently without regular practice – it cultivates technique, confidence and consistent success.

Putting Fig 61

The art of putting probably epitomizes more than all other technical aspects put together what the nature and game of golf is all about. It has been described as 'a game within a game'. No matter how successful a player is from tee shot to the green, if the ability to putt is not there then the potential and pleasure of achieving a good score is lost. It is the vital part of the game. Look at the percentages – on average it is almost 45 per cent of the game for an accomplished player – nearly half of all shots played! For a twenty handicap player it is likely to make up around 38 per cent of the round scored. High percentages indeed, but for most golfers it is a department of the game that receives little or no practice outside golf course play.

Golfers are not always keen lesson takers, but when they do commit themselves to coaching the last thing they seem to want help and advice with is their putting, even though it continually seems to be the one area that lets them down week in and week out. Of all the golf lessons a coach gives over a year,

it is doubtful that 3 per cent would be to help players with their putting techniques. The tour pros know the true value of good putting and so they spend much of their practice time on the putting green developing solid, repetitive actions. There are a number of putting coaches around these days such as Harold Swash in the United Kingdom and Dave Pelz in the USA. These coaches specialize in offering advice on just the putting aspects of the game.

In searching to identify the credentials of a successful putter we must appreciate that it is the one department of the game where we see an incredible variety of individual styles, particularly to the actual execution of the stroke. There are however, certain key fundamentals that are common to those players that perform the putting stroke with regular efficiency.

1. The putter face is square to the swing path at impact.
2. The swing path is square to the target line.
3. The ball is struck from the 'sweet-spot' of the putter.
4. The rhythm or pace of the stroke is consistent.

There are many factors that affect the making of a good putt, but the above four are the vital elements. In understanding those four elements it has to be appreciated that there are many variations of style that can produce the desired result.

Key Elements to a Good Set-up

• The palms of each hand should face one another – the back of the left hand and the palm of the right hand should be square to the target line. The thumbs point down the shaft.

Fig 61 Putting.

(a)

(b)

(c)

(a) A comfortable address position with the ball opposite the centre of the chest.

(b) A smooth one-piece back stroke.

(c) The head remains still, the stroke is from the shoulders so there is no independent wrist action.

- The club face is correctly aligned to the target.
- The body is aligned square to the target line.
- The eyes are positioned over or just inside the ball.
- The hands are level with or slightly ahead of the ball at address.
- The ball is positioned between the left instep and forward of the centre of the stance.
- The posture and set-up position are physically comfortable.

The set-up position and posture vary greatly from golfer to golfer. Some prefer to bend over exaggeratedly, whilst others tuck their elbows tight into their sides, or even spread them as far away from the body as possible. Some have narrow stances others wide, some position their feet open to the target whilst still others prefer a closed position. The parameters are very wide indeed, but usually a simple, comfortable set-up with a good grip will give a player the pre-shot fundamentals required.

Grip Options

The standard overlap, interlock or ten-finger grip can all be used effectively although there is much variation on these themes. Reverse overlap, cross-handed, split-handed, hands overlapping, right forefinger down shaft, left forefinger down shaft, both forefingers down shaft, the potential list is very long indeed.

The most popular grip used by the top players is the reverse overlap where the right hand sits

Fig 62 A square alignment, correct posture and eyes directly over the ball.

Fig 63 Some variations of grips used for putting.

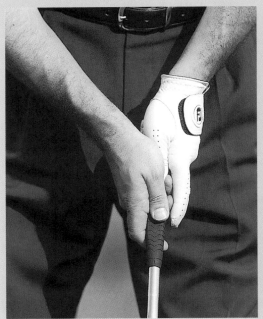

(a) The reverse overlap position is the most popular grip.

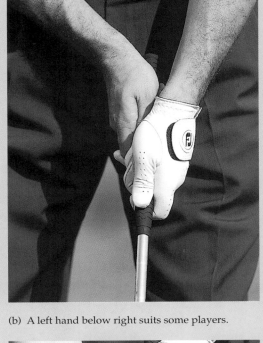

(b) A left hand below right suits some players.

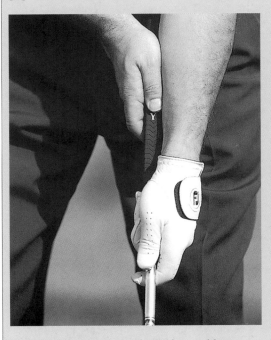

(c) The left forearm down the shaft can add extra control.

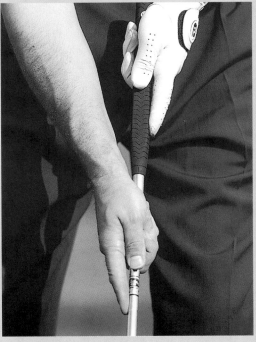

(d) A split hand position can offer more feel.

totally onto the putter handle as do the last three fingers of the left hand, then the left forefinger overlaps the knuckles of the right hand. The thumbs point directly down the top of the shaft.

Key Elements in the Stroke

• The putter head will swing backward and forward on a straight line for shorter putts, but will be on a more inside path during the backswing for the longer ones.
• The putter should be kept as low as possible to the ground during the backswing.
• The putter face should remain square to the swing path throughout the whole stroke.

• The putter should be accelerating through the impact position.
• Contacting the ball just as the upswing commences can help the strike of the putt and the roll of the ball.
• Keep the body movement as limited as possible.
• Maintain a good head position until after the ball has been struck.
• Do not allow the left wrist to bend or collapse at impact.
• Keep the stroke smooth throughout and endeavour to keep the backswing and through swing of equal distance.

There are a number of important fundamentals that go into helping a player become a good

putter – the ability to read the slope and nature of the greens, the judgement and feel for distance, good visualization and the positive attitude that leads to decisiveness and confidence – *see* Specialist Skills. Choosing the correct putter to use is also very important.

Remember what is needed – the ball must travel on the correct path to the hole and at the right speed. The putter must strike the ball well enough to allow the correct contact to take place at impact and for the ball to roll forward efficiently and effectively. Not too much else really matters. There are no prizes for how, just for how many! Good putting wins matches, tournaments, prizes and lowers players' handicaps.

Fig 64 A collapse of the left wrist is one of the more destructive actions when putting.

7
UNDERSTANDING AND CORRECTING FAULTS

The game of golf for most individuals is not so much dominated by the quality of a player's good shots as it is by the element of minimizing the number of poorer ones. The average player whose handicap exceeds 18 is likely to play a high percentage of incorrect or mishit golf shots. Fortunately, in many cases, the damage is relatively limited by a sub-standard contact between the club and the ball, but where a shot is reasonably well struck but lacks control, the adverse effects are potentially greatest as the ball is going to travel some distance. Tops, thins, skys, fat shots, can often have a relatively safe end result as the ball is so poorly struck that the distance is not so much a factor. Invariably it is the player's confidence that is affected on these occasions.

All golfers need to have a basic understanding of how or why a poor shot occurs, then how to set about improving the error successfully. Over the following pages a number of the most common golfing faults are covered with a synopsis of the most constructive ways to set about alleviating their detrimental effects on a player's game (see Fig 44).

The Slice

A slice shot occurs when at impact a player's swing path is moving across the ball to target line so that it is approaching from the outside or right of that target line and then moving in a direction that is inside or left of

it. At the same time the club face is aiming to the right, that is, open of the swing path. This out to in swing path, combined with an open club face creates a left to right side spin on the ball which has the effect of making the ball bend or move in flight in a rightward direction. The amount of slice depends on how out to in the swing path is and how open the club face is in relation to that swing path. Consequently, an exaggerated position of either will create a fairly emphatic and erratic slice shot, whereas a slight variation will only lead to a possible fade or a more controllable slice, potentially one that a player can learn to play with in quite an effective manner.

The detrimental effect of a slice is not only a noticeable lack of control of the flight of the ball, but there is also a dramatic influence on the distance the ball travels. A swing movement that causes the ball to move from left to right invariably has the clubhead approaching from too steep an angle of approach. This downward blow not only minimizes the effective forward drive the clubhead has on the ball at impact, but also maximizes the back spin because the steep angle of approach means that the clubhead contacts the ball too high up its equator and too much to the right of centre. This impact position, together with the out to in swing path and the open club face, combines to make an effective contact and control of the ball fairly limited.

Some players may find it impossible to cure their slice

problem completely, but it should still be their goal to develop a swing movement that allows them to improve their ball control and power factors. Whilst studying the swing positions that cause the slice each player must be aware of identifying their own relevant personal areas of weakness as this is critical in understanding how to go about correcting them.

The importance of going back to basics initially cannot be overstressed, almost all good things that happen during the player's swing can be related back to the most fundamental set-up and swing characteristics.

The Grip

If both or either hand is positioned too far to the left side of the handle when the golfer grips the club then the golfer will find it more difficult to deliver the club face to the ball at impact in anything but an open position in relation to the path of the swing. This is referred to as a weak grip, in effect the player is not holding the club in a natural physiological position – the left palm rather than facing slightly downward toward the right knee tends to be facing too far backward or even slightly skyward. The right palm rather than being aimed forward towards the target will be positioned facing the left knee. The grip encourages both the left and right forearms to rotate to the left at address. During the swing the forearms and hands will rotate naturally to the right into a more comfortable and natural position. This has the effect of opening up the club face and consequently increasing the effective loft at impact, which results in a high, weak slicing ball flight and one that varies depending upon the swing path characteristics. Despite a weak grip position some players are able to return the club face to the ball squarely, but the natural rotational release of the hands, wrists and forearms are far more difficult to achieve than with an orthodox grip.

Aim and Ball Position

To compensate for the left to right flight of the ball a player who slices will invariably aim the shoulders left of the target at address. This leftward position of the shoulder leads to the ball being positioned too far forward in the player's stance. If the player delivers the clubhead to the ball with the shoulders returning to the open position then the ball flight will follow the direction of the shoulders, that is, to the left of the target. A forward ball position further enhances the slice reaction and encourages the player to deliver the clubhead to the ball from too steep an angle of attack.

Posture, Balance and Swing Movement

In analysing the errors that lead to a sliced shot it is easy to see how they are all interrelated and that one fault can lead to the next and so on. The weak grip will encourage the forward ball position and lead to an open shoulder alignment at address. The weight automatically moves towards the left side and forward towards the balls of the feet, causing the posture to appear more over the ball than necessary. The swing itself now follows a predetermined route – the takeaway moves the club outside and up steeply in relation to the ball to target line. The body will struggle to rotate and turn correctly so the left shoulder tends to tilt downward, further accentuating the independent outside and upward movement of the hands and arms. The weight fails to move into the right side and the potential width of the backswing is lost. Some players try to counteract these tendencies by swinging back on an exaggerated inside path believing that this will allow them to return the clubhead to the ball correctly. This may work on occasion, but more often than not the movement is not in sympathy with the other fundamentals so the player fails to co-ordinate the swing movements as a whole and gains no reliable benefit of note.

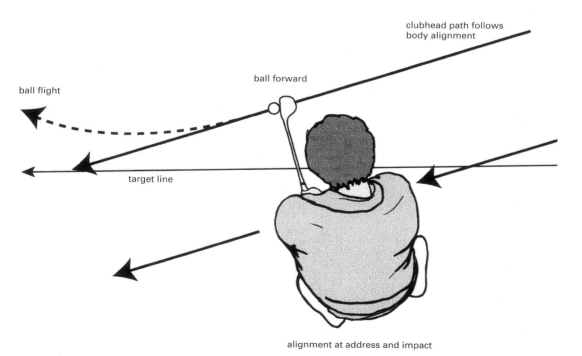

Fig 65 The club face is open in relation to the swing path, so the ball curves left to right.

With these swing characteristics there will be little chance of returning the clubhead to the ball effectively – it has to travel from an outward to inward direction with a steep angle of approach, particularly due to the poor weight distribution. The swing elements make it almost impossible for a player to correctly release the clubhead, minimizing the opportunity to square up the club face and thus leading to a classic slice position.

Set-up and swing fundamentals contrive to keep a player off balance in an athletic sense for most of the swing movement. Hence slicers of the ball tend to have poor follow-throughs and balance problems at the end of their swing movement.

Curing the Slice

The Grip

The grip should be held in a neutral or strong position, which will encourage the player to deliver the club face square to the target at impact. A stronger grip encourages the player to roll or rotate the wrists and forearms over as the clubhead approaches impact – a movement not normally achieved by the player.

Aim and Ball Position

By lining up the shoulders square to the target line the player will instinctively move the ball further back in the stance so that it will be positioned more towards the centre of the feet.

Posture, Balance and Swing

The correct grip, ball position and aim will encourage the player to feel the weight more correctly proportioned between both feet, which in turn will allow the weight distribution to feel solidly balanced between the heels and balls of the feet. This improved balance will undoubtedly lead to a better posture with the spine angle being slightly more upright, and the knees correctly flexed.

The improved set-up fundamentals allow the player to commence the backswing with a low, slightly inside takeaway movement. The shoulders are then encouraged to turn more naturally, slightly under and across towards the right side of the body. This flatter rotation of the whole body movement, combined with an improved weight distribution and balance leads to a shallower, more rounded inside swing path and flatter swing plane. The body is in effect winding up or coiling as the weight shifts into the right side.

The player has now considerably increased the chances of delivering the clubhead correctly to the ball. The downswing path should be from the inside with a shallower, more powerful angle of approach towards impact. The release of the clubhead will follow more naturally allowing the club face to be squared up more easily and effectively, delivering the loft of the club correctly to the ball at impact. The player's balance will be enhanced with the correct forward momentum of the clubhead, creating a feeling of pulling the golfer into the full follow-through position.

Positive Pointers

• To cure or to compensate for their swing faults many golfers endeavour to make an exaggerated in to out movement, but often this limits their overall chances of improvement and can lead to further errors. Understand how to swing the club from the correct inside position.

• Practise with the ball back in the stance – it will encourage a square or even closed alignment at address, thereby allowing the club to swing on a more inside path.

• Remember that if a player turns correctly and allows the

A Hit List for Slicers

• A weak grip or ineffective hand action during the golf swing is often caused by the player holding the club too much in the palms of the hands.

• A stronger grip will not necessarily cure a slice although it is likely to at least minimize the problem. Check all other set-up and swing fundamentals.

• Check that the swing plane is not too upright.

• An open club face at the top of the backswing will be one if the toe of the club points downwards towards the ground. Ideally, the toe of the club should point to the ball.

• Slicers allow the shoulders to dominate the swing movement – particularly at the commencement of the downswing balata.

• An out to in swing path and steep angle of approach accentuate the slice and consequential power loss.

• A steep angle of approach will create a deepish divot after contact with the ball, sometimes even with a wooden club.

• An open club face position at impact has the effect of increasing loft and diminishing control and power.

• Sliced shots have increased backspin, hence a loss of forward motion and distance to the ball's flight.

weight to move into the right side, the clubhead will swing more naturally from the inside.

• Any exaggeration in trying to make the backswing move on an inside path will often lead to an opposite movement at the start of the downswing whereby the shoulders and clubhead tend to be thrown outward and away from the body leading to an exaggerated out to in downswing path.

• Allow the hands and arms to swing freely during the whole movement, particularly at the commencement of the downswing.

• Try to encourage the hands to work in a more co-ordinated way – do not be frightened to feel a natural rotation of the hands and arms as you approach the impact position – allow the right to rotate over the left.

• Heavier headed clubs and more flexible shafts encourage the player to feel and release the clubhead more effectively. Irons with a more upright lie angle will also tend to help deliver the club face more closed at impact.

Drills for Slicers

1.   Practise with an umbrella or another club lying on the ground, positioned outside the ball and pointing towards the target. This will help emphasize correct alignment and swing path.

2.   Practise with a head cover or car sponge positioned 12 or 18in behind the ball to encourage an inside swing path.

3.   Practise hitting tee shots off a high peg without removing the peg at impact. This will encourage a shallower angle of approach.

4.   Take your normal address position.

Raise your left arm up level with the left shoulder and parallel to the ground.

Make a swinging movement with the right arm only.

Fig 66   Drill number 2. The clubhead swings inside the head cover.

Hold your left hand and arm in position and swing underneath it with the right hand.

This will encourage a passive involvement of the shoulders at the commencement of the downswing, a free movement of the right hand and arm and a natural release and rotational movement.

With a short iron swing gently trying to hit tee pegs out of the ground to help gain the feeling for the correct rotational movement (*see* Fig 67).

5.   First try practice swinging as if the ball is positioned above the level of your feet. Then try hitting balls from an elevated lie position. This will encourage a

Fig 67 Drill number 4. The left-arm pacifies the shoulders allowing a correct release of the right hand, arm and body.

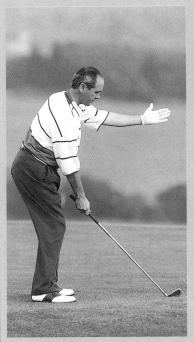

Fig 68 Drill numbers 7 and 8. The body remains passive as the arms drop downward …

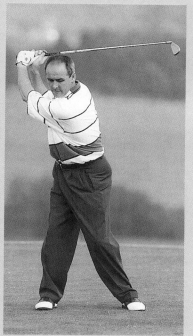

… The forearms rotate independently to help encourage a feeling for the correct clubhead release.

Fig 69 Drill number 10. The umbrella encourages a shallow inside swing path.

flatter more rotational movement of the body with an improved clubhead release through impact.
6.   To improve posture and weight distribution during the backswing movement, practise turning the upper body into a position where the spine appears slightly diagonal and to the right in relation to the lower body. The head should feel as though it is positioned over the right knee.

This will encourage a player to turn the right hip correctly during the backswing movement and allow the upper body rotation to direct the club onto the correct backswing path (*see* Fig 48).
7.   Complete the backswing movement holding the body in a relaxed but stationary position, allow the arms to drop downward towards the right hip. Repeat this action several times smoothly.

This will encourage an effective and inside commencement of the downswing.
8.   Repeat drill 7 but also allow the right forearm to rotate over the left forearm before the body begins to turn back towards the target. This will encourage the correct commencement of the downswing and a far earlier and active release of the clubhead. It also creates greater width and a

shallower angle of approach into the ball.

9.   Repeat 7 and 8 but as the club reaches its lowest point in the downswing turn the whole body through the impact position and complete the follow-through. This encourages the correct downswing movement and enhances the co-ordination of the arms and body.

10.   Position a golf umbrella in the ground 3ft behind the ball and directly on the ball to target line.

Slightly tilt the umbrella downward on the player's side of the ball to target line.

The umbrella will encourage the player to swing on a more inside and shallow path.

Make practice swings at first and then begin to hit practice shots in a relaxed easy style and until a feeling has been created for this more inside shallow golf swing.

The Hook

A hook shot occurs when at impact a player's swing path is across the ball to target line approaching from the inside side or left of that line and moving in a direction that is outside or to the right of it. At the same time the club face is aimed to the left of the swing path. This in to out swing path, combined with the closed club face creates a right to left side spin on the ball which has the effect of making the ball move or bend in flight in a leftward direction.

The amount of hook is dependent upon how in to out the swing path is and how closed the club face is in relation to that swing path. The more exaggerated the position of either or both of these factors, the more emphatic the movement of the ball and generally the more destructive the nature of the shot. The hook differs in its credentials from the slice in that it is a more powerful, aggressive type of shot

and one that most average or high handicap golfers would ideally prefer to play. It is a shot that accomplished players find more natural to their games, and one that can at times be the demise of a successful round of golf. A swing movement from an inside path creates a lower, shallower angle of approach by the clubhead toward the ball. If this combination of movement is exaggerated then it can create an excessive right to left over spin, which can cause the ball to hook leftward and to dip quickly during its flight. The ball is actually being struck below its equator and to the left of centre.

Ball striking can often be a weakness for some players who hook the ball. The shallower angle of approach causes the clubhead to contact the ground either behind the ball leading to heavy or fat shots, or it can lead to the clubhead contacting the ball on the upswing, that is, after the lowest point of the swing arc has been reached. This will lead to the clubhead contacting the ball on the bottom part of the club face causing thinned or low shots. Lesser players with these characteristics often find shots of bare lies or from thick rough difficult to execute efficiently as the angle of approach of the clubhead is not steep enough to deliver a solid downward blow into the back of the ball. More accomplished players are able to neutralize some of these downside effects of the shallower angle of approach, by making compensations such as adjusting the ball position or keeping more weight on the left side both at address and at impact.

The right to left overspin created by the golfer's swing action is a powerful one that not only gives the ball considerable travelling speed, usually on a lowish trajectory, but also causes the ball to roll on contact with the ground. The extra roll created by this ball shape can be most useful

if it propels the ball safely down the fairway, but it also has disadvantages in playing approach shots to the green where ball control on landing is a high priority. As difficult as a slice may be to cure, it is not a shot that is without some element of control, whereas a hook is far more unpredictable, often lacking finesse and control. To compensate, players who hook invariably can only resort to what is called a block shot – one that is directed straight to the right of the target. Although it is less destructive than the leftward nature of the hook, it can still leave a player in doubt as to the exact outcome of the ensuing shots during a round of golf, as this hook left/block right equation becomes very unpredictable for players with this swing action. It is not only the demise of amateur players, but is also a problem that we see certain top tournament players experience in some of their tournament play.

The Grip

If either or both hands are positioned to the right of the handle when gripping the club this is referred to as a strong grip. It is highly likely that this grip will cause a golfer to return the club face to the ball in a closed position in relation to the swing path. The left hand is likely to be positioned too far on top of the handle of the club, so that the palm faces too downward in direction. The right hand is likely to be underneath the handle with the palm facing to skyward. This position of the hands will cause the forearms to rotate to the right at address. During the swing the hands, wrists and arms rotate back to the left into a more natural and comfortable position causing the club face to close down and aim left of the swing path. The ball flight will be powerful, low and left of the path of the swing.

Aim and Ball Position

Generally a player who hooks his shots to the left of the target will aim to the right to compensate. This alignment of the shoulders to address will encourage the ball to be positioned further back in the stance. A strong grip can often further accentuate these two factors. Should a player return to this closed position at impact, then an in to out swing path and shallow angle of attack are almost guaranteed, necessitating the club face to be positioned closed to the swing path to enable the player to hit the ball towards the target.

Posture, Balance and Swing Movement

Once again it is evident that one fault can lead to a whole series of other errors that compound a player's swing problems. In this case a strong grip can accentuate poor alignment and a backward position of the golf ball at address. The weight distribution tends to be more on the right side and towards the heels, which causes the spine angle to become rather too upright at address and invariably leads to an overflexing at the knees to allow a player to drop into a comfortable position when placing the clubhead behind the ball. From this position the player is encouraged to swing the club and turn the body onto too shallow and rounded a position. A flat swing plane will be the result, with the player's arms low and positioned too far behind the body at the top of the golf swing. Conversely, some players compensate for this overly rotational and inside movement of the body by lifting their hands and arms relatively independently to a more upright position, although this is more evident in accomplished players than in higher handicap ones. The inside swing path and flat swing plane particularly, coupled with a strong grip, close the club face so that during the takeaway it 'looks back' to the ball or, even downward to the ground for too long, and at the top of the swing, it is positioned upward, looking directly towards the sky.

The downswing will follow the backswing's influence and approach the ball from a shallow inside path. The body struggles to turn back towards the ball correctly, causing a closed or blocked position which restricts the timing of the weight transfer and leaves the head set too much behind the ball at impact, and the weight too much on the right side. The right shoulder will tend to drop down and under causing the left shoulder to move upward and the hips to struggle to clear to the left. This underneath or trapped position is quite common in younger or more

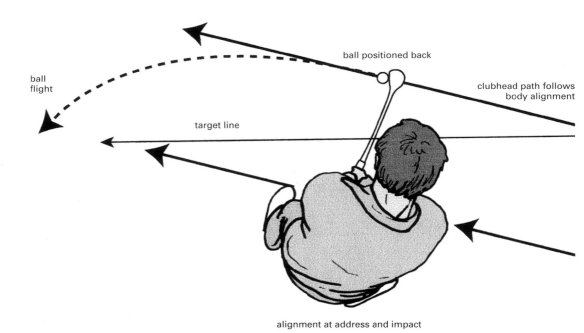

ball flight

ball positioned back

clubhead path follows body alignment

target line

alignment at address and impact

Fig 70 The club face is closed to the swing path, so that the ball curves left to right.

athletic players. A lack of sufficient forward and rotational movement from the lower body leads to the player instinctively releasing or rolling the club face to compensate, causing it to rotate over and to close at impact. The combination of the in to out swing path and the closing face sets the ball off to the right of the target with a strong right to left spin that moves the ball leftward during its flight. A strong grip will generally lead to an automatic closing of the face without the need to feel a natural rotation or release.

Control of direction is one negative aspect; the other is the angle of approach. The set-up and swing movements mean that the club can not usually approach the ball from a steep enough angle. This limits the player in terms of making a solid strike or contact with the ball at impact, particularly with the shorter shafted irons, where a

downward hit is more important. On a positive note the longer shafted clubs which require a shallower, sweeping clubhead movement, can be relatively effective in ball striking and consistency terms. Players often tend to have a relatively high follow-through caused by this more closed body position and the in to out swing path, forcing the arms in a upward direction with the club shaft angle pointing downward towards the right heel at the end of the swing movement (*see* Fig 41).

Curing the Hook

The Grip

The club should be held in a neutral or even slightly weak position to help allow the player to deliver the club face squarely to the ball at impact. This improved grip position will limit

the amount of rotation through impact, and minimize the dangerous closure of the club face. It may be beneficial for a player to feel as if the club is positioned more in the palms of the hand, which will further limit any independent roll or rotation of the club face.

Aim and Ball Position

By aligning the shoulders square to the target line the ball will instinctively be positioned more forward in the stance, possibly just inside the left heel.

Posture, Balance and Swing

The correct grip, ball position and aim will encourage the player to feel the weight more evenly proportioned between both feet with the weight distributed between the heels and balls of the feet. This superior weight distribution and balance will lead to an improved posture, with the player's spine angle more tilted over, and the arms hanging freely downward from the shoulders.

These improved set-up fundamentals encourage the player to commence the backswing with only a slight inward movement of the clubhead. Due to the improved posture the left shoulder can now turn correctly downward and across as the weight moves towards and into the right side of the body. This slightly steeper rotation of the upper body allows the player to swing the club on a more upward and steeper swing plane. The club face can now remain square throughout the takeaway and backswing movement. The player has every chance of delivering the club to the ball along the correct downswing path and with the release of the clubhead naturally

---

A Hit List for Hookers

• A strong grip position is often caused by a player holding the club too much in the fingers. It is usually an active or stronger right hand which dominates the closure of the club face at impact.

• Weakening the grip may not necessarily cure a hook, but it will help to minimize the adverse effects of a closed club face. Check all other set-up and swing fundamentals also.

• Check that the backswing plane is not too flat.

• At the top of the backswing if the club face looks vertically towards the sky it is in a closed position. Ideally the toe of the club should point towards the ball.

• A shallow downswing angle of approach accentuates the potential for hooking the ball. The clubhead will be released earlier from this position and will rotate to a more closed position prior to impact.

• A shallow angle of approach can also cause the player to hit the ground behind the ball, or contact the ball on the upswing, leading to thinned or topped shots.

• A closed face means that the club's effective loft at impact is reduced. This will create a lower, more powerful flight, but a loss of ball control.

• Lofted clubs will accentuate the movement of the ball to the left. Short irons tend to go straight left rather than with a noticeable right to left hook spin. Longer clubs have a more obvious hook, but often lose height quickly as the right to left overspin of the ball causes it to dip quicker than normal. It will also bounce and run more.

squaring up the club face at impact. The angle of approach of the clubhead will be steeper than before, with the hands leading so there is no danger of an early release prior to impact. A more solid contact will be made at impact improving the ball strike, control, flight and trajectory of the ball.

The transfer of weight can now occur more easily with the body shifting forward towards the target, and the hips and shoulders leftward and out of the way through impact. This improves the overall connection, co-ordination and control of the swing, by neutralizing any independent actions that might otherwise have been required by the hands or wrists to deliver the club face squarely to the ball. A golfer can complete the swing movement in a well-balanced position, with the hands and arms feeling lower than before and nearer to the left shoulder with the club shaft finishing more parallel to the ground at the completion of the swing.

Positive Pointers

• Practise with the ball well forward in the stance – it will lead to a square or even open alignment at address, and encourage and improve backswing movement and swing plane.
• The forward ball position will also help the player to turn the body more freely through impact.
Allow the left hand to feel more dominant at the address position, and during the swing movement itself. Left side control helps minimize if not totally eradicate a tendency to hook.
• Allow the clubhead to swing smoothly upward so that the club shaft is positioned somewhere over the right shoulder at the top of the backswing.

• Try to point the club shaft parallel to the ball to target line at the top of the backswing – most hookers tend to let the club shaft point to the right of the target or across the line at the top.
• Aim the body to the left of the target and learn to fade the ball with a left to right ball shape – try this in practice before attempting it on the golf course.
• Lighter weight clubs or less flexible shafts may reduce the tendency to close the club face at impact, but could reduce the clubhead feel during the swing movement. A flatter lie angle with the irons will help the club face to remain more open at impact.

Drills for Hookers

1.   Practise from a slope with the ball positioned below the feet. This will help develop a more upright swing plane and a steeper angle of approach into the ball.
2.   Practise with an umbrella lying on the ground positioned just outside the ball and pointing towards the target. This will help emphasize the importance of correct alignment and swing path.
3.   Practise with a head cover or sponge 12–18in behind the ball, but slightly inside a line pointing from the ball to the target. If the clubhead makes contact with the head cover or sponge as it approaches impact then the downswing is on to inside a path and too shallow an angle of approach.
4.   Take a normal stance and then draw the right foot back about 6–10in. Feel the arms swing upwards freely during the backswing and let the upper body turn smoothly to the left during the downswing and through-swing movements.

Fig 71 Drill number 3. The clubhead will travel from an improved swing path and angle.

Fig 72 Drill number 4. The arms are encouraged to swing upward correctly during the backswing. During the downswing, the upper body rotates more aggressively over the lower body.

the downward angle of approach and ball striking skills.

8 Position an umbrella or old golf shaft in the ground about 3ft behind the ball on an imaginary line midway between the ball and your toes. Slightly tilt the umbrella towards your right hip. Practise the downswing movement in slow motion allowing the club shaft to travel over the top of the umbrella which will encourage a less inside swing path, a steeper angle of approach of the clubhead and an improved position of the right side of the body. With a little practice and confidence it is then possible to try hitting the ball with some smooth 7 iron swings to develop the correct feel and movement.

9. Practise from a downslope to encourage a more left-sided weight distribution at address, a good swing plane and the correct down and through feeling. Remember to hit the shot smoothly as good balance should be maintained at all times.

10. Try hitting half shots with an open position of the feet and hips; this will encourage the club to move on an upward path and plane during the backswing. Turn the body freely in both directions feeling an improved relationship with the hands, arms and body.

Fig 73 Drill number 5. A steeper angle of approach is guaranteed.

Summary of the Hook and Slice

It is difficult not to make a major topic of these two types of shot, as they are the most dominating and prevalent in the games of all golfers. It is not easy for a player to accept that often the evasive measures they take to eradicate these problems sometimes serve to compound their swing weaknesses. Golf is often a game of opposites – a player aims to the left but the

5. Place a tee peg or head cover about 6–12in behind the ball. Hit irons shots endeavouring to strike the ball without the clubhead contacting the tee peg or head cover. This will steepen the angle of approach and encourage divots to be taken after impact with the ball. It will also discourage an inside downswing path.

6. Place a tee peg in the ground, 2–3in in front of the ball. Practise striking the ball and removing the tee peg from the ground as the clubhead continues downward after contact with the ball. This will encourage a good downswing path and improved angle of approach.

7. Practise hitting some shots from bare or tight lies to improve

Fig 74 Drill number 8. The umbrella encourages a more down the line swing path.

player a first class lesson, but it is ultimately up to that player to understand and practise the correct movements.

The Pull, Push, Fade and Draw Shots

The pull and push shots are closely related to the slice and hook in that the player's swing movements have almost identical characteristics. None of these shots has the destructive potential of the other two, but by the same token they can develop into either a slice or a hook with the smallest of changes.

The Pull

A pull can be simply described as a shot that goes straight left of the target. A player's swing movement might match those of a regular slicer of the ball, but the main difference is the direction the club face aims at impact. A pull shot is executed when the swing path of the clubhead is travelling from an out to in direction in relation to the target with the club face square to that swing path. The ball travels in a straight line. If the club face is not square to the swing path then the ball will deviate one way or the other – if the ball starts left in the same direction as the swing path, but then bends further to the left in the air, the club face must have been closed to the path creating a right to left side spin on the ball. This is a pull hook or pull draw depending on how much deviation there is on the flight of the ball. If the ball starts left, but bends to the right then the club face must have been open to that swing path creating a left to right side spin on the ball. This is a slice or a fade depending upon how much deviation there is on the ball's flight.

ball goes to the right. The simplest cures are usually the easiest – to help cure a slice aim to the right – the grip, ball position, swing plane and path and natural release of the clubhead will change automatically. It is a matter of time and patience until the swing becomes more natural and instinctive. A player who

has grooved one regular movement should not expect any change, particularly one of an opposite virtue to take place in a short-term period. Regular and disciplined practice, combined with a clear understanding of how the swing path and club face positions affect each shot are usually necessary. A coach can give a

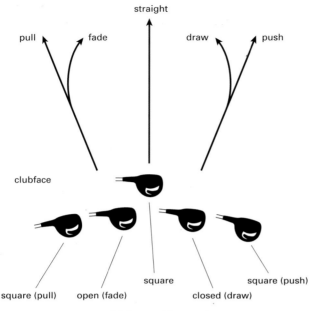

ball flight

straight

pull   fade   draw   push

clubface

square (pull)   open (fade)   square   closed (draw)   square (push)

note clubface positions are in
relation to the swing path

Fig 75 Ball flight during a push,
pull, fade or draw.

The Push

The push is the opposite of a pull. The clubhead is travelling across the target line from inside to out with the club face square to that swing path. The ball will travel in a straight line to the right of the target. If the club face is not square to the swing path then the ball will either bend further right in flight due to the left to right side spin created by an open club face – this is called a pushed fade or pushed slice. Or it will bend from right to left because the club face was closed to the swing path and so imparted the opposite side spin. This will either be a draw or a hook depending upon how much right to left deviation there is on the ball's flight.

Fade or Draw

The fade or draw basically falls into a position between the slice/ pull or the hook/push relationship. A slight out to in swing path with open face or in to out with a closed face dictates the shape and description of the shot. The more controlled the club face and the swing path factors the more likely a player can develop a fade or draw which will offer improved ball striking, increased distance, greater reliability and consistency and regular accuracy as the outcome of each shot is far more predictable.

The fade shot is effective when the ball commences its flight slightly left of target and moves gently left to right as it heads back towards that target. The draw starts towards the right of the target but moves gently left during flight.

All four of these shots pull, push, fade or draw are more obvious in the games of accomplished players. Higher handicap players need to improve the direction or path of their swings first which, in turn, will improve the angle of approach of the clubhead towards impact. Control of the club face is in many respects the easiest of aspects to improve or put right, particularly if swing path and angle of approach are reasonably acceptable. Golfers must assess their personal swing characteristics, some must work to develop their basic fundamentals whereas others might simply refine them to gain more effective golfing potential.

Mishits

The type of shots that could be included in this category would be tops, thins, skys, heavy shots, shanks, toed or heeled shots. In most cases a poor result is caused by relatively obvious swing breakdown – a lack of confidence is often the original cause of the error creating a reduced swing or shot commitment. It is not possible to say that a particular mishit shot is only caused by one specific swing error – a player who slices may, on occasion, top the ball as easily as one who hooks, or a low handicap player may hit the ground before impact as does a novice. In assessing the potential reasons for playing a mishit shot it is simpler to summarize a selection of swing movements and to categorize the poor shots that might result accordingly.

Incorrect Grip

1. Strong grip – hands positioned to the right side of the handle. A lack of club face control with this type of grip can cause a player to release or roll the club face more actively during the downswing. The clubhead can move ahead of the hands prior to impact or the club face can close too quickly. The angle of approach is shallow in most cases.
Result – Tops, thins, heavys, skys, toed, hooks, low shots.
Shots most difficult to play – From bare lies, out of the rough, bunkers, high lobs, fades, ball below feet, downward sloping lies.
2. Weak grip – Hands positioned to the left of the handle. Again a lack of club face control with this type of grip encourages the player to open the club face during the swing, restricting the wrist action and limiting clubhead release. It also encourages players to use their upper bodies more actively. A player's divot may be long, thin and aim well left.
Result – Tops, thins, heels, slices, skys, weak shots.
Shots most difficult to play – Straight face clubs, low shots, a draw, ball above feet.

Posture, Balance and Weight Distribution

These are three of the key aspects in helping to play successful golf, particularly weight distribution and balance. Without them control of the club face and consequently consistency of performance are unlikely as a player will continually have to make some form of correction or recovery movement during the swing prior to impact. The position of the head is most vital as it dictates the potential for good timing and co-ordination. Poor head position leads to incorrect or excessive body movement.

Head Low at Address or Impact

The head is positioned too low at address it will restrict or limit the entire swing movement. In an attempt to keep the head still golfers may feel the necessity to maintain this original head position restricting the other swing actions from correctly taking place during the swing itself. This will undoubtedly affect the overall balance and timing of the swing. Should a player's head drop down at any time during the swing itself, it is likely that the upper body in particular will be out of position restricting the correct rotation and overall balance, both during the backswing and forward swing movements.

Players should seek to position the head correctly at address and to maintain a similar position at impact although it is not correct to assume that the head should remain still throughout the whole swing movement.
Result: Potentially any poor shot.

Weight Transfer

The golf swing operates most effectively for the majority of

players when the weight transfers naturally towards and into the right side during the backswing, and back towards and onto the left side before, during and after impact. Without this sequence a player may hit shots with too much weight remaining on the left side during the backswing, which will either lead to a reverse pivot movement whereby the weight reverts towards the right side during the downswing, or possibly a player will be unable to make the correct lateral weight shift towards the target and to clear the left side out of the way prior to impact. This may also lead to a loss of balance with the weight falling forward towards the toes or back towards the heels prior to impact.
Result – Tops, thins, heavys, skys, toed, heels.
Shots most difficult to play – Sloping lies, almost all non straightforward shots, longer or less lofted clubs.

Swing Path: Out to In

In most instances a golfer can survive quite effectively if the swing path is out to in. The angle of approach of the clubhead is usually quite steep, which limits the player in some areas, but it does prove an advantage on short irons or around the green when the natural swing characteristics can be an asset.
Result – Heels, tops, high weak ball flight.
Shots most difficult to play – Ball above feet, uphill slopes, low shots, low running chips, draw or hook shots.

Swing Path: In to Out

An in to out swing path promotes a shallow angle of approach by the clubhead towards impact. A combination of this swing path and the angle of approach can lead to erratic play for some golfers. A natural down and through rotational movement is lost and one that promotes a more outward pushing action prior to impact is implemented. Often the player's hands tend to be positioned behind the ball at impact, with the result that there is little or no divot taken, even with short irons or sometimes the divot is taken prior to contact with the ball.

Result – Tops, thins, heavys, shanks, toed, scooped-up shots, pushes, hooks.

Shots most difficult to play – Bare lies, heavy rough, ball below feet, downhill lies, short irons, fades, bunker shots

Club Face

It is unlikely that the club face on its own could be positioned in such an open or closed way as to cause a particularly mishit shot. If the swing path or angle of approach is correct it is doubtful if the player would have insufficient club face control to execute some form of tolerable shot. If the player has relaxed or let go of the club prior to impact then perhaps the contact with the ball would be particularly poor, but this is unlikely to be a regular swing fault as a player would surely recognize these symptoms by noticing the unusual movement

and position of the clubhead in the hands at the completion of the swing. Often players struggle to make contact with the centre of the club face, but hit the ball more towards the toe or heel of the club. For an average golfer shots struck from the toe often move off quickly to the right of the player and lack any real forward motion. Shots struck from the heel are equally as mishit, but tend to go low and left in direction with poor forward motion.

The Shank

The shank is more diverse than just a heeled shot. It comes when playing an iron shot, usually a pitch or chip and the ball is struck from the hosel or neck of the club. It is usually caused by the player swinging the club on an exaggerated inside path leading to a flat, shallow swing plane. From this position the club can either be returned back to the ball on a similarly exaggerated path, or usually will be thrown outward and away from the body as a reaction to the backswing movement. Either way the clubhead swings in a direction that moves outside or away from the centre of the ball. Contact is off the neck and the ball shoots

violently to the right, and more often than not into trouble. Players who shank will verify that it is a fearsome shot to be afflicted with and it can become very psychological with a loss of confidence affecting the player's whole game. Misguidedly players tend to aim more to the left, swing inside on the way back and try to push the clubhead towards the target. This usually compounds the problem. The solution is basically simple – stand correctly to the ball with the shoulders square to the target, swing the clubhead back and up on the correct path with a steepish swing plane. Swing the club down and through feeling the hands move smoothly leftward and past the left hip.

Summary

One of the truest statements in golf is that a player is not measured by the great shots they hit, but by the quality of their bad ones. This should give all golfers a clear guide as to their priorities with regard to improving their technical abilities. A reasonably solid swing action will give a golfer the opportunity to play enough good shots to an acceptable level. Should a player wish to upgrade his level of performance, then faults must be improved and errors minimized. As a player obtains more control of the ball, so the number of good shots increases. The more a golfer can position the ball in a straightforward, playable position on the course, the more often effective quality shots can be played. This leads to an increase in quality experiences and confidence and, in turn, offers further opportunity for progress. There is no such thing as perfect golf or the perfect golfer. Appreciating and evaluating faults whilst endeavouring to improve them will promote future development.

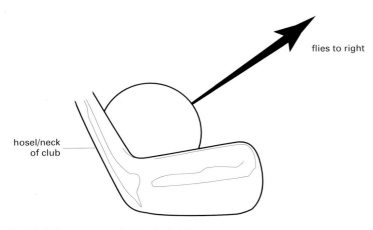

flies to right

hosel/neck of club

Fig 76 Ball contacts neck/hosel of club.

8
IMPROVING YOUR SKILLS

Skill is defined as 'something acquired by training'. There are two basic options when it comes to gaining a skilful ability, firstly acquire it naturally or instinctively through practice and play, or secondly train to acquire a skill, then work to enhance it effectively. Each of these may work better for certain types of golfer. The first alternative for example would be favoured by youngsters, natural ball players and those who dislike having to learn the logic of how and why. The second option is a more planned approach particularly as golf is a game taken up by people at such a variety of ages, and so understanding how and why to do the correct golfing actions is necessary to help make forward progress. All golfers or would-be golfers would far prefer to just hit the ball and learn the more important fundamentals as they go along, but regrettably golf is a game full of bad habits, and once these become ingrained the opportunities for developing a controlled, skilful game become more and more difficult to achieve. The perfect solution is a good natural feel for the game, tempered with a desire and ability to learn and adapt one's own potential for improvement.

Learning to hit a golf ball is not particularly difficult. Adapting an individual swing technique to suit the wide variety of shots that golf requires us to play, often in competitive circumstances, is a true test for a player, not to mention its significance in the overall pleasure of the game. In this section of the book some of the more obvious skills are looked at together with a few ancillary ones that help complete a golfer's shot-making repertoire.

For any golfer to be able to play skilful golf shots they must be able to use or adapt their swing technique in a versatile way. Generally the more orthodox a player's technique the easier to adapt a swing to the correct style for playing a particular shot. In the previous section a variety of faults were evaluated, and it should have been clear that from certain individual habits, golfers significantly limit their chances of success, for example a strong grip would make playing a high, soft fade shot particularly difficult, as would the weight on the right foot at impact when attempting a low shot into the wind. Golfers should be aware of their own particular weaknesses both technically and in shot-making terms. It is possible to improve the latter without developing the former, but more likely it will need an improvement of both knowledge and swing sense to accomplish quality and consistency.

Understanding the principles of swing path, angle of approach, club face and ball flight are all significantly relevant when developing shot-making skills. There are few golf shots that cannot be executed to some level of competence with the control of these attributes. Top professionals such as Seve Ballesteros have famous reputations built on such skills. They not only have solid, repetitive techniques, but also have developed their ball control skills through practice, application and tournament experience. They all have a high level of feel and mental imagery for the shot they are about to play, and this helps them to adapt and position themselves correctly at both address and during the swing itself.

Uneven Lies

Any variation of sloping lies will affect the way a golfer returns the clubhead to the ball. The set-up, posture and aim, and more than likely the swing itself, will need to be adjusted to suit the stance and lie conditions.

Side Hill – Ball above the Feet Fig 77

Understanding the following factors will help a player appreciate the relative simplicity of this shot. The ball is positioned above the feet so accept that:

1. It will be necessary to stand a little further from the ball at address.
2. The posture must be as perpendicular to the slope as possible, but the weight must not be too far back towards the heels.
3. Hold the club lower down the handle to help maintain control.
4. The lie of the ball and the player's posture will make the body turn more rotationally, and the swing plane flatter. Position the ball more in the centre of the stance.

Fig 77 Ball above the feet – the position of the ball dictates a flatter swing plane and more rotational swing action.

5. Balance is more difficult to maintain, so swing smoothly and well within your capabilities, maintaining your original spine angle throughout.

6. The ball flight will be to the left as the set-up and swing characteristics cause the club face to return to impact in a closed position. N.B. The aim, therefore, must be to the right of the target to compensate.

7. The closed club face at impact also has the effect of reducing the loft of the club. This will make the ball flight lower, which in turn will reduce the ball control and increase roll on landing. It can add some extra distance to the shot, which must be accounted for in terms of club selection.

Side Hill – Ball Below Feet Fig 78

This is generally a more difficult shot than with the ball above the feet, perhaps due to the fact that the swing is less rotational and relies more on a controlled hand and arm swing.

With the ball position below the feet accept that:

1. It will be necessary to stand closer to the ball at address.

2. The posture will be more over the ball and as near perpendicular to the ground as possible. The weight will feel more towards the toes. This is natural but good balance must be maintained during the swing as any movement forward or

backward is likely to have an adverse effect on the result of the shot.

3. Hold the club at the top of the handle to help minimize the need to lean over towards the ball, but be aware that this can limit control.

4. The position of the ball and posture will cause the shoulders to turn more down and under during the swing and as a result the club will move more vertically on an upright swing plane.

5. Balance is critical and must be a high priority. Maintain good posture throughout the swing.

6. The ball flight will tend to be to the right as the set-up and swing characteristics lead to an open club face position at impact.

N.B. aim to the left to compensate.

Fig 78 Ball below the feet – the posture is far more over the ball and creates a steeper swing plane and body action.

7. An open clubface has the effect of increasing the loft of each club, which will weaken the flight of the ball, and require a player to choose a more powerful club to compensate. In allowing for this distance factor the player must bear in mind that less lofted clubs further exaggerate the slice spin on the ball.

Uphill Lie Fig 79

Most golfers have little fear of this shot, as getting the ball into the air is relatively easy. In fact the difficulty is often that it flies too high with a lack of forward momentum. The following points are most relevant:

1. The body should be set up as perpendicular to the slope as possible. The weight will naturally favour the right side, care should

Fig 79 Uphill lies – the body is perpendicular to the slope and a slightly wider stance helps maintain balance.

103

be taken not to have too much weight favouring the right foot. Having said this, it is important not to lean into the slope.

2. A slightly wider stance will help maintain stability and balance.

3. The slope encourages a low takeaway and inside arc, which in turn will lead to a shallow angle of approach towards the impact position.

4. It can be instinctive to position the ball more towards the centre of the stance, but players must be careful not to overexaggerate this temptation as it will encourage the weight to remain on the right side at impact.

5. Gripping down the handle offers more control, but does restrict the width of the swing arc.

6. Transferring the weight forward will be more difficult, which limits the potential of

clearing the hips both before and during impact. This will encourage the hands to rotate and release earlier, closing the club face and possibly causing the player to pull or hook the ball to the left of the target. N.B. Aim to the right to compensate.

7. The slope is creating a swing movement that adds loft to the club face at impact, and so the increased height of the ball flight can limit the player's ball control and distance objectives.

8. Choose a stronger lofted club and remember to maintain a smooth rhythm and balance throughout the swing.

Downhill Lies Fig 80

This is probably the most difficult of all the sloping lies. The slope ensures that the ball

will fly on a lower trajectory which, unfortunately, causes golfers to feel that they need to help the ball into the air, and in doing so they often fail to execute the necessary swing movement that ensures a successful result. The following points are most relevant:

1. Set up to the ball with the shoulders as perpendicular to the slope as possible. The weight will be on the left side – resist the temptation to lean to the right either at address or during the swing.

2. Holding the club lower down the handle can help maintain control.

3. Play the ball more in the centre of the stance, to help achieve a solid contact with the ball.

4. The slope and player's posture will cause the swing to

Fig 80 Downhill lies – the weight favours the left side throughout the swing. The ball is positioned well back.

move the club up more steeply during the backswing with the left shoulder moving down and under and the body turn more limited than normal.

5. Try to maintain a centred, well-balanced position throughout the swing. If the player's weight slides too far forward towards the target, a topped or thin shot could be the result. If it falls backwards, a heavy shot is more likely to be the result.

6. The steep downswing will cause the club face to remain open, and so the ball will move to the right after impact. N.B. Aim to the left to compensate.

7. Allow the clubhead to swing down and through the ball at impact, feeling as if it is following the natural contours of the ground.

8. Remember to choose a club commensurable with the slope, that is, sufficient loft to get the ball airborne, and to control the flight of the ball.

Pitch or Chip Shots off the Sloping Lie

In theory the technique remains the same as for the full shot except that the margin for error is often more critical for a player the nearer the shot is played to the flagstick, as any error at this point in playing a hole is likely to cause the player to drop an extra shot to par. In actual practice the technique may be slightly different from that of the theoretical one, particularly for more accomplished or advanced players. Rather than aiming up to the right or left to allow for swing variations, it may be preferable for a player to develop more control of the alignment of the club face at impact. For example when pitching with the ball position above the level of the feet, the player may choose consciously to ensure that the club face is square or even open

at impact to counteract the natural tendency to rotate it closed. The stance and alignment will also be more square to the target. It is very much a personal preference and one based on ability, confidence and levels of skill.

Summary

Uneven lies undoubtedly create an additional challenge for the golfer, and understanding how the ball will react off the club face in each individual situation is a necessity as well as an obvious advantage. Even the very best players make errors of judgement, but they will always look to minimize these to a large extent.

Playing off slopes requires understanding, clear thinking, rhythm and balance. It is also important to practise off these uneven positions, just as a player would practise a 3ft putt or 250yd drive. No golfer can predict the outcome of such a shot without some sort of regular practice and understanding.

High and Low Shots

The need and ability to be able to vary the height of the ball flight is an essential aspect in any player's repertoire of shots. Where the ensuing shot needs to be high over the top of a tree, or low under its hanging branches, a golfer must possess the necessary understanding and skill to bring about the required result during a round of golf, particularly in competitive situations. In many instances it is a simple lack of knowledge or practice that costs the golfer dearly in scoring terms. In an attempt to play this more unorthodox shot the golfer is immediately under increased pressure which can lead to some rather illogical thinking and course management at times, and

Fig 81 All golfers need to be able to play under or over trees.

a failure to control adequately the swing action in the execution of the required shot.

The High Shot Fig 82

A key element in playing a high trajectory shot is to visualize and feel that the swing action is long and wide. The clubhead must approach the impact position at a shallow angle so that it sweeps into the ball making contact as nearly as possible to the lowest point of the swing arc. Even with an iron shot the player will take little or no divot. A more skilful player may feel as if the ball is being 'clipped off' the top off the turf.

In essence it is as if the player is making a similar swing motion to that used when playing a fairway wood shot. The loft on the club face must be used to create maximum elevation, whilst the wide swing action provides the necessary clubhead speed to hit the ball high and far enough for the requirement of the shot.

The higher trajectory may help the golfer gain distance through the air, particularly if the shot is wind assisted, but it will minimize any forward roll of the ball on landing. Into the wind the distance that the ball will carry through the air may be considerably reduced, and so once again club selection is an important criterion.

The high shot will be of great use when playing certain shots downwind, when it is necessary to carry the ball over a mound,

bunker or water hazard, or just to play to a difficult or tight pin placement.

At Address

1. Position the ball more forward in your stance than normal, for irons near to the left heel, for woods the left instep, but not too far forward so that contact might be made on the upswing.
2. A slightly wider stance will help provide a solid base for the necessary rotational full turn and shallower angle of approach to the ball.
3. The hands and body will be positioned more behind the ball than normal, particularly for an iron shot. The weight will be more on the right side.

Fig 82 A high shot – the ball is positioned more forward, the backswing a wide, full movement.

4. If a particularly high shot is required it may be necessary to adopt a more open stance and alignment, but with the club face aiming square to the actual target. An out to in swing path with the club face open to that swing path will cut the ball up into the air on a higher trajectory. There will be an increase of left to right side spin causing the ball to slice, which must be allowed for in directional terms. The distance the ball carries will also be reduced.

For the Swing

1. The takeaway should be smooth and wide with a delayed or limited setting of the wrists.
2. The weight should feel comfortably into the right side, with the shoulders making a full turn so as to accomplish fully completed backswing movement.
3. The transition from backward to forward swing should be smooth and unhurried, encouraging a wide sweeping angle of approach towards the ball.
4. The temptation to help get the ball airborne must be resisted as any attempt to lift the ball will only result in the hands propelling the clubhead forward too early, so that at impact it is likely that the clubhead would have passed the lowest point of the swing arc and would be moving in a more upward direction. This will either cause a heavy shot, one where a divot is taken before impact or a thin shot with the leading edge of the club face making contact too far up the ball's circumference. Both will limit ball strike potential, flight characteristics and distance.
5. Allow the club to sweep under the ball, there may be a sensation of clipping the ball off the turf.
6. A good rhythm is very important throughout the whole swing action.
7. The weight should be fully transferred onto the left side.

Any attempt to stay back on the right side to help get the ball airborne will limit success and lead to some very inconsistent results. The follow-through should feel high and wide.

The high shot requires particularly good visualization, timing and confidence. A slight mistake in the swing action reduces the chances of contacting the ball and turf at the critical time and at the correct point in the swing arc. To be successful under pressure it is important to practise not only the technical execution, but the mental rehearsal and visualization to help build confidence.

The Low Shot Fig 83

The execution of the successful low shot could be construed as being the opposite of the high one, but this is not entirely correct. The player is seeking to deliver the club face to the ball with a slight decrease in its effective loft, but any attempt to achieve this by making it an exaggeratedly downward blow, that is, a chopping down action, is likely to result in an increase in the ball's height and a loss of distance. The appearance and feel of the swing will be that of less than a full movement with the ball being knocked down and forward more than with an orthodox shot. The width and length of the swing will be limited and it will be necessary for the hands to lead the clubhead at impact. The lower trajectory will reduce the distance at which the ball travels through the air and increase the amount of roll on landing. These characteristics need to be taken into account with regard to club selection and course management, particularly if there is a bunker or other hazard guarding the target, or if the flag is positioned close to the front edge of the green.

A low shot is also of great use in windy conditions or if a player wishes to play a low-flying running shot, which will prove particularly useful when playing on a seaside course, or when ground conditions are essentially dry.

At Address

1. Position the ball more towards the centre of the stance, and just inside the left heel for woods.
2. The stance can be as normal although the weight should feel slightly towards the left side, mainly due to the adjusted ball position.
3. The club should be held slightly down the grip with the hands feeling more forward of the ball than normal.
4. If a particularly low shot is required then the player could choose two alternatives, either select a low numbered club or, possibly to play the ball even further back in stance with the shoulders aligned right of the target and the club face aimed directly at the target. This position at address will lead to an in to out swing path with the club face slightly closed at impact. The result will be a right to left hooking shot with a low flight, relatively short carry distance and excessive run characteristics.

The Swing

1. The takeaway should be smooth with minimal wrist-set.
2. The shoulders should turn to about a three-quarter position with the weight remaining fairly central – feeling more over the ball than normal.
3. The wrists should remain passive throughout the backswing, which will limit both feel and actual length of the completed movement.
4. The transition from backward to forward swing needs to be

Fig 83 The low shot.

(a)

(b)

(c)

The ball is positioned back in the stance (a), the weight remains in front of the ball at the top of the backswing (b), and the follow-through is limited (c).

smooth, and the temptation to 'lean into' or to drive forward too early should be resisted as this will result in a mishit or miscontrolled shot due to the exaggeratedly steep angle of approach caused. A deep divot will usually provide the evidence of such a movement.
5. Allow the weight to remain over the ball with a progressive weight transfer as the impact position approaches.
6. The clubhead should feel as if it is 'squeezing' the ball against the turf and that the ball is flying off fast and low towards the target.
7. The whole swing should be smooth, rhythmical and well-balanced.
8. The body should turn fully through so that the chest faces the target, but the swing movement itself will be shorter and more limited than normal, with the hands finishing no higher than shoulder height on completion of the swing.

A low shot is not as difficult to play as a high one, but even so it requires an acceptable level of skill established with practice and experience. Once again good visualization and feel for the shot are of vital importance.

No matter how high the level of a player's ability, playing a controlled low-flighted shot with a wooden club is more difficult than with an iron off a tee-peg. Some experts recommend teeing the ball high, so that a shallow downswing approach of the clubhead sweeps the ball away on a low trajectory, whereas others suggest teeing it lower to help encourage the clubhead to contact the ball with the bottom part of the clubface, which promotes a more penetrating ball flight. From the fairway it is only the more lofted woods that tend to create a high trajectory so a simple option may well be to choose a less lofted wood club

and to play the shot with a smoother rhythm.
A golfer who is successfully able to play both high and low shots can be sure that their swing action is technically solid enough to provide increased shot-making skills, which will offer the potential for lower scoring if combined with sound course-management skills.

Playing in the Wind

In the United Kingdom it is a rare occurrence to play golf when there is no wind at all. Golfers must accept that the wind adds to the challenge of the game and that without the ability to adapt to the conditions brought about by its presence the player will rarely be able to perform to a satisfactory and consistent level.
Courses are often constructed with the wind in mind. Rarely will a golf course architect design a long and difficult hole into the direction of the prevailing wind. In many cases what appears to be a relatively easy or tame hole in calm conditions can be transformed when the wind begins to blow, so that suddenly bunkers and other hazards influence play more than anticipated and what might on occasion be a simple mid- or short-iron shot becomes a demanding longer one. Par fives that sometimes play as short as a par four become their true test of golf and the greens appear to shrink in size on par threes as a greater degree of ball control is required to play onto the green in one shot. One of the best examples of this is the 'Postage Stamp' – the eighth hole at Royal Troon.
The wind blows from four general directions:

1. Behind or following.
2. Against or into.
3. Across wind from left to right.

4. Across from right to left.

There is obviously a whole variety of combinations of these wind factors that golfers will experience during even one round of golf and it is important that a player has the judgement and skill to assess how to play the ensuing shots correctly.
It is worth noting that playing into or down the wind requires certain similar swing characteristics to hitting the ball on a high or low flight, and so the following information may be slightly similar to the previous section. It is important to identify the relevant points and endeavour to keep the execution of each shot as simple as possible.

Wind Behind

A following wind, depending on its intensity, will affect the ball's flight in several ways:

A ball will be helped forward more with the amount and effect of backspin on a ball being reduced by the wind pushing forward and down on the ball and the trajectory being lower. This causes the ball to travel further in total distance particularly due to the extra run on landing. Most golfers will appreciate the help of a following wind in certain circumstances such as when playing a drive from the tee on a long par 4 or par 5 hole, but there are times when playing downwind is often a disadvantage such as when hazards, that is, bunkers, water or out of bounds are reachable with the help of the wind or, playing an approach shot to the green when controlling the ball on landing is an absolute necessity.
A player has several options in terms of course management and these are dependent upon the

player's skill level and his confidence or preference:

1. Increasing the height or trajectory of the shot to improve the distance the ball travels through the air and to reduce the amount of forward roll of the ball on landing. This can apply to tee shots as well as approaches to the green. From the tee a player may prefer to choose a more lofted wood than a driver so that the ball is elevated more easily. Alternatively, teeing the ball higher and sweeping the clubhead upward so that the ball is struck slightly underneath its circumference is another option to increase the trajectory.

2. On approach shots the ball may be positioned more forward than normal causing the player's weight to remain behind the ball at impact. This will lead to a higher flighted shot and less roll on landing. Opening the club face and aiming the body slightly left of target will allow the player to fade the ball slightly (although the amount of fade will be reduced downwind) again improving the control of the ball on landing.

3. Should the player not have the skill or preference to play a high shot, a ball played with its normal trajectory will mean that a player has to simply allow for a slight increase of distance through the air and extra roll on landing.

In certain circumstances it may be preferable to actually play to decrease the height of the shot, so that the ball is hardly affected by the wind at all. This would mean that the player has to appreciate the carry and roll distance factor fairly skilfully, but it may be the only option when playing in extreme downwind circumstances, particularly if the golf course is dry with hard, running fairways.

A player's choice or options may most often be influenced by the nature of the shot he is about to play. Length of the hole, width of the fairway, hazards or position of the flagstick all require the player to calculate the risk factors, and to decide upon the most suitable shot in the circumstances. The usual rule of thumb applies – a player should favour his strengths and only play the more risky type of shots when necessary.

Wind Against

The majority of golfers find playing shots against the wind one of the most difficult aspects of golf. Depending on the intensity of the wind the flight of the ball will be affected in two ways – the distance it travels and the direction of its flight.

The contact that the clubhead makes with the ball is more critical than normal as any mishits or extra side or back spin will be exaggerated by the wind and cause the ball to deviate from its normal trajectory. Hence a small slice becomes a big one; a pull turns into a pull draw/hook, a high trajectory becomes even higher. Unfortunately it is natural for a golfer to try to hit the ball harder than normal in an endeavour to beat the effects of the wind. This, in almost all cases, will work in reverse having more detrimental effects than good ones. The harder a player swings the more errors are likely to occur, such as a tendency to lean too far forward at impact in an effort to keep the ball low. This actually creates a steep angle of clubhead approach into the impact position, which is more likely to send the ball higher rather than lower than normal. Also leaning forward, even if contact with the ball is successful, often makes it difficult for the player to square up the club face. In the majority of cases the face remains open so that the ball flies off to the right, which will be further exaggerated by the effects of the wind or, alternatively, the golfer makes a last split-second attempt to square up the club face and the reverse happens, the club face closes and de-lofts at impact so that a low, mishit shot usually struck from the heel side of the club face and moving to the left of the target is the result.

Finally, a harder, faster swing action can often cause the golfer to throw the clubhead towards the ball too early during the downswing movement. This leads to a deceleration of the speed as impact approaches with the clubhead moving past the hands before contact is made with the ball. The result is that the club strikes the ground before the ball or the club reaches the ball as the upswing commences so that the ball is hit off the bottom of the club face causing a topped or thinned shot.

The message is relatively simple – the harder a player swings, the greater the errors experienced. A normal swing is generally all that is required, although this may make the player feel that the swing is in fact slightly slower than normal as the influence of the wind invariably increases the pressure of playing the shot, so that a golfer's feel and judgement in executing the swing and shot require more discipline. There are several options a player can use in terms of execution and course management, and once again these will be dependent upon skill levels and preference. The details covered earlier in the chapter regarding the technique for low shots also apply to shots into the wind.

Although players instinctively tend to tee the ball low for tee shots, this can often have a detrimental effect for less skilful players who will generally be tempted to hit down too steeply onto the ball when it is positioned at a low height, and it also encourages the club face to remain open at impact. Many prefer to work on the theory that if the ball is teed higher than normal rather than lower, the clubhead approach towards impact will be shallower, which widens the swing arc and helps drive the ball more forward rather than upward. In this case it can be a positive aspect for the player to feel as if the clubhead is travelling level to the ground as it approaches the ball. Positioning the ball back in the stance can help lower the flight of the ball but only if the player controls the timing of the forward weight shift – the detrimental effects of an early slide forward and steep clubhead approach into the shot have already been fully explained.

Utilizing the style of swing that suits a draw or hook is often successful for many players. The technique required for this shot perfectly suits the low shot requirements – alignment a little closed, aiming to the right of target, ball slightly back in stance, swing path relatively shallow and from an inside path. The results – a low, right to left ball flight.

To summarize, the key elements are to keep the swing speed smooth and controllable, position the ball further back in the stance, grip lower down the handle of the club for control, restrict the length of the backswing and follow-through to about three quarters of normal, particularly for mid- and short irons – long irons and woods fly lower anyway, and finally maintain good balance at all times.

Cross Winds

Cross winds cause players some confusion at times because they are never quite sure whether to play a shot that works with the wind or try to play one that holds up against it. If there is any doubt or a lack of skill, the simplest solution is always to play shots allowing the wind to move the ball.

The difficulty, and sometimes danger, is that the wind can overemphasize the movement of the ball so that although there may well be the benefit of some additional length to the shot, the ball could end up missing a green, finishing in the rough or in a hazard. A player must assess the situation and the risks

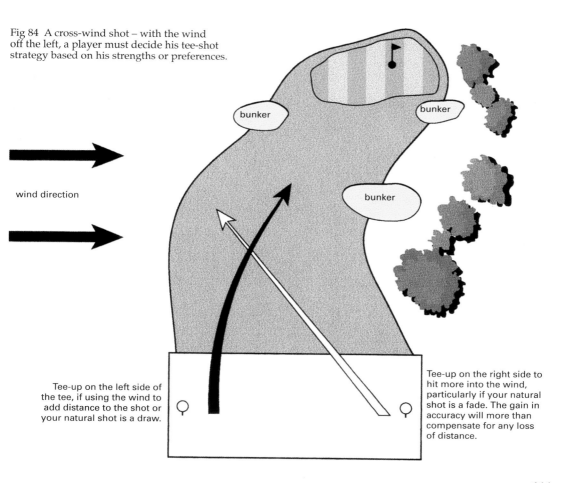

Fig 84 A cross-wind shot – with the wind off the left, a player must decide his tee-shot strategy based on his strengths or preferences.

wind direction

bunker

bunker

bunker

Tee-up on the left side of the tee, if using the wind to add distance to the shot or your natural shot is a draw.

Tee-up on the right side to hit more into the wind, particularly if your natural shot is a fade. The gain in accuracy will more than compensate for any loss of distance.

involved and with some sensible course management, play the simplest and most effective shot.

It is not advisable to play higher flighted shots in a crosswind. A normal or low trajectory will offer better ball control. From the tee a player who decides to use the wind to help shape the shot may well choose to tee up the ball on the side from where the wind is coming, that is, in a left to right wind, tee up on the left side, aim for the left side of the fairway and allow the ball to slide from left to right – a fade shot – on the wind. Conversely, a player may feel increased confidence by playing a shot more into the wind and would rather choose to tee the ball up on the teeing ground on the opposite side to the direction of the wind, that is, with the wind off the left side, the player would tee the ball up on the right hand side of the tee, aiming for the left side or left half of the fairway and driving the ball more into the wind so that the side-effects would be minimized to some degree. In this case the shot would be likely to lose some of its length, but the control and accuracy factors would more than compensate for that.

The Psychology of Wind Play

The major challenge of playing golf in the wind is very often psychological. Rarely do players enjoy playing in the wind, but to succeed is mainly a matter of good attitude. The best players are those who are able to make the mental adjustments necessary to maintain their emotional equilibrium in windy conditions. It is likely that more fairways and greens than normal will be missed due to the conditions, and so a player must mentally prepare for these disruptions to his game. It is vital that a player does not get frustrated or down on himself as the wind is

unpredictable at best. Anger must not enter the player's emotional state as it can only put more pressure on the player himself. Sticking to the normal pre-shot routine and keeping good timing and control of all movements is an important aspect. The game of golf is about being able to take on the challenges thrown at us both in a physical and physiological sense. Technical preparation and a positive mental approach go a long way towards helping a player to perform better in the wind.

Summarizing Wind Play

There is no denying the relevance and influence of the wind on the game of golf. Rarely is golf played without its presence to some extent. The key element in wind, as it is in golf as a whole, is control. The wind will minimize control by increasing or decreasing any spin the player's clubhead makes on contact with the ball. To reduce this loss of control, one must always play within one's capabilities keeping the swing movement as near normal that is possible. The speed or rhythm should be smooth and natural. Some coaches and wind specialists advocate a policy of swinging softly into the wind, and hard downwind. Balance is a high priority so that a player's weight distribution and control are increased. Choose a club with a stronger loft where necessary, beating the effects of the wind with controlled ball flight rather than putting emphasis on an aggressive, attacking shot.

Remember, the wind will encourage a player to hit the ball harder, reducing the likelihood of consistent success. Making a good swing movement and striking the ball with a solid contact will more than compensate for most negative aspects of the wind.

The Effect of Wind on Ball Distance		
Wind (mph)	Distance through the air (yd)	Total length (yd)
0	200	230
Behind		
10	206	237
20	211	250
30	225	269
Into		
10	191	215
20	181	195
30	160	165

Shots from the Rough

It is inevitable that all players will be faced with playing a number of shots from either the rough or semi-rough. The type of recovery shot to be played will be very much dependent upon the lie of the ball and the situation in which the golfer finds himself on a particular hole. There will be times when the player must face the truth that taking the shortest route back to the fairway is the only option, whereas on other occasions it may be possible to actually play an attacking shot and aim directly at the flagstick.

Understanding the technicalities of playing from the rough is an important element of success in these instances. When the ball is lying in light rough it is inevitable that a certain amount of grass will be collected between the club face and ball at impact, and this will have more influence on the distance the ball travels rather than the direction it goes in. The amount of backspin is reduced and consequently it is very easy for the player to experience 'flyers' where the ball comes off the club face much faster than normal and has increased distance factors both through the air and once it lands and begins to roll. This is particularly true when the grain of the grass is in the general direction of the shot. It is obviously important that the golfer takes these potential flyer situations into account when choosing the correct club selection for the shot. For heavier rough or when the grain of grass is lying away from the target the player must be fully aware of the importance of getting the club face correctly in contact with the ball. Long grass wraps itself around the hosel of the golf club, and once this happens the club face closes so that at impact it aims more left and the loft is decreased. To counteract this the player must increase the steepness of the angle of approach so that the club contacts the ball with a more descending blow. To further increase the potential for a solid contact it is possible for a player to adapt to a more open stance and alignment, and to aim the clubface a little more to the right at address. These two factors help increase the angle of approach and ensure that even if the club face closes slightly it still remains relatively square to the target. The ball position should always be played from near to the middle of the stance so that there is less likelihood of any long grass wrapping itself around the clubhead or shaft. It may be advisable to feel that weight is positioned more to the left, to encourage a steeper swing action, with a more active wrist set. A firm, but not tight grip is also a benefit.

For shots played from heavy rough around the green it may be better to adopt a bunker type technique where the club face is laid considerably open and the stance and shoulders aim well left. This will create an out to in cutting action of the swing path moving from across and to the

Fig 85 Even the best players visit the rough frequently. Here Bernhard Langer executes a superb recovery shot.

left of the flag stick. More accomplished players attempt to actually let the club enter the long grass slightly behind the ball so that they are in effect taking a divot of grass underneath the ball. This will cause the ball to pop up quickly into the air and allow a far more attacking shot to

be played than would normally be possible if a player were endeavouring to get the club face cleanly in contact with the ball.

The essence of good play from the rough is to ensure as solid a contact as possible between the club face and the ball. A swing path that is from an in to out

113

direction will tend to approach the ball from too shallow an angle of approach which will not only have the risk of collecting too much grass between the club face and ball, but will also encourage a player to close the club face prior to impact. The rough will reduce the clubhead speed, distance and control factors, therefore the club must approach the ball from a steep angle. The feeling of slicing the shot increases the player's potential to execute a successful recovery. The extent to which a player adapts his style to suit the situation is very much a personal preference and based on experience and previous success.

Bare Lies

Most golfers tend to react in a very negative way when they find their ball sitting on a bare or tight lie as they fear not being able to make solid contact with the ball. The shot has to be played with a fair amount of precision for the golfer to enjoy control of both distance and direction. The greatest temptation for any golfer is to endeavour to try to help the ball to get airborne from a bare lie which is a major mistake and one that creates more poor results than playing the shot in a relatively straightforward fashion. It is possible that the clubhead will bounce off the bare surface with the result that the shot may be rather low and squirty with no control. To compensate this the player must attempt to hit the ball with a steeper angle of approach by positioning the ball further back in the stance and, if anything, turning the club face slightly inward so that it appears a little closed, as these adaptations will certainly help ensure more consistent contact and overall success. From here the club face is able to squeeze the ball

against the hard surface and continue its downward descent into the ground with the leading edge cutting through so that a divot can be taken, and there is no danger of the flange of the club bouncing off the hard surface. If the player addresses the ball with a closed club face, it will be necessary to aim slightly to the right to compensate, and possibly to choose a more lofted club for increased control.

This is not a shot that allows the player much margin for error and as such must be played in a sensible fashion. Accomplished players do not fear the shot in the same way as a middle or higher handicap golfer. Control is increased with practice and confidence, although all players must be fully aware of the dangers should the shot not be executed correctly.

Improved Bunker Play

Although most golfers have some form of proficiency when playing a shot from a green side bunker, most have reduced or little skill when playing a longer bunker shot. Whereas fairway bunker shots are relatively straightforward generally, playing from sand from 30 to 60yd tends to be the most difficult to execute. In fact even the most accomplished players including professionals find this distance the one they least relish.

Approach Shots from Bunkers

As with all bunker shots there are some very relevant assessments a player must make before attempting to execute the shot – choice of club (usually a wedge or sand wedge) depending upon the lie of the ball, the nature and depth of the sand, the levelness of the stance, how close the ball

is positioned towards the bunker face and how physically high that face is, the distance the ball has to carry to reach the green, the position of the flagstick, how much green the player has to work with, the direction and intensity of the wind, the slope and nature of the ground around the bunker and the green and finally, the type of difficulties and dangers near to, or around the green that could be an influence should the execution of the shot not be correct.

A few general rules apply in judging and playing this type of shot.

Distance is controlled by the following factors:

• The length of the backswing and speed through impact.
• Ball position – forward = higher with less power, back = lower and more aggressive.
• The position of the club face at impact – an open face will decrease the distance the ball travels, a closed or hooded face will increase this factor.
• The angle of the clubhead approach to the ball – a steep angle will generally reduce distance, a shallow one will help increase it. The direction of the swing path will also be an influence here.
• Contact of the ball or sand – the less sand contacted between the club face and the ball at impact the further the ball is likely to travel. It is worth remembering that an active hand action is likely to make judging the correct amount of sand taken more difficult. Passive hands are preferable.
• A player must be careful when taking the stance. As vital as it is to get a firm footing in the sand, it is also important not to dig the feet down too deep as the level of the base of the feet will become too exaggeratedly low in relation to the level of the ball. A solid footing is all that is really required.

114

A player may have certain individual preferences, for example, a longer than recommended smooth swing action may be preferential for relatively short shots, but requires a proficient level of skill and feel from the golfer. Others may choose a shorter more aggressive swing action, preferring to drive the ball forward towards the target. Generally it is best to keep the length of the backswing and follow-through about the same, with the combination of the other influencing factors making up the whole movement and execution of the shot.

Direction is controlled by:

• The club face – square, open or closed.
• The swing path – in to square to in, out to in or in to out. A player's aim and alignment factor have a considerable influence on the swing path.
• An out to in swing path will reduce the forward momentum at impact and will therefore be a factor with regard to distance as well as direction. This swing path direction will also tend to steepen the angle of approach, so that the clubhead digs more deeply into the sand. To counteract the effects of the swing path a player will need to open the club face somewhat, which will add loft and consequently height to the trajectory of the shot.
• An in to out swing path is not one particularly recommended or favoured in playing bunker shots of this type of distance. This swing path encourages a low or shallow angle of approach, which will keep the clubhead moving more parallel to the sand rather than travelling down, and through. The ball will be contacted more cleanly than normal with a divot of sand being very shallow or almost non-existent. There is a danger that the clubhead might

contact the sand too early or behind the ball, causing the player to scoop up too much sand between the club face and the ball, or that the contact on the ball may be rather thin so that the ball flight is low, aggressive and uncontrollable.
• If the swing has a pronounced in to out path, the player will have to compensate for the directional influence by closing the club face at impact. This closure will reduce the effective loft of the club face creating a lower trajectory and more aggressive shot with less backspin. It is a dangerous and difficult swing balance and not a shot for the faint-hearted or less skilful player.
• A relatively normal in to square to in swing path is quite acceptable for many of these mid-distance bunker shots. A square or slightly open stance allows the player to maintain a normal swing path. The angle of approach should be fairly neutral with the clubhead hitting into the sand an acceptable distance behind the ball. The player does not need to compensate by adjusting the club face alignment in any way.
• The mid-distance bunker shot causes players great confusion at times – it is neither a straightforward splash or explosion shot nor is it quite the committed full swing action required for fairway bunkers. The factors described above give a player several options with regard to height, distance and control. Each player will have a preference, probably founded on his or her own swing strengths or, and just as importantly, based on confidence, generally born from previous successes or failures. All the usual factors play an important role, the correct set-up and ball position, length and rhythm of the swing action, weight distribution and balance, but above all feel and confidence for the shot about to be played. It

is not always easy to practise this shot regularly, yet this is a vital factor, as visualization and knowledge can only be enhanced by practical experience.

The Fairway or Long Bunker Shot

The fairway bunker shot should to all intents and purposes be a relatively straightforward golf shot, which requires a few customized adjustments by the player. The main criterion is to ensure that the clubhead contacts the ball first before the sand, otherwise distance and control will be reduced. The player must go through the same series of pre-shot assessments as were summarized in covering approach shots from bunkers.

The correct choice of club is fairly critical as the necessity for distance must be counterbalanced with the reality of ensuring that the loft of the club is sufficient to elevate the ball over the lip of the bunker face. The lie of the ball dictates the player's following moves as the poorer this is the greater the loft of the club required, plus the more benefit there is to be gained by increasing the angle of attack and opening the club face to ensure a higher launch angle at impact.

The depth of the sand in the bunker is slightly less relevant if the ball has a good lie, although the player must establish a solid footing as the increased swing movement of the fairway bunker shot in comparison to that of a green side one, means that there is more likelihood of the feet, particularly the right one, moving during the swing.

The ball should be positioned towards the centre of the stance to help ensure a clean strike prior to the club contacting the sand. Keeping the hands forward of the ball at impact will ensure solid contact with the ball.

Fig 86 Nick Faldo demonstrates the correct technique for playing fairway bunker shots.

A useful tip is to remember to grip down the handle slightly as this not only increases control, but helps counteract the usual necessity for a player to shuffle their feet down into the sand in an effort to improve stability, which in turn lowers the level of the base of the feet in relation to the level of the ball itself.

The swing should be kept relatively short and simple, with as little unnecessary or excessive movement as possible. There should be a limited lower body action, as too much will lead to erratic and unreliable results. The quieter lower body action also helps reduce the full swing movement in most cases leading to a three-quarter position, which may well prove quite sufficient for most golfers. The transition into the downswing movement

needs to be smooth and flowing, as any attempt to rush back to the ball will affect the balance, co-ordination and control of the downswing.

The ball should be swept fairly cleanly off the sand, although few players are skilful enough to contact the ball without taking at least a small divot of sand. If the lie is not ideal, or the player has any doubts as to the outcome of the shot, then it is advisable to hit more downward into the ball to increase the percentage of success. The clubhead will take a longer, deeper divot of sand after contacting the ball. In playing this shot with a steeper angle of approach it may be necessary for the player to change the club selection, as the hands tend to lead the clubhead driving the ball more forward with a lower

flighted trajectory. The rhythm or pace of the swing are important elements as they help the player to maintain one of the most important aspects – that of balance. Without good balance the player's centre of gravity is likely to move leading to inconsistent results. Confidence is once again a vital factor. Some players prefer to focus their eyes on the front of the ball to ensure that their thoughts are positive, and the swing movement is working to help contact the ball before the sand.

As confidence and proficiency are increased a player will become more positive in playing these shots. Overaggression will often cost more than conservative play. Appreciating the maximum distance possible and then gearing down a little more will lead to no great overall loss as

Tips from Sloping Lies in Bunkers

Key Aspects
1. Good contact with the ball.
2. Swing within yourself.
3. Balance.

Ball on Up Slope
1. Shoulders parallel to slope – ball more in centre of the stance.
2. Ball flight higher, and so choose an appropriate club – possibly 1 or 2 clubs stronger.
3. Limit the length of the swing to help balance and control – sweep ball off the sand.
4. Weight transfer difficult due to limited leg action – ball may travel left from this slope, therefore make allowances.

Ball on Down Slope
1. Shoulders parallel to slope – ball in centre of stance, grip down handle slightly.
2. Ball flight lower – choose appropriate club, possibly 1 or 2 clubs weaker.
3. Restrict length of backswing for control and balance. Hit down in direction of slope.
4. Maintain balance – follow-through will be short of full position.
5. Ball may move to the right – take this into consideration.

Ball above Feet
1. Grip down handle slightly depending on severity of slope.
2. Ball towards middle of stance – adopt more upright posture.
3. Ball will be swept more off the sand and may move to left in the air.

Ball below Feet
1. Posture more over ball – dig feet well into sand and limit the length of the swing maintaining balance and rhythm.
2. Keep leg actions quiet – divot slightly deeper than normal.
3. The ball may move little to right. Take this into consideration.

positional play is part of executing a sound recovery and good course management.

It is also an advantage to appreciate the characteristics of ball flight and distance with certain clubs, particularly when playing on different courses with different types of bunker design and sand conditions.

Finally, and by way of repetition, a player should never hesitate to select a more lofted club or play the shot with a technique that elevates the trajectory of the ball quicker as the most important rule is to get the ball out, particularly when in deeper fairway bunkers.

Improved Pitching and Chipping

The importance of the short game in scoring terms means that to lower scores and improve a handicap level a player must dedicate sufficient time to specific pitching and chipping practice. An improvement of skills leads to a greater scope and variety of shots available to the player in scoring terms. A player must not only seek technical improvement, but be fully aware that balance, feel, co-ordination and rhythm, all work together to produce consistent, high-quality short game results. Before a player can

develop skills to accommodate some of the more advanced shots, it is generally fair to assume that they will have established a satisfactory level of success with the basic essentials for the short game shots. These are:

1. A correct address position (Fig 87) – feet closer together than for a normal shot, feet and hips slightly open to the target, weight forward of the ball favouring the left side, hands positioned slightly down the handle and forward of the ball, grip pressure not too tight, arms fairly close to the body.
2. The swing length and speed are controlled well enough to provide sufficiently consistent results.
3. The balance and co-ordination of all movements allows consistent ball striking and adequate ball flight control.

Playing High Pitches Fig 87

There are a number of ways for a golfer to increase the effective club face loft at impact which will lead to a higher flighted shot than normal. These are:– open the club face, move the hands and consequently the butt end of the club further behind the ball at address, and finally and perhaps most simply move the ball more forward in the stance. All have particular implications, but the extra height and control on landing can be sourced from one of these alternatives or a combination of two or three of them.

The Standard High Pitch

By moving the ball forward the body is in effect being positioned more behind the ball at address. This will lead to a slight opening up of the upper body to adjust to the ball position, but not enough to affect the swing path to any

The Lob Shot

This is really an adaptation of the cut-up shot. The ball is positioned forward; the hands are kept level with the ball at address. The backswing becomes more of a movement with the arms and therefore is longer, with the hands and wrists remaining relatively passive throughout. The downswing is smooth and the club glides underneath the ball sending it on a high trajectory with a soft landing.

The longer, wider swing action creates a shallow angle of approach to the ball and so a relatively good lie is needed before attempting this shot.

The Soft Shot

The essence of this shot is not that of a high spin, high-flighted one, but of a controlled flight and soft landing. The ball is positioned just inside the left heel, but can vary depending on the height of shot required, and the hands can be positioned opposite the back of the ball. The club face aims to the target and the body is relatively square, but with the feet open. This set-up position helps limit the amount of wrist action and keeps the club face square or even slightly closed to the path of the swing creating a low, wide shallow backswing arc.

The arc remains shallow on the downswing, the hands and clubhead feel as if they move at a relatively similar speed, with the right hand sliding gently under the left at impact, allowing the increasing loft of the club face to 'pop' the ball forward and up. The flight of the ball is one of a low spin, gentle, medium height trajectory due to the slow, smooth swing action. The ball drops down gently onto the surface of the green and rolls

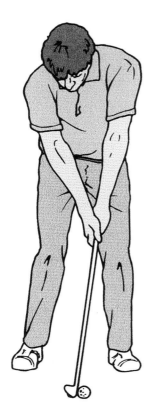

Fig 87 The standard pitch – the ball is positioned opposite the centre of the chest, the weight favours the left side and the hands are slightly ahead of the ball.

Fig 88 Playing high pitches – the ball is positioned well forward in the stance, the weight fairly even between the feet, the hands set back slightly behind the ball. Note the subsequent shaft angle.

great extent. The wrists do not need to be particularly active allowing the club to slide under the ball from a relatively shallow angle of the approach. The overall length of the swing is dependent on the length of the shot required and the weight will remain slightly left-sided throughout the swing action.

The Cut-up Shot Fig 87

The ball is positioned opposite the left heel with the club face aiming slightly right and the body aligned a little left. This open position, similar to a bunker shot, allows the clubhead

path to follow the direction of the body to cut across the ball from out to in. The open club face neutralizes this swing direction and also adds effective loft at impact. The hands and wrists will be more active with this style of shot so a steeper angle of approach and firm crisp strike at impact, combine with the set-up factors to give the ball a high launch angle with the ball having an increased amount of backspin, both of which stop the ball quickly on landing. This is a particularly good shot from difficult lies as the steeper swing action allows the club to reach the bottom of the ball more easily.

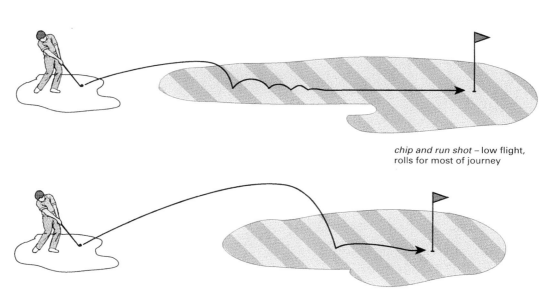

chip and run shot – low flight, rolls for most of journey

pitch – medium height, backspin helps limit roll on landing

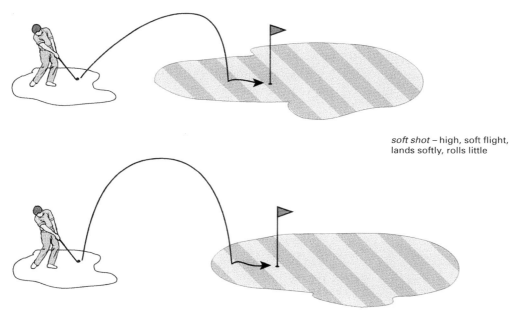

soft shot – high, soft flight, lands softly, rolls little

lob – very high flight, lands and stops quickly

Fig 89 Chip and pitch – flight and roll characteristics.

only a limited distance. The skill required to play this shot is far higher than with most pitch shots. The difficulties of keeping a smooth rhythm, combined with striking the ball with the hands positioned level, add greater risk overall. The shallow angle of the arc means a lie must be a good one to ensure that the clubhead can get efficiently to the bottom of the ball.

It is important that all golfers are proficient with at least one technique that allows them to stop the ball on the green. Players with greater short game skills can adapt or combine these

119

techniques to play a greater variety of shots, and therefore offer themselves far more scope in scoring terms.

Useful Lower Shots

Fig 90

In seeking to hit the ball on a lower trajectory around the green there are several basic ways of decreasing the effective loft of the club, so that the ball begins its flight at a lower launch angle. These are:– Move the ball further back in the stance, increase the amount of weight positioned on the left side, move the butt end of the shaft forward of the ball at address or finally, most simply, choose a straighter-faced club. Most lower-flighted shots can be mastered with these options or a combination of them, particularly with regard to ball position and weight distribution, which is very much a personal preference and dictates much of what happens with the following swing action. Whichever technique is chosen the player must be aware of the amount of hand and wrist action used during the swing itself. Too active an action may cause the club to be picked up too quickly and delivered back to the ball as steeply, sending the ball forward too aggressively with a lack of overall control. Too limited a hand and wrist action could mean that the clubhead will swing on too shallow an arc making it difficult for the player to squeeze the ball forward. This will lead to mishits or mistimed shots and a lack of consistency.

By moving the ball back in the stance, the body is effectively being positioned more in front of the ball. This will automatically reduce the effective loft of the club face at impact and help to hit the ball on a lower-flighted trajectory. With the weight positioned more onto the left side

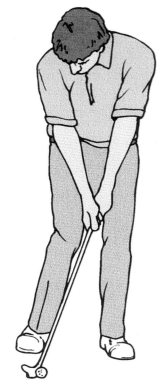

Fig 90 The ball is positioned back in the stance, the weight and hands forward of the ball. Note the subsequent shaft angle.

at address the player helps ensure that the hands arrive at impact in front of the leading edge of the club limiting the height of the shot and assuring a relatively consistent contact with the ball.

A player may simply choose to move the butt end of the shaft forward at address, which is in effect just positioning the hands further forward of the ball. This will reduce the effective loft of the club at address and as long as the player is able to return his hands to this same position at impact, the ball flight will once again be low and the ball will run on landing. Many higher handicapped players prefer to play this type of shot with this one adjustment, but it can have some disadvantages because at

address the player's weight is often positioned too evenly between both feet causing inconsistencies in ball striking terms with players contacting the ground behind the ball rather than being able to 'squeeze' the ball towards the target.

On a more positive note an advantage in playing the shot with this simple adjustment can be that with the hands a little more forward the wrists are already pre-set. All the player then needs to concentrate on in order to achieve the correct move is to allow the arms to swing backward and forward fast enough to generate the necessary amount of clubhead speed. More proficient players favour this type of adaptation, but will ensure that sufficient weight is positioned onto the left side to make sure that the clubhead is returned to the ball on a steep enough angle of attack to make crisp contact with the ball. It is a simple adjustment that allows a player to get consistent ball strike and reliable ball flight.

With these adaptations the position of the body will be one slightly different from a normal standard pitch or pitch shot in that the player will feel as if they are more over the ball address and that the left shoulder is far lower, so that the shoulders appear more parallel to the ground.

Higher handicap or less accomplished golfers may benefit by moving the ball more backward in the stance as this is the simplest option, and although to some extent there can be a slight loss of overall control this may be more than compensated for them by the improved confidence they gain from knowing that the ball position does incorporate a certain amount of margin for error with regard to actually making a decent contact with the ball.

Finally, the simplest option of choosing a straight-faced club should not be forgotten. It can provide the most consistent and reliable option as set-up and swing do not need to have any great adaptations to any particular extent and the variation of club chosen offers the differentials in ball flight and roll characteristics required for most shots that any player will be called upon to play.

The 'Knock it Forward' Shot

This is not strictly from the textbooks, but proves a useful shot in certain circumstances such as a recovery shot from the trees or rough, pitching from under a tree, or for running a ball up a steep bank around the approaches to the green. The basic technique is as for any low-flighted shot, but the player must allow the wrists to cock or set more than normal during the backswing. The clubhead must then be encouraged to strike more downward onto the ball so that the clubhead speed is increased. The hands will be more in front of the clubhead at impact which reduces club face loft still further, and creates an aggressive type of shot that should land on a predetermined spot and chase through to the target. Control will be relatively limited due to the lack of finesse, and so a player must be fully aware of the higher risk element that this shot could produce if it is does not come off.

The Hook Spin Chip

This shot is not really as complicated as its title may suggest. With the ball position slightly back in the stance, the body aligned square or even a little closed and the club face aiming to the target, the player should feel that the clubhead is swinging on an inside path both backward and forward towards the ball. Just

before impact the player must sense that the clubhead is slightly closed to the swing path, so that it feels as if the chip will be played like a mini-hook shot. It is unlikely that the ball will actually move right to left in flight, but the swing action has the effect of de-lofting the club at impact creating a low-running shot, which is particularly useful if the pin is positioned a long way onto the green or the shot is to be played up hill.

The Putting Chip Fig 91

This little shot is not one particularly favoured by most amateur golfers and is yet one that offers excellent control and increases the options for any player who has the technique and confidence to play it. The technique itself is relatively simple – the swing is similar to that of a longish putt using a set-up that looks more like a putting stance than that of a chipping one. The player must stand close to the ball, holding the club with a normal putting grip. This will cause the shaft of the club to appear more vertical than normal at address and for the club to sit on the ground resting on the toe side of the clubhead – the heel side will be off the ground completely.

The putting grip encourages the player to hold the club more into the palms of the hands, limiting unnecessary hand and wrist action and reducing any clubhead rotation during the swing itself. The hands will be positioned slightly ahead of the ball at address, the elbows relaxed and set in towards the body. The weight will tend to favour the left side. The swing should feel like a long, positive putting stroke, with the clubhead gently accelerating through the impact position. The set-up ensures that the ball is contacted just before the bottom of the swing arc, with the passive hands and wrists helping to pop the ball forward without too much

contact with the turf. The follow-through should show no signs of an independent hand action, with the left wrist remaining as it was at address and finishing square to the flagstick. The flight of the ball will be relatively low and soft whichever club is selected, with the amount of roll relatively predictable. It is a very useful shot particularly if the ball is positioned close to the edge of the green, or if the green is fast or sloping away from the player. It enhances control and with regular practice can prove an important addition to a player's repertoire of shots. One final point to note, it is not a shot to be attempted from a poor lie, and it is also a more difficult shot to play with the more lofted clubs.

Tips For Increased Skill and Improved Versatility

1.   Remember to adapt the ball position and set-up correctly to improve feel, control and versatility, that is, the set-up rehearses the impact position.
2.   Do not be frightened to grip down the handle to improve control, even if it means the right hand touches the shaft of the club.
3.   Grip adaptations – a weak left-hand position, that is, to the left, will often allow the player to feel that the hands are working together more as the palms of each hand face one another. Also a weak left-hand position will encourage a player to increase club face loft at impact leading to higher, softer shots. This is particularly useful for the more accomplished player who requires greater versatility from his short game.

A strong left-hand position, whilst likely to take some loft off the club face at impact, does help the player to feel that the left hand leads the clubhead through the impact position. This usually generates a crisp, effective contact with the ball and is

Fig 91 The putting chip.

(a)

(b)

(a) The posture and stance are similar to a putt. Note how vertical the shaft is positioned.

(b) The short backswing is a one-piece movement.

(c) There is no breakdown of the wrists through impact.

(c)

particularly useful with a high handicap or weak wristed golfers when playing shots that do not require a higher flight.

4. Remember, soft hands for gentle shots, a firmer grip for crisp, knock forward ones.

5. Ball position is not just related to the stance, it must be in relation to the position and weight distribution of the body, that is, the centre of the chest should always be forward of the ball to create a low flight shot, whereas if it is positioned behind the ball at address, this will help the elevation of a shot.

6. The position of the hands at address and their actions during the swing control the trajectory of the ball. Appreciating this point, plus practice and experimentation will all help increase the player's knowledge and understanding of his own capabilities.

7. Always try to match the length of the backswing and through-swing for greater consistency.

8. Higher flighted shots are easier with longer, slower swing actions with limited hand action; lower shots with crisper hands and wrist-controlled actions.

9. The more upright the swing arc, the higher the ball will fly. The flatter the arc, the more the ball will travel on a lower running trajectory.

10. Visualization of shots is the key to the short game ability.

11. There is no substitute for practice. It not only increases the player's feel and skill, but also enhances confidence which plays a very important role in all shots around the green.

Improved Putting

The basic fundamentals of a putting stroke have been covered earlier so now it would be appropriate to look at what distinguishes those players who putt particularly well from those who putt poorly. In general terms it can be summarized as follows: the putting stroke, a player's mental attitude, reading of the greens, or possibly the putter, that is, the club.

Players often confuse the sheer importance of the mechanical aspects of putting. Of course without them it is extremely difficult to develop a reliable stroke, but really the mechanics are only a small percentage of the overall aspect. Feel is the key element; without it players will not be able to judge the speed of a putt, or the effects of slopes on the green. Good feel helps to develop a player's confidence, which, in turn, is always another feature in any good putter's armoury.

Mental Attitudes

It is important to accept that putting plays a key role in making up the score for a round of golf, and as such it is a department of the game that all golfers should learn to enjoy. There are many who appear to have excellent putting strokes and in fact can often prove the quality of their actions on the practice putting green and in friendly rounds of golf, yet in competitive situations when the pressure of the event plays a key role some players lose their ability to hole what would be in different circumstances a relatively straightforward putt. Those that can hole out on a regular basis when it matters most are the most successful putters, and indeed often the most adept at winning events and matches. In other words the player with the strongest attitude and belief will in most cases prove to be the best putter, and will surpass a player with a superior technique, but an inferior mental approach.

The putting element in golf is one of precision and superior touch, yet it requires the player to be decisive and positive with no room for fear or negative thoughts, otherwise once on the green this will restrict the commitment to making a good putt. The way that golf is played educates a golfer to appreciate the vital importance of putting and indeed the lack of opportunity to

---

A Reminder of the Key Fundamentals of Putting

1. Eyes over the ball at address with the ball position opposite the centre of the upper body.

2. The hands should be positioned under the shoulders for a more consistent swing path.

3. The putter face must be square to the target at address and impact.

4. The stroke itself is a pendulum motion, with the clubhead accelerating through impact and the body movement kept to a minimum.

5. The swing path of the putter head must be square to the line of the putt through the impact position.

6. At impact the putter head should be either at the bottom of the swing arc or just beginning the upstroke. Avoid contacting the ball at a downward angle of approach.

7. Generally the backswing and through-swing will be of equal length.

8. The rhythm or speed of the stroke must be consistent and smooth.

9. The ball should be struck from the sweet spot of the putter to obtain solid contact, thus offering consistency and control on a regular basis.

Fig 92 Bernhard Langer with the long putter. A possible solution to the putting woes.

successful career, he has been able to conquer most difficulties through sheer willpower and application. Once again attitude proved the key element – it makes a player able to control any nervousness and allows the components of a strong stomach and great heart to rule the emotions.

Developing Feel, Accuracy and Judgement

The two key elements in holing a putt or at least making a successful one will always be the ability to roll the ball along the correct path towards the hole and to do so at the right speed. This may seem relatively simple, and yet all golfers will appreciate the difficulties of achieving these two factors on a regular basis.

Pace versus Attacking Style

Fortunately putts can be holed without having to have a one only combination of both perfect pace and accuracy. For example a putt of 15ft that has 12in of turn or break assuming that the player rolls the putt at an average speed or pace, might be holed in two alternative ways – a more firmly hit putt travelling at an increased speed, but aimed more directly at the hole or, a more gently hit pace putt which will travel at less speed, albeit enough to reach the centre of the cup, which will start out more than 12in wide of the hole. In the first instance the ball will travel a straighter line route, but will need to make accurate contact with the back of the hole otherwise it will be travelling too quickly to drop in from either the left or right hand sides of the hole. This style of putting suits the aggressive type of player who enjoys attacking the hole with his putts, but it does have a greater element of risk should the ball

recover, and the consequences of missing makeable putts. No department of the game is quite so critical in a player's score – a mishit drive can be made up for by a good recovery shot, a missed green does not rule out the potential of a par, even a birdie, should a good short game be used effectively. Yet invariably a player still has to make an important putt to save the score at any hole. There is no escape; the putter can be 'the beauty' or 'the beast' in a player's

bag. Look at today's great players such as Tiger Woods, Nick Faldo, Ian Woosnam, Colin Montgomerie, Phil Michelson, José Maria Olazabal, they all putt with a different style or technique, yet when we watch them winning important championships, it is on the putting green where we see them consolidating their successes. Even though the great German golfer Bernhard Langer, has had severe putting problems on and off throughout his highly miss the target as it will travel several feet past the hole and the player may be gambling on his ability to hole the return putt. Conversely, the lag or pace putter feels greater confidence knowing that the first putt will slow down or 'die' around the hole, so that if the break has been assessed correctly the ball can drop into the hole from the front, sides or back edges. This style of putting generally proves more effective for most players, particularly on faster greens, and also the risk of three putting is minimized – a strong psychological boost for most players.

The Pros and Cons of Pace Putting Style

1. Requires a good ability to read the speed and break of the green.
2. Requires a good feel for distance and direction.

3. Requires a soft or gentle grip of the putter handle to enhance feel and allow the player to make a controlled stroke.
4. Requires a smoother more rhythmical putting style, generally with a longish pendulum action.
5. Requires consistent quality ball striking as the slower forward roll of the ball is more likely to be more affected by any irregularities on the surface of the green.
6. A patient, controlled attitude, as any temptation to hurry the stroke will minimize the chances of success.
7. Is most effective on fast greens with a good quality surface.
8. Suits golfers with even temperaments and patience.
9. Offers the most consistent form of putting, particularly for longer putts where distance rather than direction is the key criterion.

The Pros and Cons of Aggressive Putting Style

1. Requires good understanding for break and direction with slightly less emphasis on feel for distance.
2. The putter can be held tighter and more aggressively to offer a positive feel to the player.
3. The putting movement can be quicker and more of a hitting action with a limited follow-through.
4. Putting green tension can be reduced through a more positive, aggressive approach to the putt.
5. Slower pace greens may be easier to putt on successfully. Quicker greens will need more patience and a common-sense approach.
6. Suits golfers with a less patient, more aggressive attitude.
7. A more exciting style of putting but possibly one that is less consistent and reliable.

Summary

Pace putting is generally regarded as the safest, most consistent style with players maintaining a regular average of total putts per round. Putts for long distance prove easier to leave close to the hole leaving a safer, shorter distance for the second putt. Even on shorter putts the pace putter will still have to account for speed and break. The bold attitude and attacking style allows a player to straighten out most medium and short putts, which makes reading the green a little less precise and demanding, but on longer ones the player must adapt to more of a pace putting style otherwise the number of putts per green and per round can be higher than acceptable – unless that is, the player has an unique ability to hole most of the return putts!

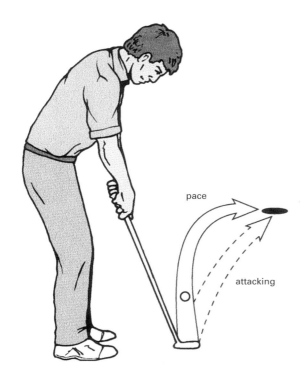

Fig 93 Aggressive putting calls for a more direct route to the hole.

Direction and Distance Factors

Learning to hit a putt in the correct direction should be relatively easy when we appreciate the limited movement of the clubhead in golfing terms. Distance control is often a factor that troubles most average players. This is where feel, combined with confidence and belief are key roles. Deceleration of the putter just before impact is the most common fault generally caused by a golfer's lack of belief in his own judgement or a fear of commitment to the putt. An important aspect of consistent distance control is the ability to smoothly accelerate the putter head through impact. Contacting the ball in the sweet spot of the putter, preferably at the commencement of the upstroke and with the swing path and face square are extremely relative, but distance control cannot be successfully achieved without the ability of the player to control the acceleration of the clubhead.

Directional Control

The following information and tips should prove useful for developing direction control and consistency.

1. Putting requires a minimal percentage of independent hand and wrist action and as such it is far more beneficial to grip the handle of the club into the palms of each hand. Although this may reduce the amount of feel a player senses from the fingers, it has the effect of limiting the amount of independent movement of both the hands and the wrists, offering a player the opportunity to build a far more 'one-piece' style or technique, integrating a more successful relationship between hands, wrists and shoulders.
2. On shorter putts the clubhead travels straight back and through, whereas on longer ones the backswing is on a more inside path allowing the putter to stay lower to the ground until well into the through-stroke.
3. Some players like to feel the left forearm is an extension of the putter shaft, and so a palm-dominated left-hand grip works very effectively in allowing the forearm to be positioned correctly and comfortably.
4. Positioning the left hand below the right is popular with many golfers. The actual position of each hand is in effect the same as with the standard grip except that the player lowers the upper hand and it now becomes the lower hand position. The feel of

the putting stroke will differ considerably as this grip adaptation tends to make the left hand more dominant so the player has the sensation that the putter is being pulled through impact rather than being pushed through. The left wrist is also far less likely to break down prior to or during impact, and so the face of the putter can remain square to the line of the putt more easily.

Aiming Correctly

It is perhaps a simple but obvious point that unless the putter face is aimed correctly to the target and the player positions his body correctly in relation to the alignment of that putter face, it is doubtful that any form of regular success can be achieved.

Tips for Aiming

1. To help line up the putter face correctly, pick a spot on the line of the putt which is between the ball and the hole, but nearest to the ball. Use this spot as an aiming point. On straightish putts it need only be a few inches in front of the ball, but on putts with a definite break, pick a spot where the ball turns towards the hole. This not only helps with the

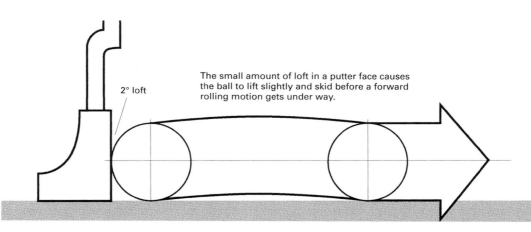

2° loft

The small amount of loft in a putter face causes the ball to lift slightly and skid before a forward rolling motion gets under way.

Fig 94 When putting, the ball lifts at impact.

Fig 95 The coin indicates the exact line to the hole. Practise putting over it.

wall, board or wood. For longer putts the toe would move slightly inside during the backswing movement, but would follow-through on a straight line after the impact position.

2. Position two clubs on the ground with the shafts parallel to one another, but just far enough apart to place a putter head into the gap. Practise stroking putts keeping the putter moving between the shafts. A line of tee pegs can be used as an alternative to the shafts.

3. Tie two pencils together with a reasonable length of string. Stick one pencil into the ground just behind the ball to be struck and the other to the opposite side of the hole. Swing the putter head under the string so that the stroke remains square to the line of the putt and low to the ground. The string will illustrate and help to develop both of these factors (Fig 96).

4. Place ten balls in a circle 3ft from a central tee peg. Putt to the peg endeavouring to hit it with each ball. This will improve accuracy and touch. Progress to a 6ft circle when the 3ft test has been accomplished successfully on a regular basis. Try this drill around the hole (Fig 97).

aim, but also enhances the feel and visualization for the curve of the putt.

2. When practising place two tee pegs about 4in apart at right angles to the centre of the hole (for a straight putt). Aligning the toe and heel of the putter head opposite each peg ensures a square club face when addressing the ball.

3. Remember that most people have one dominant eye and so it is worth finding out which one it is as this could affect the reading of the green and the aim of the putter and player when addressing the ball.

4. Keep the head level at address. Tilting it to the left or the right effects a player's aim and perspective of the putt.

The Stroke

To develop a square on an online putting stroke a few simple drills can be followed.

1. Place the toe of the putter against a wall, skirting-board or piece of wood with a straight edge. Swing the putter as with a normal putting stroke ensuring the toe of the putter glides smoothly along the edge of the

Distance Control

Distance is the one factor affected by a lack of correct acceleration of the putter and an off-centre strike, and so to help develop the feel for distance and to improve a player's judgement for longer putts several factors need to be developed and improved if a player is to achieve consistent results.

The Feel Factor

Feel is described as 'having a physical or emotional sensation of something'. To putt well a golfer must experience both physical and emotional

127

Fig 96 The string helps the player keep the blade and stroke square to the hole.

Fig 97 A great drill – the more putts holed in a row the greater the pressure.

sensations. Without these there will be a limited amount of judgement and consequently little development of the confidence required in successful putting. In a physical sense feel comes from the contact the player has whilst holding the putter plus the rhythm of the stroke itself. The emotional sensation is simply the mental response to this, together with the information supplied through the eyes about the shot in hand.

Tips to Improve Feel

1. Try putting with either the left or right hand only. This will also improve control.
2. Hold the putter with only the last three fingers of the left hand and the thumb and forefinger of the right hand gripping the putter handle. There may be a lack of control at first when making an actual putting stroke, but this exercise is a sure way to develop correct grip pressure, a smooth stroke and the feel factor.

Improving Ball Strike

Striking the putt from the sweet spot of the putter is a high priority for all golfers, yet proves to be a relatively difficult task despite the limited movement of the putter head itself. If a ball is not struck from the correct part of the putter face, it not only deviates in direction, but also fails to roll correctly forward. In most cases the player will have made some other technical error in the stroke which will accentuate the failure or inability to strike the ball correctly.

The most common mistakes are to deliver the putter head on to downward or descending an angle of approach or the opposite trying to hit the ball too much on the upswing. Either can cause the ball to be struck from the toe or heel side of the club face

Fig 98 The ball is struck from the centre of the putter face.

Fig 99 To find the sweet spot of your putter, tap the centre of the face with a tee-peg. It should swing backward and forward with the face remaining square.

dominated by a slight rocking action from the shoulders, but also encourages a player to feel the correct co-ordination of the whole movement.

2. Place two elastic bands around the putter head or alternatively position two coins or some Blu-Tack on the putter face on either side of the sweet spot and about 1in apart. This should leave a sufficient gap to strike the ball correctly from the centre part of the putter's face (Fig 98). Start by practising 3ft putts and then working further away from the hole, as you become more proficient. For longer putts the gap between the elastic bands or Blu-Tack will have to be widened as a longer putting stroke decreases the margin for error making the drill more difficult to carry out successfully.

3. Place a tee-peg slightly outside the toe of the putter when addressing a ball. Practise making putting strokes, allowing the toe of the putter to swing past but as close as possible to the tee-peg. This should ensure a strike off the sweet spot of the putter face.

reducing the ball's forward momentum.

A putter head travelling low to the ground, swing path on line to the target and face square to that swing path are all required to enhance the ball-striking skills.

Tips for Improving Ball Strike

1. The elbows should remain close to the sides of the body throughout the stroke. This not only allows the movement to be

The Distance Factor

If all the qualities of a decent putting stroke are evident then learning to control the distance

129

factor should not be too difficult a task. There are many ways to develop the control of distance, but bear in mind the close relationship with the ability to read the nature of the greens.

Tips for Improving Distance Control

1. On shorter putts, where a firm positive putt is required, it can be beneficial to putt to a point several inches past the hole to encourage a firm strike of the ball.
2. Place five tee-pegs at 6ft, 12ft, 18ft, 24ft and 30ft distances. Putt one ball to each tee-peg in turn. Repeat or work in reverse. Try to leave the ball as close as possible to each tee-peg every time. Move the tee-pegs closer together – 9ft, 12ft, 15ft, 18ft, and 21ft to make the drill more difficult and to enhance the feel for distance still further.

3. Place a tee-peg 10ft from a hole. Move a further 10ft away from the tee-peg so that you are 20ft from the hole itself. Using six balls putt the first one to the peg and try to place each of the remaining five balls a little further past the previous ball, but progressively nearer to the hole. Try to keep the balls between the peg and the hole at all times (Fig 100).
4. Place a golf club flat on the ground about 2 or 3ft behind the hole. From 15ft or more, try to putt three balls past the hole but not touching the shaft of the club (Fig 101).
5. With six balls, putt towards the edge of the green without allowing the balls to roll onto or touch the fringe bordering the edge of the green. Aim to different parts of the green to help enhance feel and control.
6. Place some string in a circle of about 3ft in diameter. First from 10ft, then from 15, 20, 25 and 30ft

try to putt six balls consecutively into the circle.
7. Try putting with your eyes closed – lining up the putt to the hole correctly, closing the eyes, visualizing the putt and feeling the stroke itself. As an additional practice drill you could make a comment out loud on whether the ball has reached or gone past the hole, or has finished to the left or right of the hole before you open your eyes.

On Reading Greens

This may be something that most golfers take for granted, yet it is a skill that not only has to be learned, but one that has to be done successfully, otherwise all other factors whether they are done to a high quality or not are in a sense made redundant. To be an effective putter a player must be able to read greens well – the speed, slope, gradient, grass

Fig 100 Distance control tip 3.

Fig 101 Distance control tip 4.

type, length, grain, texture, moisture content, wind speed and direction are all part of the equation and must be taken into consideration by the player on every putt. The amount of break a player judges to allow for on any sloping putt has to be balanced with the speed at which the ball is travelling and the contact with the putter. It is useful to remember that in effect 'all putts are straight putts', that is, a player must putt in a straight line to a point at which the slope and gravity affects the direction of the ball as it is travelling towards the hole. It is not the actual putting stroke that redirects the ball, it is the green and natural forces.

Some greens have what is called 'grain' due to their type of grass. This, in most cases, often has only a minimal effect with regard to speed and direction, but on greens with Bermuda grass for example, there can be quite a dramatic difference when the grass grows in a particular direction. With the grain, the ball will roll quicker and turn slightly less to the left or to the right. Into the grain the ball will roll slower and will turn slightly more in the appropriate direction, that is, a left to right putt will turn slightly more to the right than normal. Side hill putts follow the same rule. Two simple ways of reading Bermuda type greens are to look if the grass is shiny as it means the grain is in the same direction as the putt itself, and so it will be quicker. If the grass looks dull or dark it is the reverse situation and the putt will be much slower. Secondly, the grain usually follows the direction of the nearest water supply or the setting sun.

Tips for Reading Greens

1. Faster greens will require a player to allow for increased break, as a putt must be hit more gently, therefore exaggerating the effect of the slope and gravity.
2. Putts travelling more slowly will be more easily affected by any imperfections in the green than those travelling at a faster speed.
3. A putt generally breaks most as it nears the hole and is slowing down.
4. Putting to a point past the hole is useful on uphill putts: to a point just short of the hole on fast downhill ones.
5. Always attempt to putt to the high side of the hole, as not only will there be more chance of holing the putt, but it is likely that the ball will finish closer to the hole.

Putting it All Together

The more instinctive and natural a player feels about the putting stroke the more likelihood of consistent success. A correct technical action is very important. Without it a player is limiting the amount of success possible. Successful putting is ultimately all about attitude. If a player has confidence and belief, then fear is abolished and the attitude is totally positive. Developing this approach and making putting a key strength in the game allows a player great access to establishing a consistent and competitive ability.

The Putter

All equipment is based upon personal preference, but poor putters, that is, those who lack feel, rhythm or technique will benefit by using a heavier type of putter and one with a cavity back designed to improve mishits. Players with proficient putting techniques or greater feel normally prefer to use lighter, well-balanced putters. A putter must have a pleasing appearance, the correct grip or handle size, sit correctly on the ground when the player addresses the ball, be the correct lie and length, be easy to line up and above all offer the correct feel for the player. Some players change regularly, whilst others stick to the same putter for many years through success and failure. Obviously, it is very much a personal choice, but it is a very important one. Players should always take sufficient time when choosing a new putter and should, if possible, compare with other types. It is the one club that will be used on many occasions on every round of golf and must offer the player the maximum potential to be proficient at short, medium and long ranges.

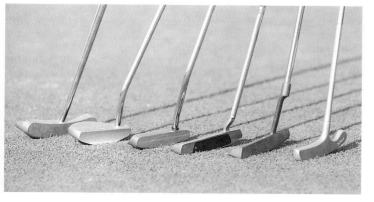

Fig 102 Just a few of the vast array of different putters available for golfers.

9

INDIVIDUAL NEEDS

Before breaking down priorities with regard to women, seniors, juniors and disabled golfers, it is useful to comprehend the differences that physical stature and size make to golfers as a whole. We are all fully aware of the diverse variations in human beings relating to height, build, weight and strength. These variations can have a fairly dramatic effect on the golfer in relation to the way they go about swinging the golf club and, consequently, the way they play their games.

Variation in height does not generally prohibit the golfer, although particularly short or tall people may experience areas of limitation, which need to be accommodated if they are to get the best from themselves. Short people find balance an easier factor in golf because their centre of gravity is lower. They can maintain their balance better particularly in more awkward stance situations, or when the wind is more forceful. Their height helps to combine co-ordination and control fairly naturally. They

will stand fairly upright at the address, with a tendency for their weight to sit more towards their heels. This, combined with a need to stand physically further from the ball, will encourage them to swing on a relatively flat swing plane. Tall players, whose centre of gravity is higher, will find establishing good balance on slopes and in high winds more awkward and a need for greater discipline will be required. They must maintain more control of their body movements than a shorter player, as longer arms and

Fig 103 Ian Woosnam (short), Greg Norman (tall).

legs and a naturally wide swing arc can be more difficult to co-ordinate. At set-up, their weight is likely to be more towards the balls of their feet due to the angle of their body being more bent over, or tilted towards the ball. They will also stand physically nearer to the ball, which will encourage them to swing on a more upright swing plane.

These natural reasons for the swing plane to be so different, make it logical that short players should hit the ball from more of an in to out swing path due to their flatter swing plane, that they should draw the ball more easily, hit the ball on a lower trajectory and, possibly, find the longer clubs easier to use. A taller player assuming that the swing action is not too long or uncontrolled may find the irons easier to use due to the more upright swing plane creating a steeper arc. Consequently more backspin can be created at impact which offers greater control but leads to a higher trajectory of ball flight. Often solid, long hitting with the woods is not combined with sufficient control due to this steeper swing arc.

The build of a golfer has a number of implications. A slim person would have the advantage of more potential mobility and freedom. At the set-up there would be no physical bumps or lumps to affect the natural hanging position of the arms. The swing action itself might tend to be longer and looser, but this would ultimately depend on the physical strength of the individual. A more rotund golfer may find mobility and overall movement more difficult to achieve. At set-up, the arms would hang more naturally outward and around the upper body. Good rotation might prove difficult, so that the swing would tend to be shorter and quicker in rhythm. Not only would good weight distribution and balance be definite assets, an improved

body turn might need to be developed and it would also be of benefit if the player were able to create a controlled, but relatively active hand and arm action to help increase clubhead speed.

Actual body weight itself is not always a relevant advantage or disadvantage. If a player has a light body weight then it is clear that they are going to have to compensate for the lack of extra muscle bulk with another swing factor such as mobility, coil, leverage or a fast hand action.

Strength definitely has its advantages but as was mentioned earlier sheer brute force counts for little if there is no flexibility, discipline, co-ordination or

control. Adequate golfing strength is all that is required.

Women

Women would appear to be at a disadvantage in playing golf due to the fact that their physical strength is, in most cases, less than that of male golfers. This strength factor often makes creating sufficient clubhead speed difficult to achieve, and not only affects ball striking and distance, but also shots from the rough and awkward lies, or in being able to

Fig 104 Laura Davies driving.

play a shot with a controlled flight such as a draw or fade or one that goes high or low. With regard to the swing movement there are some important points to note:

Keys to the Set-up

1. It may be advisable to strengthen the grip slightly to aid the control and speed generated through the hand action. The left hand might well show three to four knuckles, with the right hand moving more underneath the handle so that the Vs formed between each thumb and forefinger are pointing to, or just outside the right shoulder, rather than between it and the head.
2. It may be beneficial to play the ball in a more central position between the feet. This will allow the hands to be positioned more forward and the shoulders to aim a little more to the right of the target, potentially encouraging a full rotational turn of the shoulders and the opportunity to swing the clubhead on a more inside path for additional power.
3. The posture will be fairly dependent upon the individual lady's build, but most have a habit of standing to the ball with their backs relatively upright, their bottoms pushed inward, the knees overly flexed and their weight favouring the heels. From here they tend to turn their shoulders on too flat a plane or angle with an independent and relatively weak upward lifting of the hands and arms during the backswing movement.
4. This upper body should tilt or lean slightly forward, allowing the arms to hang freely down from the shoulders. This will tend to pull the weight slightly more forward towards the toes, and so to counterbalance this, the lady player should feel that her bottom is pushed slightly outward. The weight should feel central between the heels and the balls of the feet.

Keys to the Swing

1. The takeaway should be kept low and on a slightly inside path.
2. The turn of the shoulders and hips needs to be well co-ordinated. Lady golfers sometimes find turning the hips correctly a difficult action – some overturn them so that they lose balance and control, whilst others tend to push their right hip outward rather than rotationally around, which leads to a poor weight distribution and balance and an incorrect shoulder turn.
3. In most cases their shorter height gives women a lower centre of gravity which they can utilize by using controlled lateral as well as rotational movements – into the right side during the backswing and back onto the left side through impact and to the finish position. It is important that a good lateral movement does not become a sway of the body.
4. At impact many lady players tend to have a slightly collapsed or folded left wrist position. This is generally due to their weaker hands and wrists not being able to maintain the backswing wrist set position long enough in the downswing movement, which causes the clubhead to be released early so that it in fact passes the hands prior to impact. A stronger grip can be of benefit although good body turn and weight transfer through the ball can also balance out much of the potential disadvantage. The failure to keep a straight left wrist position at impact limits ball striking potential as the clubhead cannot 'squeeze' the ball forward effectively due to the angle of attack becoming too shallow prior to impact. These factors also cause the effective loft of the club to be increased, which can lead to weaker flighted shots. This is a difficult fault to cure and not one that lady golfers should put too great an emphasis on without consulting a coach for advice.

5. Maintaining good balance and rhythm is important, as it will increase accuracy and consistency. Also, should the player have need to strike the ball harder on occasions, there will always be the good discipline of this regular balance control to back it up.
6. With a slower clubhead speed most lady golfers hit the ball on a relatively flat or low trajectory which will at least create more roll upon landing and is something that the lady golfer should take advantage of.

Course Management

If distance is not a natural asset then control and consistency have to be seen as beneficial replacements. Most lady players have a reputation for accuracy so they should take advantage of this, and of the best course-management tactics to suit their style of play.

The shortest route may not always be the best one – plotting a realistic path towards the hole, keeping out of trouble, and playing within personal handicap limitations should be a high priority. Avoiding dangers like deep bunkers or high trees that block the next shot to the hole are important factors, particularly if a lack of strength or control of the ball trajectory are going to make the next shot more difficult to play. Playing to individual strengths and, wherever, possible steering away from the weaknesses is a major source of good course management skill.

Skills and Equipment

The long irons are usually the least favourite clubs that any lady golfer possesses. Woods are far easier to hit and offer that extra bit of confidence to the player. Lofted woods, such as 5, 6, 7, or 9 are often great assets. They will elevate the ball from all sorts of difficult lies and situations, and so lady players should not be frightened to use them regularly. These woods should be seen as score savers – a valuable boost to achieving low scores and making the game more enjoyable.

Many ladies seem to lack good technique and regular consistency on and around the green. This would appear odd, as the short game does not require strength or power. It requires at least an ample technique, but more importantly good touch and feel, with visualization an important extra. Touch and feel can be worked upon by good practice routines, technique through tuition and practice and visualization needs developing by watching successful short game players and professionals, and by seeking a little extra advice from a coach as and when necessary. A good wedge or sand wedge should be selected – one that suits the player's technique. A well-balanced and correct length putter is essential and will always be a good investment whatever the initial costs. Finally, endeavour to keep practice sessions shorter but more effective and do not forget the advantages of an electric golf trolley, which can help to minimize fatigue – the extra energy saved will certainly help increase the potential to maintain or lower scores, particularly towards the end of a round.

Fig 105 Lucy Ambrozey Czyk, a keen junior golfer.

Juniors

This short segment of the book cannot hope to cover all aspects that relate to junior golf and the junior golfer, but it is an opportunity to highlight some of the more relevant points.

As a junior golfer some of the difficulties and technicalities of the game are of no relevance whatsoever. In most cases juniors benefit from the advantage of a 'no fear' philosophy which is one that allows them to see only the positive side of the game – for most of the time at least!

With regard to swing technicalities everything should be kept to a basic, simple level. Sound fundamentals are important but not the highest criteria in the early stages of swing development, when one bears in mind the big differences in weight, height, strength, maturity and understanding of young players whose ages may range from six to eighteen years old. In fact, it is often impossible to compare one player of a particular age with another of like age, due to these differences. In general terms, the more progressive or mature the junior the greater the need to adhere to sound fundamentals. Bearing these points in mind there are some suggestions that can be of benefit, particularly to those who are new to the game, or at the higher end of the handicap scale.

Keys to the Set-up

1. The grip can be a little stronger than orthodox to compensate for any lack of strength – the left hand may show three to four knuckles, and the right hand may be positioned slightly around and under the club handle so that the Vs formed by the thumb and forefingers of each hand point towards the right shoulder.

135

2. In terms of height, shorter juniors should stand as tall as possible, whilst taller ones should bend a little more over the ball, but each must develop a correct and comfortable posture and balance at address.

3. Depending upon overall size, smaller built juniors may benefit by using a slightly wider stance. In adults this could potentially limit mobility, but in a young golfer flexibility is one of their strengths. In fact there tends to be a danger of overactivity within the swing action and so it can be of help if the stance is wide enough to limit any unnecessary movement. There is an added bonus in that it also creates a lower centre of gravity, increasing balance and stability throughout the swing itself.

4. The ball should be positioned in one consistent position if possible particularly for all irons, as this will simplify the set-up procedure. The woods may have to be played slightly more forward towards the left heel.

5. The aim should be square or even a little to the right of the target to encourage a good rotational turn during the backswing and the clubhead to travel on an inside swing path.

6. Young players will, by instinct, and correctly so, keep some form of movement and flow going throughout their pre-shot routine. These natural movements are of great benefit and will help of course if they are of a constructive nature such as eyes to target and back to the ball, or rehearsing takeaway movements, or releasing tension with the correct waggle or movement of the clubhead. Everything must be natural and follow an instinctive pattern for the junior golfer.

Keys to the Swing

1. It is also natural for young players to want to hit the ball as hard as they can and why not, since power is an essential factor in the modern game. Hit it hard, but endeavour to maintain good rhythm and balance.

2. Sufficient flexibility to turn fully will not generally be a problem. The body should rotate and turn correctly with the weight moving towards and into the right side during the backswing.

3. It is important not to keep the head absolutely still – the head may move or rotate a little to the right during the backswing and back to the left during the down and through movements. The head should not go upward or downward, but a little movement sideways is of no real consequence. In fact it can be a bonus as it allows the junior to gain more freedom and hence a more natural swing action.

4. The length of the swing may be on the long side due to a lack of physical strength and control. Within reason this is not a problem but the sooner the club can be controlled at the top of the backswing, the sooner, more solid, consistent and enjoyable golf can be experienced.

5. Taking a divot with the irons is not that vital at this stage. Some will not have sufficient strength or technical expertise to hit down on the ball correctly, so there is no harm in feeling that even the irons are 'swept away' like the woods. The short irons will require the clubhead to make more of a ball/turf contact so that the ball elevates on a correct trajectory, but even for smaller juniors the shorter shafted irons should help to provide a sufficiently upright swing arc to achieve this.

6. If a junior lacks the strength to create enough clubhead speed then their ball striking will be on the weaker side, and an inability to apply sufficient backspin onto the ball at impact will mean that the ball will have a relatively low trajectory with more roll on landing.

Course Management

The principle to playing to the strengths of the individual apply to juniors, especially if they lack the power to hit the ball far enough to reach holes in a reasonable number of shots. Having said this, there is a natural confident aggression in young players that dictates that they must take more risks than their adult counterparts. This should not be discouraged, particularly under normal playing conditions. Young players will progress more quickly, as their mistakes offer them feed-back, so that any failures can provide a positive source of information, particularly as most juniors will enjoy the challenge of trying again and again until success is achieved. Not only is this a great asset, it provides the motivation to improve their capabilities, and the stimulus that allows them to play many exceptional and match-winning shots during play.

Club selection can often lead to unforced errors – the temptation to underclub means that they try to hit the ball too hard to compensate, whilst sometimes their swing development is so rapid that some shots are so well struck that the ball 'sails' over the green.

Learning to play the course correctly is important, as is an understanding of how climatic and course conditions can affect play. Wind, rain, dry or wet conditions, slopes of fairways and greens, depth of sand plus many other factors will be learnt through experience and from watching, listening and playing with low handicap players or professionals.

Skills and Equipment

Younger, high handicap or physically weaker juniors will have to use their equipment industriously. They will not favour the longer irons or perhaps even the number 1 wood off the tee. Juniors will benefit by learning to control effectively the flight of the ball and shape of their shots. There is no need for them to have a full set of clubs. A 3 and/or 5 wood plus 4, 6, 8 p.w. or 5, 7, 9, s.w. irons are sufficient, along with a reasonable putter and small bag. This limited selection of clubs will encourage them to play a wide variety of half or three-quarter shots to compensate for the length potential of the missing clubs. The ability to manufacture shots and to have control of the ball in doing so is one of the key fundamentals in the development of a junior's golf. In learning shots with extra skills such as making the ball roll an extra few yards, hooking low under a tree, a high trajectory shot over a distant tree plus many others, youngsters are developing the ability to play every conceivable shot that the game of golf might confront them with. There is no substitute for this skill as it helps to develop natural visualization and imagination and increases the feel and clubhead control needed. It elevates the player's confidence and self-belief.

These are instinctive skills that come naturally to the young golfer yet may never be successfully cultivated at a more adult age. Juniors evolve from an instinctive 'play all out', 'no fear' attitude.

Almost all juniors are very good short game players, particularly once on the putting green. Their lack of length with the long game leads to them not being able to reach some greens or missing more of them with their approach shots, so that they have actually more on-course short game practice, and under pressure too! Also, off the course they enjoy the stimulation and competitive challenge of the short game practice. Their touch, feel and flair

are superior to most adult players and, ironically, possibly only deteriorate as they gain increased physical strength, which, in turn, helps them to hit the ball further and provides the opportunity to hit more greens in regulation.

With regard to equipment there are some golden rules that all parents should follow when buying clubs for juniors. They must be properly suited to each youngster and should be an acceptable length and design, plus the grip should be the correct thickness for the individual hand size. Seek professional advice whenever possible as choosing the wrong equipment can often restrict the progress and success of young golfers. Clubs that are too long or too heavy will create swing faults that may never be fully eradicated in the future, or may frustrate the youngster whose interest and motivation may diminish to the extent of losing the desire to play altogether. We are advised to buy our children the appropriate shoe size to allow their feet to develop correctly – the same principle should apply when buying junior golf equipment!

Although a youngster's attention span is relatively short, instruction should be made available to all young golfers. There should not be a need for too much information in the early stages, but all should at least have the opportunity to start the right way.

Advanced juniors will have sufficient ability to use a full set of clubs, to understand the more detailed aspects of the game and to participate in golf at higher competitive levels. Their coaching will be more advanced although simple in content and they will practise almost as much as they play on the golf course. They will establish their own identity and will undoubtedly go through the growing ups and downs of physical and emotional turmoil at times. It is all part of

the learning curve. Golf provides youngsters with some wonderful life-educating opportunities – the satisfaction and pleasure of experiencing progress and development; the effort needed to develop and improve skills leading to positive successes and rewards whilst, at the same time, accepting that failure is always an imminent factor; fairness and honesty with regard to other players and to the Rules of Golf. Fortitude, courage, perseverance and self-control are all there to be learnt and experienced. A sense of humour, the ability to have fun and a realistic understanding of what is achievable and pleasurable will surely enhance any young player's ability and future success.

Seniors

For the senior player, golf can offer a wonderful opportunity to provide useful healthy exercise, a sporting competitiveness and a social environment with like-minded individuals. There are a number of disadvantages for seniors which may be more acutely accentuated the older or less physically fit the individual.

It is a fact that as a person ages the body experiences a gradual loss of strength, flexibility, speed and co-ordination. Eyesight may also decline significantly, which contributes to poor co-ordination and to a potential loss of balance. Judgement of distance and the ability to read the line to the hole may be considerably affected. Glasses or contact lenses may reduce the problem but beware of bifocals, as the split between the lower and upper lens sections may well not be an asset with regard to focusing both on the ball at address and watching it on the way to its target in the distance.

As muscles shorten and flex less easily a senior player will begin to notice that their tee shots lose distance and that they may

Keys to the Set-up

These will be similar to those for the lady player and are as follows:

1. A strong grip whereby the hands are positioned more to the right of the handle. By moving the left hand over in a clockwise direction three to four knuckles may be visible, with the right hand moving more underneath the shaft. This is quite acceptable and will allow the golfer the potential to deliver the clubhead to the ball at impact in a more powerful position with the club face less lofted.
2. A more centred ball position may allow the clubhead to contact the ball in a more solid fashion, particularly if the player has a lack of mobility limiting any lateral movement or drive from the lower body.
3. The posture may need a regular check-up as poor positions and body angles will become second nature as the muscle strength and flexibility diminishes. Standing 'tall', with a posture that allows the arms to hang freely away from the body will be of great benefit particularly with regard to allowing the body to turn more easily and the arms to swing more freely.
4. Making a full ninety degree shoulder turn may be quite difficult, so by slightly narrowing the stance or turning the right foot a little further outward, the hips can turn more freely and this will help increase the length of the swing. Alternatively, a closed stance, one aiming to the right of the target, will create more freedom during the backswing by improving the potential rotational movement, and helping the clubhead to move on a more inside path.

Keys to the Swing

1. The takeaway should be kept low and as wide as possible. A

Fig 106 Gary Player, one of the fittest senior golfers in the world.

have to select a more powerful club than previously to cover the same given distance. The ability to create the same clubhead speed as enjoyed in earlier times diminishes as does that of being able to deliver the clubhead to the ball from such a powerful and correct angle of attack, resulting in less solid and consistent ball striking capabilities.

Beginners may find learning the basic fundamentals more taxing than if they had taken up the game in their younger years. The ability to create and co-ordinate certain swing movements may be a slower process, as may be the inability to copy or imitate certain swing demonstrations.

A similar scenario applies to seniors as does to lady golfers. Less power leads to the disadvantages mentioned previously which, in themselves, cause the golfer difficulty in playing shots from sloping lies and the rough, from playing into the wind and in manufacturing hooks or slices and controlling the height of the shots – most seniors will flight the ball relatively low due to a lack of clubhead speed and ball-strike characteristics. Practice sessions should be of a quality level rather than quantity with plenty of emphasis on the short game, especially shots close to the green and on the putting surface itself.

lack of turn can lead to a player swinging the club up too steeply during the backswing, whereas a good takeaway movement encourages the hips and shoulders to turn more naturally and to the maximum position possible.

2. The wrists may not be flexible or strong enough to attain the ideal wrist set position. Although it is also advisable to exercise to maintain as much wrist strength and mobility as possible, it is not unacceptable or a major disadvantage to allow the left arm to fold or bend just slightly, as the backswing nears completion. This will help increase the length of the backswing and will provide the potential for increased clubhead speed at impact. N.B. A bending of the left arm at the elbow does potentially add another 'lever' to the swing action which, if released, that is, the arm straightens correctly during the downswing, could be of benefit. It can, of course, be a distinct disadvantage if the timing is incorrect, but for many it may well be worth trying, as it will allow the whole swing to feel more loose and free offering potential for additional hand and arm release.

3. The left wrist may 'collapse' slightly at impact, which weakens the ball striking potential. A stronger grip may well help, as will a good turn and weight transfer through impact.

4. Endeavour to maintain good balance, rhythm and co-ordination throughout the swing. It may not be possible to achieve a slight lateral movement towards and into the right foot during the backswing or subsequent one to the left as the club travels forward and through impact, but maintaining balance is a vital attribute when combined with good rhythm and good co-ordination.

5. There is generally a lack of leg action from most senior golfers, so the upper body will nearly

always be more dominant. Allow the shoulders to move more freely and try to complete the follow-through with the weight transferring to the left side at the end of the swing movement.

6. If the player has the required levels of skill or control to play a draw or slight hook shot then distance can be increased. The swing path must be from an in to out direction with the club face aiming left on this path. A strong grip and closed stance will certainly play a part in helping this to work.

Course Management

The old adage of short, but straight, might apply more to senior golfers than to any other category. If distance is not the asset it once was, it is imperative to keep the ball in play and to make the most of a strategic game. Course management is therefore vital with an awareness of good club selection. It helps, therefore, to know exactly how far you personally hit the ball. Good course strategy will alleviate the danger of coming up against deep or difficult bunkers, thick rough, shots around or over trees, and uncomfortable sloping lies, or even leaving the ball on the most dangerous side of the hole once around or on the green itself. Having the ability to shot-make or manufacture shots as and when required will undoubtedly lead to more consistent and lower scoring. Over clubbing, that is, choosing a 6 instead or 7 iron should be favoured rather than under clubbing.

Skills and Equipment

Many seniors are unable to strike the ball solidly enough to allow them to hit long irons with any degree of consistent success. It is sometimes a difficult fact to accept particularly if a player has

enjoyed the pleasure of striking powerful long irons on past occasions, but it is, nevertheless, one that almost all older players have to come to terms with. The ideal replacement can be a lofted wood ranging from a number 5 right through to a number 9. Ego must not be a factor – the emphasis should be on making the game easier to play and ultimately keeping the round score as low as possible. The lofted woods provide the ideal long iron replacement off the tee on par 3s, or out of the rough, or semi-rough and from sloping or difficult lies. Most golfers also find them relatively easy to shape shots with, so that the fade or draw can add an extra dimension or skill factor to a player's game.

A senior player must see the short game as a major asset as quality shots both on or around the green will more than make up for any loss of power or distance in the long game. Regular practice in these departments is almost a necessity so that any difficult pitch or bunker shot can be played with confidence and correct technique.

Sometimes senior golfers experience deterioration in their putting ability particularly on shorter putts where a steady hand plays a vital role. Improving the long putts will certainly release some of the difficulty if a tap-in distance is all that is needed after the first attempt. If a player's eyesight deteriorates then reading certain putts can be difficult so the player must improve and develop a better feel for distance and direction through regular practice.

Off the tee a driver or number 1 wood with more loft, perhaps up to 12 or 13 degrees, should be chosen. This will not only improve confidence but also offer the additional benefits of carrying the ball longer through the air and increased control. Lighter clubs, perhaps with graphite shafts would usually be of benefit, as will the advantage of mid-size iron heads with a cavity back design feature. Thicker grips will feel more comfortable as the hold of the club weakens with age. Many golfers who suffer from arthritis benefit greatly with these oversized grips. Using a lighter bag, waterproofs and shoes are all energy-saving during a round of golf as are electric golf trolleys which are very popular and certainly make the game more pleasurable in walking terms.

In the winter keeping warm is imperative, particularly the hands and wrists, as poor golf can be disappointing enough without the additional hazard of a cold body.

No option should be ignored including seeking the knowledge of a good PGA teaching professional, who will be able to offer some valuable swing and equipment advice that is likely to make a significant difference to the quality of golf and therefore the pleasure and enjoyment from it!

Disabled or Handicapped Golfers

It is important that the individual player is fully aware of his or her limitations and should, within reason, set realistic personal goals for themselves. The help of a knowledgeable and understanding golf coach should not be overlooked. The experience and expertise of a good PGA professional will undoubtedly allow the player to learn and potentially develop far more enjoyable standards of play. It is fairly logical that a person with only one arm or leg will have severe limitations with regard to mobility and strength, but a clearer appreciation of simple swing mechanics can only be of benefit when adapting these unfortunate disadvantages into an acceptable enough swing

movement, which allows a reasonably satisfying and enjoyable level of success.

Poor eyesight must be one of the commonest of all complications for golfers, particularly those above the age of forty. Many wear bifocal glasses which is usually a major mistake as the split between lenses distorts vision at address and often causes the player to lift or drop the head into an unnatural position when setting up to the ball. It really is a matter of individual preference, but as long as a golfer's vision is good enough to judge distances (making more use of course planners could be one idea), and to take a correct aim to a target, then the priority must be on being able to focus clearly once inside the distance of 100yd approximately from the hole. The short game is vital and so poor-sighted players cannot afford to misjudge short chips or pitches, or perhaps more importantly, to misread/misjudge shots once on the putting green.

This latter point is relative to all disabled or handicapped players. The limitations on developing a good short game are likely to be far less than those regulating the opportunities to develop the sound long game technique, so this is the obvious

department to spend most available practice time.

Lofted woods, shorter clubs, more flexible shafts, thicker grips, lighter equipment, electric trolleys or buggies are but a few suggestions that may allow the disadvantaged that extra element of success.

Throughout the country there are numerous golf events especially staged for the handicapped player. Many blind golfers enjoy the exhilaration of the game – usually with the aid of a friend to line them up correctly and to select the appropriate club. Limbless golfers compete against one another at times to very high standards, with national championships being played annually. Interestingly enough, Joe Nicols, a one-armed golfer competed in six US Opens.

Whatever the disability, within reason, the game of golf is playable to an acceptable standard. If just being able to hit the ball forward and get it airborne allows a golfer to achieve personal enjoyment and satisfaction, or if perhaps a wheelchair-bound enthusiast is able to putt a ball regularly into the hole, then it shows that experiencing the pleasures of golf is possible for almost anybody.

Fig 107 This one-armed player illustrates an excellent top of the backswing position.

10
DEVELOPING YOUR GAME

It is fair to say that quite a high percentage of golfers are looking to improve their standards of play. The potential for development is dependent on a whole variety of circumstances, but a player must take into account the following factors:

1. Current ability and handicap level.
2. Current age.
3. The number of years playing the game.
4. Physiological capability and limitations.
5. The desire to practise.
6. The amount of time available for practice.
7. The desire to receive regular coaching advice.
8. The availability and quality of that coaching advice.
9. The accessibility of adequate training facilities.
10. A realistic understanding and acceptance of what is achievable.
11. A realistic investment of both time and money.
12. Finally, two key elements – a genuine desire to get better, coupled together with a realistic and patient attitude with regard to the timescale required make established and permanent improvement.

Beginners and Novices

This section relates to those players who are just learning the game from the basic elements upward, and those who have as yet not been able to apply effectively those basic elements in practical terms. Many golfers might refer to themselves as novices even though they may have played the game over a number of years. Here we will look at certain elements that relate specifically to helping inexperienced players gain the opportunity to make sound, forward progress.

Mastering the Fundamentals

Newcomers to the game fall into two categories – one is those individuals who prefer to get hold of a golf club and learn the basic rudimentaries by trial and error. After a certain period of time they may decide that professional coaching is an advantage, if not a necessity. The other category is the one that prefers to learn the basics of the game through a programmed learning environment, and as such would only consider progress effective if aided by the advice and direction of a professional coach.

It is unrealistic to say that golf cannot be successfully self-taught. Any person with a reasonable level of hand–eye co-ordination will undoubtedly have a fair chance of striking a golf ball with some sort of effectiveness. Some can, in fact, over a period of time become very proficient, and achieve a low handicap status. Generally though golf is a sport that favours an acceptable level of technical correctness. A player that ignores technical necessities or fundamentals can find themselves losing out by learning positions and movements that feel initially comfortable, and which may prove effective in the shorter term, but all too often limit ongoing development over the longer term. Regrettably many self-taught players fall prey to the instant success they often achieve.

When after a period of time their standard of play levels off, and they then wish to progress to a higher level, they often find that no matter how much time and effort they dedicate to the task, their progress is minimal. At this time they often decide to seek coaching help, appreciating that their technique is the obvious reason why they are struggling to develop the necessary extra skill required for progress, and so begins a potentially tough and physical phase to the development of their golf, as not only do they have to come to terms with understanding and appreciating the importance of correct fundamentals and technique as explained to them by a professional coach, but they also have to be resilient enough to have their current swing technique critically assessed and sometimes 'overhauled' as part of the potential for improvement. It is at this time that a poor grip, set-up or swing idiosyncrasy prove all the more difficult to correct, and above all the player becomes increasingly frustrated and demoralized as instant results rarely occur due to the fact that the new movements are unlikely to be effective whilst the old ones are

141

still prevalent or in any way continue to have a dominant effect over the proposed changes.

The coach is often in a no-win situation with some players. Good advice and recommendations may be welcomed in the first instance, but when progress is not relatively instantaneous some self-taught players lack the patience and fortitude to continue applying the correct swing procedures. This backward to go forward process is often difficult to come to terms with for those who have previously enjoyed an acceptable level of improvement and progress. Others will patiently stick with the improvement programme and are dutifully rewarded with improved and consistent progress. Yet others take a regressive step to their original technique acknowledging that they are more comfortable in accepting their previous standards rather than taking on further frustrations from the recent innovation.

Needless to say there are fortunately those players who adapt quickly and efficiently to the coach's suggestions, and find change quite painless in overall terms. It really is an individual thing, but it does seek to emphasize the important point that all beginners and novices should be fully aware of – there is no better way to learn the game of golf than through the correct system. It is a great benefit to receive sound, simple advice right from the beginning. There is no real effective alternative unless age or natural skills allow otherwise. Seeking qualified advice and accepting a coach's recommendations are important – this is a game that can be played for many, many years, and so sacrificing longer-term gains and pleasure for short-term success is unnecessary.

Tips for the Beginner/Novice

1. Seek tuition from a professional coach.
2. Learn primarily to perform the fundamentals of the game. These are:
   (a) The grip or hold of the club
   (b) The set-up and posture
   (c) Aiming to the target
   (d) Balance and weight distribution
   (e) The turn-back and turn-through movement
   (f) The basic co-ordination of movement
   (g) The rhythm or speed of the swing.
3. Accept that there is a proven successful sequence to learning the game of golf and work to this formula.
4. Dedicate sufficient time to worthwhile practice.
5. Do not always measure technical improvement through initial ball striking success.
6. Be patient and accept that learning the golf swing can be a challenging task.
7. Do not be influenced by poor advice – stick to the important aspects outlined by the coach.
8. Practise a little and often, rather than infrequently or excessively.
9. Practise with the more lofted clubs for easier progress, that is, 5–9 irons, 3–7 woods.
10. Accept that you will not always experience positive progress and that you may sometimes have to go back one step to progress forward several.
11. Remember you will not lose the skills you have been taught or practised to perfect, but they may disappear momentarily – even though this moment can feel like an eternity!
12. Build your confidence – It is a vital element for success!
13. Finally – above all, enjoy the experience of learning.

Middle to High Handicap Players

In this section golfers between the handicaps of 13–27 (for males) and 16–35 (for females) may recognize certain characteristics that are covered. There will generally be an obvious difference between a 13 handicapper and one of 27 handicap, but it is simpler to condense these general aspects for the benefit of golfers in this group.

This category of player includes the highest percentage of golfers in the world, and encompasses relative newcomers right through to those who have played for many decades, as well as many who have, at the same time during their golfing lives, achieved a considerable level of success at the game, but for a variety of reasons may not be able to maintain their once acknowledged standards. In reality the majority will be those who have played on a regular basis, and have found a playing standard that satisfies their ambitions, or perhaps one that now appears more difficult to improve upon. Many will be self-taught players as I referred to a little earlier in this chapter of the book. Others may have a regular golf lesson, not only because they wish to lower their handicap level, but because the challenge of learning and perfecting new skills, combined with the pleasure of enhancing their current ones, provides great satisfaction and enjoyment.

Progress from higher handicap levels downward usually begins to slow down around the 16–20 mark. The handicap system is more generous at the higher levels, with golfers receiving the benefits of up to 2 shots per hole allowance. As the handicap reduces, the player acknowledges that any score of 2 over par or more on a hole – a double bogey – will require a suitable complement of lower figures to balance out the final round score if playing to or even below the individual's handicap is to be achieved. The margin for error becomes less and less as the handicap decreases. The challenge and pressures of the game become more emphatic. Players become more aware of their own strengths and weaknesses, often culminating in their developing a golfing strategy that endeavours to minimize or leave out of their on-course play any of the elements they least enjoy or experience less practical success with. The emergence of the mental and fitness aspects of the game not only become more obvious, but also in many cases dominate a player's potential for improvement, or sometimes even the enjoyment derived from playing on the golf course. This unique combination of physical and mental skills begins to become more apparent as players seek to overcome the challenge of their own individual game, particularly in competitive situations.

Confidence dominates many playing aspects and, as all golfers will acknowledge, with it they feel unbeatable, without it the game is a veritable minefield of disaster!

Golfers in this category should learn to evaluate their physical and technical capabilities realistically. Improvement and progress is possible through a variety of means, but these have to be correctly recognized before any effective solution or game plan can be put into action. For example, in some instances it might be an obvious technical fault or weakness that is holding back a player's potential, whereas for another golfer their skill level in one particular department of the game may be the area that is holding back the progress. It has to be correctly identified before effective improvement can be implemented. Professional advice and qualified instruction are once again vital elements in helping select the best route forward. This not only applies when a golfer reaches a stalemate with their game, but also when they experience losses of form or poor scoring on the course. If a player acknowledges the need for a quick fix or a swing overhaul, then at least they can begin to establish a greater and more enjoyable understanding of how they are capable of making positive progress.

The coach will initially analyse the pre-swing fundamentals of the player, as this is, in most cases, where core errors emanate. As a player revitalizes these fundamentals invariably the more dynamic and difficult movements of the golf swing begin to fall into place. There is rarely an instant formula to alleviate a golfer's problems, although many, through trial and error, or a one-off tip, believe that they have found the golfing 'secret', only to find that a day or so later normality returns relatively easily! There is no substitute for solid, simple, reliable basic swing fundamentals. Some top players appear to be very unorthodox, but swing analysis shows that they all possess an uncanny ability to deliver the clubhead directly to the ball at impact through sound downswing movement.

Tips for Middle to High Handicap Golfers

1. Endeavour to build sound set-up and fundamentals. These are:
   (a) A good grip or hold of the club
   (b) The correct aim of the club face and body
   (c) The correct ball position
   (d) A good posture and weight distribution
   (e) Check your body turns correctly back and through
   (f) Swing the club on plane
   (g) Maintain good rhythm and balance
   (h) Always complete your backswing and follow-through movements
   (i) Work to build the co-ordination of your swing.
2. Seek professional advice on a regular basis, or as often as possible, not just when playing poorly.
3. Accept that swing errors are easy to develop or may have been developed through a self-taught phase. Acknowledge the need to make patient improvement and progress for game development.
4. Practise all short game departments regularly.
5. Never underestimate the mental aspects of the game – build your confidence and self-belief.
6. Finally, learn to play within your capabilities – when executing a shot or when using your course-management skills.

Accomplished Players

It is probably a little unfair to categorize all players between handicaps of 4–12 (Men) or 5–16 (Ladies) into an accomplished player status, but it is beneficial to recognize that from these handicaps downward players have reached an above-average standard of play, and generally have the potential scope for further development. A variety of factors will have become apparent by the time a player has reached this level. Technically players will have succeeded in incorporating a high percentage of the accepted pre-swing and swing fundamentals into their individual styles. Should any of these fundamentals not be a part of the player's style, some form of compensational recovery movement will have been integrated into the swing action to counterbalance any negative 'side effects'; for example a strong grip which may cause a closed club face position often leads to a player using excessive body action, usually the legs, to neutralize a potential pull or hook shot. Weaker departments of a player's game will be minimized by some form of evasive measure such as an alternative style of shot, or the inclusion of a danger-minimizing additional piece of golf equipment, such as a 7 wood or similar, rather than a reliance on a 3 or 4 iron.

Whichever way the individual equation is worked out, a golfer will establish a relatively consistent style of play, and to a relatively satisfactory standard. It is of course important that a player is able to recognize the strengths and weaknesses of their own game. All too often a player whose tee shots are a strength, but who has a weak short game will dedicate a large proportion of practice time to hitting tee shots mainly due to the pleasure derived from striking the ball well with a wooden or metal club. These weaker elements of the game will not put themselves right without an organized remedial course of action that must be adhered to by the player. Once again the help and advice of an accomplished coach will be of great benefit, not only in providing the necessary technical information, but in clarifying the simplest, quickest and most effective way to solve the problem.

It is from this category of golfer that the desire for 'consistency' is most mentioned. Ask a player what part of their game they would most wish to develop, and more often than not the answer is not specific, but a general reply of 'it is the inconsistency that spoils my golf'. This consistency factor is

not an easy one to come to terms with. All golfers desire consistency whether they are tour professionals or weekend players. Why is a golfer inconsistent? There are a whole variety of reasons, some of which are relatively out of the individual's control. As was stated earlier, in pure technical terms one idiosyncratic movement or fault will lead to another to counterbalance it. This is in itself not a major disadvantage, although it is dependent upon which fault or idiosyncratic movement is applicable, or to what extent it influences the other movements in a player's swing action. What is relative is the ability of the individual to integrate successfully these movements into their swing actions, and to be able to repeat their best swings on a regular and reliable basis particularly under pressure. This comes down to a high level of feel and confidence from the individual. For a golfer to play once a week and expect consistency is almost impossible. Few human beings could possibly feel the exact same physiological sensations from day to day, let alone from week to week – as is shown by the variation in scoring of the top professionals and by the variation of tournament winners week in week out. The confidence factor increases a player's potential to feel physically comfortable with the swing movements by virtue of a no-fear positive attitude status, but confidence alone cannot conquer the strive for consistency, as ultimately there has to be a high percentage of physical repetition to a player's swing action – this repetition is an individual factor whereby some players will achieve it through more natural and instinctive measures, perhaps due to a high level of hand–eye co-ordination, whereas others

will seek the benefits of improved technical aspects, working on the premise that the more correct or neutral their swing action, the less likelihood that they will make unnecessary errors when playing their golf shots. A golfer's perception of consistent play is often hard to evaluate – for some it will be the ability to maintain good ball-striking skills, for others it will be about their eventual score.

No one swing action will work for everybody, and ultimately it is the control of the flight of the ball that dictates the potential to score well or consistently, and as such, as long as a swing action repeats itself often enough, then a player has the potential to improve his scores on a reasonably regular and consistent basis.

Whatever quality of long game the player possesses, it is invariably the short game and putting that dictate the quality of scoring during a round of golf. Developing feel for the short game through regular practice is essential. Putting can be improved through coaching and practice.

Tips for Accomplished Players

1. Check out and improve your pre-swing and swing fundamentals on a regular basis. These are:
   (a) Develop a reliable pre-shot routine
   (b) A correct grip or hold of the club
   (c) The correct aim of the club face and body
   (d) Understand ball position
   (e) Develop a good posture and balance
   (f) Seek to co-ordinate the movements of your hands, arms and body
   (g) Maintain consistent rhythm and balance through-out the swing movement.

2. Use the help and advice of a regular coach.

3. Establish an understanding of your weaker game points – work to minimize or alleviate these.

4. Learn to understand the flight of the ball – that is, hook, slice, draw, fade, high and low.

5. Practise to control the flight of the ball or at least to improve your current standards.

6. Practise the shots you use or need most on the golf course itself.

7. Improve your short game and putting through practice and tuition if need be.

8. Develop a greater range of chipping, pitching and bunker shots.

9. Improve your course management skills.

10. Play within your limitations during a round of golf.

11. Remember that it is quality and not quantity that counts.

Advanced Players

What constitutes an advanced player? For these purposes, a handicap of below 3 (male) 4 (female) will suffice. There are, however, many players in the 4 – 6 handicap bracket who play to an excellent standard, but miss out by not consolidating the art of scoring during a round of golf. The art of achieving a good advanced level or standard of play is to be able to put more than just one good round together at one time, and to be able to shoot a number of good solid low-scoring rounds of golf consecutively. To achieve a low score over two rounds of a competition is more measurable than over one. Indeed, to do it over a four-round event, which is the format of all major tournaments, is even more measurable, yet again. It is, therefore, quite relevant that as an advanced player develops his game and improves his ability to score, he should endeavour to

test himself out under more severe competitive conditions. This not only means playing against similarly advanced golfers, but competing in high level events played over more challenging golf courses and for a greater reward or status should the player ultimately win.

This competitive thrust is the very essence of what drives the ambitious golfer forever onward and upward. Playing while in a competitive situation is the ultimate test for all advanced golfers, and as such puts a different emphasis on the priorities that now become the major focus. At this stage the pre-swing and swing fundamentals should have become well established, and although some of the leading players in the world have their own individual idiosyncrasies the core of all swing movement is based around sound repetitive actions that have been tried and tested under some considerable pressure. For a player to make continued forward progress from the early stages of advanced status then there must be a gradual easing out of the weaker or more destructive elements of the individual's game.

This might be a technical aspect identified as a swing movement causing too many erratic golf shots, or it might be a skill factor, such as a lack of ball control, or even more common amongst advanced golfers is an inability to perform quality shots in a competitive environment. Pressure affects all good players, but it is the ability to handle this efficiently and effectively that helps to define those who achieve success and those who do not. The mind plays a tremendous role in golf, particularly at more advanced levels of play, and as all golfers will have experienced at some time or another a lack of confidence or self-belief, will make even the most

straightforward of shots into ones not to be relished. This change of emphasis from a high percentage of physical priorities towards an even higher level of psychological ones makes the game the ultimate challenge. Later in the book psychological aspects are dealt with in greater depth, but suffice it to say at advanced levels of golf no matter how good a swing action a player has, without a strong mental attitude and competitive edge, players are likely to underperform except in the less relevant events.

The advanced player must look at every aspect of the game from technique, right through to course management and equipment, not forgetting the physiological and psychological points. Young players benefit by working regularly with a trusted coach, particularly one who has watched them develop their game over a number of years. The player/coach relationship thrives from mutual faith in one another. Communication is easier and more comfortable. There is a natural response from the player, and the coach benefits by being able to watch the player in competitive situations observing the best and worst of their game.

It is very easy for a good player to fall into the trap of practising incorrectly by either working to develop the less relevant department or departments of the game, or by aimlessly hitting hundreds of practice shots in the mistaken belief that quantity counts over quality. A player must seek to develop the widest depth of skill possible, and to enhance this task by understanding the relevant information, then working to achieve and consistently repeat the necessary swing movements.

No matter how high the standard of the long game or full shots, the emphasis on golf is being able to achieve the lowest score possible, and so the short game and putting once again play a huge part. For advanced players up to 65 per cent of the final score can be classified as coming from their short game – an incredible percentage when one looks at the average amount of effort and practice put into this department by many players – possibly only 10–20 per cent of their time. Observing the top tour players only seeks to emphasize this point. We are all in awe of such players as Tiger Woods, John Daly or Laura Davies, but the winner is invariably the player that holes the most putts, particularly the ones that really matter at the most critical of times.

There is an endless amount of information and advice available for advanced players. Much of it has been passed down or learned from the very best players in the world. Each player needs to identify the relevant points that affect his or her ability to make progress, and which will lead to

ongoing development and improvement. The key priorities are based around performance and results, so that no matter what preference a player has, their ultimate goal must be to achieve their lowest potential scores as regularly as possible.

Tips for Advanced Players

1. Keep a regular check on your pre-swing and swing fundamentals. These are:

(a) Consolidate your pre-shot routine
(b) The grip or hold of the club
(c) The set-up and aim to the target
(d) The rotation of the body coupled with the positions the club moves through during the swing
(e) The rhythm, balance and co-ordination of the swing movement

(f) The quality of ball strike.
2. Use a regular coach – learn from his or her skills.
3. Appreciate your strengths and weaknesses as a player.
4. Consolidate and improve where possible your technical aspects.
5. Understand the importance of the short game and putting.
6. Identify your mental strengths and weaknesses; improve these whenever and wherever possible.
7. Do not ignore the physiological/fitness aspects.
8. Practise correctly and effectively – quality not quantity.
9. Good course management is a priority.
10. Assess your equipment needs.
11. Finally, success is measured by the ability to score in competitive situations – this is the ultimate test and one that almost all sportsmen relish.

PART 3
SUPPORT SYSTEMS

11
MANAGING YOUR GAME

It is the intention of this final section of the book to focus on aspects that allow golfers to convert knowledge, understanding and ability into playing successful golf. There are certain skills that are unique to golf itself, but much of what differentiates a successful player from a not so successful one is often a fundamental appreciation of rational and obvious basics that must be an integral part of any player's makeup. Golf can provide a player with immense satisfaction and pleasure even at a relatively poor standard, but in analysing a winning formula there are many other qualities involved of which a high percentage are clearly evident in those that have achieved success.

How Committed are You?

The first step to achieving success as a golfer is to come to terms with what is possible given the daily commitments an individual has in all areas of normal life. It is very easy to underestimate how education, business, social or family commitments affect the potential to plan and carry out an effective development programme. It may not be necessary to reconsider reorganizing one's whole lifestyle just for the sake of the game, but it is important to come to terms with what are realistic personal limitations or the need to restructure schedules to offer greater scope for game enhancement.

Every golfer should be aware of how much available time per week they have solely for the purpose of playing or practising golf. A once-a-week golfer with little or no spare time must accept the lack of opportunity to develop his or her skills. One with the potential to play twice a week plus an hour or two available for practice has a far greater scope to develop and improve his golf game. A player who has ample opportunity to play, perhaps four or five times per week, plus almost daily practice has a wonderful opportunity to enhance and develop his skills and overall game, but must

endeavour to manage this time efficiently, otherwise so much of the potential will be wasted. There is no ideal equation for all golfers; it is recognizing these opportunities that offers each player a chance to develop their own personal programme – one that can lead to improved levels of skill, performance and enjoyment.

There are common areas that all golfers should acknowledge when analysing their opportunities and potential for developing their game.

- Assess how much golf you would like to play.
- Realistically, how much time is available per week solely for play or practice?
- If you decide to change your golfing routine how realistic are the chances of sticking to it on a regular basis.
- How important is solely playing the course as opposed to dedicating specific time for practice?
- Are you prepared to learn to practise correctly – even those departments of your game that you least enjoy?
- Will you be prepared to work within the guidelines advised by a coach even if your golf and scoring appear to take a backward step initially?
- Are you prepared to miss out on certain competitive opportunities whilst giving your game a fair chance to develop?
- Course management, psychological and physiological aspects must also be assessed.
- You may need to assess your current golf equipment, possibly adjusting where appropriate or upgrading as and when necessary – particularly if your new golf regime alters your physical requirements.

Efficient and Effective Practice

Practising efficiently and effectively can be broken down into a number of categories, each of which need to be clarified and clearly understood. Technical aspects, the mental attitude, course-management skills, practice rounds and tournament preparation are all separate aspects that need to be fully appreciated. The following details provide a fairly intense resumé of what is involved in each category.

Regular Practice

The comment 'Play to Practise, not Practise to Play' is so relevant when it comes down to regular practice for all golfers. In other words learn from what you do on the golf course, identify your weaknesses and go to the practice area to work to improve these aspects. Do not spend valuable time practising things that you are unable to achieve or do not use when you are playing the course itself. A typical example of this might be a player who identifies an inability to play successfully shots with a number 3 iron. Regular practice may well improve the technical ability to play this club, and just as importantly, build confidence, but what the player should first identify is the absolute need to be able to hit regular, quality 3 iron shots, that is, does the course the golfer plays on demand a regular number of these shots to a highish standard or is it just a belief by the player that without the ability to hit solid 3 iron shots he is not a competent or complete golfer!

Perhaps some of that practice time might have been better invested in other ways – learning to control a lofted wood shot as a replacement club for a 3 iron distance; working on general ball-striking skills or, more obviously, increased short game practice to improve the ability to get up and down from around the green more often, particularly as few players are proficient enough to hit a green regularly with a 3 iron anyway.

Each golfer must establish a duration for practice that does not create fatigue or a loss of concentration as practising past an effective stage will only lead to retrograde results. Although tiredness may be more recognizable in a physical sense than a mental one, it is this mental aspect that will have the most detrimental effect on a player's swing. A lack of concentration or focus can easily lead to poor results. It is generally accepted that a human being concentrates best for periods of up to about forty minutes at any one time. After this they should rest for a short period before resuming the task for a further duration. Invariably these concentrated sessions will need to be shortened or become shorter if longer periods of practice are planned or if a player is in any way physically or mentally fatigued before commencing practice.

All practice sessions should have a routine to them, although this may vary dependent upon the length of the session or the type of practice to be included.

The long game practice will be more physically demanding than the short game, which has rather less emphasis on athletic movement and requires more feel and rhythm from the swing movement. A player should seek to build a suitable routine, which fits into a regular time slot. Within that routine slight changes would be acceptable, but must still allow the player to keep to an established pattern of swing maintenance and/or development. The routine should be adhered to for long enough to establish its effectiveness – Four or five regular practice sessions will not be enough for any player to seek great benefit, whereas sticking to something over two or three months will begin to establish a golfing routine, and one that benefits through feedback from and back to golf course play.

The reason to practise is to establish a regular swing action that a player is able to repeat time and time again no matter how important the situation, and how pressurized the moment. The more a swing is repeated correctly the greater the chance that a player will adapt to it naturally.

For most players hitting shots on the range is relatively easy, but on the golf course they find things far harder to keep under control. Practising in a way that stimulates course play is the most effective form of practice, and one that should be integrated into a golfer's practice sessions as much as possible. The nearer a golf situation can be recreated in practice the greater the benefit.

- Do not always roll the ball onto a good lie; drop it and play it as it lies as often as possible. This is particularly important with regard to short game practice, where the ball rarely sits on a perfect piece of grass – play shots off uneven or sloping lies.
- Play one shot at a time, with any one club and then change to another club to help recreate what actually might happen on the golf course itself. Enhance the benefit of this type of practice by using good visualization and imagination skill, plus a regular pre-shot routine.

• Always aim for a specific target. It is often beneficial to choose a different target for each practice shot to help to develop a sound pre-shot routine and enhance aiming skills.

• Set standards or goals – hitting ten balls, say, with a club to a target with a mental stipulation that six must be within a certain more realistic distance of the target. For bunkers it may be beneficial to set a goal of getting three balls inside a distance of three feet from the flagstick from ten consecutive shots.

What to Include

Simply what will bring about a positive development of an individual's game! To repeat, it is not difficult to work at any one aspect of the game, it is the correct identification of this aspect that matters most. It is obviously not so difficult if a player can correctly assess their own game requirements, for example, a short hitter may feel that the majority of time should be spent hitting long irons and woods in an effort to increase length, accuracy and consistency with this type of shot. This may be partially true, but if this player accepts he is already hitting a high percentage of these shots on the course anyway then developing a reliable, proficient ability with approach shots, the short game and putting will improve the potential to score well and release some of the long game pressures.

Quality practice is about combining the right ingredients. For instance, if a technical position in the swing is incorrect and a new one needs to be worked at then it may be far better to isolate that one part of the swing so that effective practice can be gained rather than putting too much of a priority on ball strike and ball flight characteristics. It is not possible to spend a whole session working at technical development anyway. A good routine will include some technical work and some specific club practice, combining an acceptable standard of accuracy and ball control, an appreciation of ball striking qualities and also the important aspects of rhythm, balance and feel. Including all these aspects aids positive progress. It is the quality of the practice not the quantity that dictates success.

Tips for the Long Hitter

1. Accuracy and consistency from the tee.
2. Alternative clubs off the tee to provide reliability if required.

3. A regular ball shape – straight, fade or draw and improve general ball control skills.
4. Whatever your normal ball shape always be able to hit the other options.
5. Longer drives will mean shorter shots to the green – accuracy with approach shots particularly from the middle and short irons is essential.
6. The ability to reach most greens in two puts an emphasis on accurate approach play.
7. Hitting greens in regulation usually means that a golfer has a higher percentage of longer first putts.
8. Longer hitting generally means greater inaccuracy – practising shots from out of the rough will improve the skill factor and also the scoring potential from these positions.
9. Longer hitters often lack the feel of finesse of shorter hitters. Develop routines that improve these aspects.

Tips for the Medium Hitter

1. Accuracy and consistency in all departments, particularly from off the tee.
2. As regular a ball shape as possible.
3. Accuracy and ball control with approach shots to the green particularly with the middle irons.
4. Being able to shape the ball both left to right or right to left will improve scoring potential, as will being able to hit the ball higher or lower when required.
5. 40–80yd shots will be regularly required on the course. These half or three-quarter shots need a high percentage of practice.
6. Steadiness rather than dynamic qualities will be a strength, so look for a repetition of shots.
7. The number of greens hit in regulation may not be high so tighten short game skills and improve reliability in mid- to longer-length putting distances.

Tips for the Short Hitter

1. Accept that distance is not the key priority.
2. Most short hitters are relatively accurate but should develop consistency of ball strike as poor ball-striking skills will shorten shots further.
3. Be proficient with lofted woods, as long irons are more difficult to be reliable with.
4. Accept that there are some greens that are not reachable with any two clubs so positional play is vital.

5. Short hitters must know their most reliable clubs when under pressure – they will invariably make most use of them.

6. An above average short game is required so a high percentage of practice time must be dedicated to this aspect.

7. A good short game will offer the player far more opportunities of converting shorter putts into par scores. A high percentage must be holed – practise putting from 3ft–6ft diligently.

8. Rhythm and balance help all swing aspects – erratic golf is not acceptable for the shorter hitter.

Generally

Remember practice is only beneficial if what a player practises is not only technically correct but incorporates important aspects such as balance, feel, control and rhythm.

• Practice is about creating habits – good ones that is! Most golfers have to rid themselves of old or bad habits initially by adopting new movements that help them to develop improved habits.
• Practise with clubs that build rhythm, feel and confidence. These will usually be the player's most favoured clubs. Be disciplined as practising with the long clubs may lead to too much aggression and a loss of control.
• Work on your weakest elements once a more satisfactory swing action and confidence have been established.
• The short game accounts for at least 50 per cent of a golfer's score – a high percentage of time should be given to it.

Enhancing Practice At All Levels

• Do not be tempted to hit too many balls in too limited an amount of time. Often with a reasonable number of practice balls in front of the player, the temptation is to hit them in rapid succession without enough thought for the true purpose of the session.
• Always place the ball first and then go through a regular pre-shot routine for the address position.
• Do not practise when you are physically or mentally tired. If you do, keep it as short, simple and as effortless as possible.
• Do not continue to practise if things are going badly and improvement and progress seem

unattainable. Be patient and wait until a more opportune time when things are sure to go better.
• Only practise for short periods of time in adverse weather conditions such as strong winds – consistency will be far harder to achieve and errors can compound or creep in unnecessarily.
• In windy conditions should practice be necessary, try to practise into the wind as this will tend to emphasize any ball flight errors and offer valuable feedback. A right to left wind will minimize a slice spin, but shorten the length of the shot although it does encourage the correct in to out swing action, which can prove extremely beneficial. A left to right wind will accentuate a golfer's slice or open club face error – not always a good psychological idea! Downwind the ball spin is minimized so errors are neutralized often giving false feedback to the player.
• Always practise shots that are relevant to your own game, for example, fairway woods rather than long irons if you rarely use or need to use them.
• Practice on the golf course can be very useful – on your regular course it is a good idea to select an alternative club to the one you might usually use from a particular tee. This enhances your concentration, widens your club selection for future use, offers additional practice for tee shots on other holes or courses and sets up alternative approach shots to the hole, which further enhances a player's knowledge and experience of his own capabilities.
• Practice is to help build up repetition and confidence. Always finish on a positive note – if possible after several good shots.
• Remember it is quality not quantity that counts.

Pre-round Practice and Preparation

All players should warm up their muscles with some form of simple exercise routine prior to hitting the first shot of the day, as the individual's feel, mobility and balance will benefit greatly. On the practice range:

• Commence with half wedge or short iron shots to develop rhythm and feel immediately.
Build up to full swing shots, continuing to develop rhythm, balance and consistency.
• Find your shape of shot for the day – it is not always possible to hit the same shape day in day

151

out. Do not fight the shape for the day, but accept it and work with it ready for the golf course play. Work through a variety of clubs – short, mid- and long irons, a few woods and then back to short irons again.

• Try to maintain a consistent system and number of shots hit.
• Include some mental rehearsal – select clubs and execute shots as if playing the first few holes to help encourage a good start to the round.
• Practise some finesse shots around the chipping green and in the sand bunker.
• On the putting green develop a feel for the longer 'lay-up' putts and hole out some putts from around 3ft to develop confidence.
• Allow a few extra minutes to check your equipment and to walk to the first tee in a correct and positive frame of mind.

Each golfer must establish some pre-round routine even if it only involves some loosening-up exercise and a few putts before play. Top players have a regular pattern, which commences with eating arrangements prior to arriving at the golf course, time of arrival at the course itself, duration of warm up, content of warm up, spare time for any personal routines before stepping onto the first tee. Perhaps the most relevant and important point has yet to be emphasized. The pre-round warm-up and practice is not about working on the technical aspects of the swing, but it is simply to prepare the golfer for the ensuing challenge for the round of golf in hand. It is too late to make any radical changes to the golf swing itself and so whatever characteristics the golfer has on that day are the ones that he/she must use as effectively and efficiently as possible to help produce the lowest score for that round. In other words, if a player's regular fade shot appears to be more of a slice on that day rather than use the pre-round session to try to cure the problem, it is far more effective to adapt to playing with the slice for that round itself, leaving all technical work until after the completion of the round. The key priority is to concentrate on making a good score for the round itself.

This is very much a matter of the correct mental attitude, but one that enables any level of player to respond positively to golf course play. The player must appreciate that there will be certain shots that he may not, on this occasion, be as proficient at as he would have been under normal playing circumstances. A percentage attitude must be adopted, possibly plotting a safer route from the tee to the green, looking to position the ball in the most sensible and reliable of places from which to play the next shot.

This pre-round preparation contributes greatly in terms of round success. Leading golfers appreciate that they cannot play their best golf every day. They accept this and rather than fight it they simply choose to play with it, preferring to make the most use of what they are doing well and to minimize the negative effect of what they might be doing badly on that particular day.

Building a Routine

There are many other aspects involved in helping any golfer to learn, develop and improve almost all areas of their game. Identifying personal requirements is vital and the help and co-operation of a willing coach will enhance a player's development by offering direction as well as qualified knowledge. Nevertheless a player should enhance his own game through the development of good routines, understand and be able to carry out a number of drills specific to personal swing requirements, consider the use and value of some sort of regular skills or shot-making test, and be prepared to possibly invest in purchasing relevant practice or training aids should they offer the potential for swing development.

Building a Pre-shot or Pre-swing Routine

The importance of a good pre-shot routine cannot be overemphasized and is not only covered in this particular chapter, but also again later under mental aspects of the game. Observing top players illustrates this philosophy – Tiger Woods in the 1997 US Masters Tournament gave a perfect example – whilst playing the last few holes there was incredible noise and excitement from the spectators, yet he was able to carry out his familiar routine on each shot, blocking out the distractions and playing his shots to his normal high standard. He was obviously nervous and excited at the prospect of winning his first major championship. His adrenaline level must have been very high, his heart pumping faster than normal, but he still maintained great discipline. This was due to an established routine – the set-up routine and the routine built around on course play – walking speed between shots, time taken to assess the shot in hand and club selection.

The pre-shot or pre-swing routine is probably one of the most significant factors of playing golf. Without an established pre-shot routine golfers are in effect relegating themselves to playing golf at a lower standard than they are capable of. All golfers have to prepare themselves for the shot in hand but without a regular pattern to this preparation it is almost impossible to establish a consistency to the golf shots that follow. Golf is a game that requires a player to establish correct pre-swing positions – aim of club face and body, position of the ball, hold of the club, posture and weight distribution. The swing itself – the direction and movement of the clubhead, plus the winding up and unwinding of the body – are all influenced by this set-up position. It stands to reason therefore, that the significance of the pre-shot routine cannot and should not be underestimated. Players must establish one that suits them, one that they feel comfortable using and most importantly one that allows their swing actions to be most effective when executing the shot.

'The better the player the better the routine'. This tends to be an obvious fact. Look at the top players in the world of golf – Tiger Woods, Greg Norman, Ian Woosnam, Nick Faldo – all of them have a regular sequence of movements to their pre-shot routine. So regular in fact that should they be viewed from a distance they would still be instantly recognizable by this sequence of movements prior to playing a shot. All of them have practised and developed their routines over their years of competitive golf. Why the great deliberations and effort to establish this as part of their playing style? Because they know how important it is, and fully appreciate that if they do not have a disciplined series of pre-shot movements their ability to perform shots on the golf course in competitive situations will be seriously affected. It is the whole foundation of playing while under pressure and it ensures that the player sets up physically and mentally with a totally focused and decisive attitude to the target.

When to Start the Routine Fig 108

Most amateur players wonder why they are so inconsistent and unable to play shots with any real reliability. Identifying when to start a pre-shot routine is import. A good routine does not necessarily begin once a player has the club in his hand – it can commence far earlier – sometimes as early as when the player lets go of his trolley handle or drops his bag on the ground. Some players will go immediately into a regular sequence of assessing the shot in hand – possibly throwing some grass into the air to test the wind direction and strength; studying a yardage chart and assessing other outside factors such as hazards, ground conditions and climate; choosing the appropriate club selection. These may be the early stages of the pre-shot routine and they may vary on certain shots, but most golfers will already have commenced what unbeknown to them is a routine of sorts. For the top players these preliminaries are often as set as the final moments before the swing begins.

The majority of golfers would still not recognize that their routine has commenced even when eyeing the target, but this is when those that visualize the shot in hand spend some of their most important seconds. Perhaps it is as the physical movements of creating the grip and stance get under way that most feel that they are into some form of regular pattern. This procedure triggers the golfer's final physical and mental state prior to the swing commencing. This mental focus has to be achieved no matter how reliable the physical aspects as success is ultimately reliant upon the correct mental attitude.

Some Pre-shot Suggestions

• Recognize the pre-shot routine as commencing with a regular pattern of movement such as taking a club from the bag or perhaps adjusting the tightness of the golf glove.
• Build your personal movements into the routine and ensure that they are comfortable to repeat and effective as regards to your results.
• Pre-shot routines include:

    Standing behind the ball looking towards the target to help alignment.

Fig 108 The pre-swing routine.

(a)

(b)

(c)

(d)

(a) Approach the ball from behind, building a good visualization and feel for the shot.

(b) Set the club face square to the target with the feet still close together.

(c) Widen the stance, set alignment square to target.

(d) One last look to check all's well.

(e) Swing with confidence.

(e)

It may be beneficial to focus on an intermediate target, perhaps just in front of the ball itself, so that the club face can be aimed to this point with less chance of an error as the player moves further into the routine.

Some players use visualization at this time to help build a strong mental picture of the shot in hand.

Grip

It is common for the hands to be positioned after the club face is set towards the target, although some players position their hands in line with the club face and then step into the address position.

Stance

With the feet positioned fairly close together, it is easier to move each foot in turn to establish the correct distance between the feet for the appropriate shot and, of course, the ball position and the aim. More accomplished players tend to move the left foot first and then the right one.

Ball Position

The movements of establishing the stance do in effect dictate the final ball position. By positioning the ball in the centre of a narrow stance and moving the left foot first the golfer is establishing the exact position of the ball in relation to the left heel. A minimal movement sets the ball up off or just inside the left heel, whilst a greater movement positions the ball more towards the centre of the stance. The right foot moves to accommodate the correct width of stance for the shot.

Pre-swing Movement

Golf is a dead ball game that does not require fast reactive reflexes. It is however important not to 'freeze up' over the shot and so some form of tension-relieving movement keeps the muscles flexed and primed for the swing action.

Looking from the ball to the target and back to the ball again helps build a decisive mental attitude. Waggling or lifting the clubhead, controlled relaxing and regripping of the club, wriggling the toes, flexing the knees all help to prepare the golfer ready for the swing.

Getting Under Way

Either a forward press of the hands towards the target, a kick inward of the right knee or a slight lateral or rotational movement of the head are popular ways to commence the actual swing movement.

• Remember simple is most effective and easiest to repeat. Always keep the same routine on all shots, particularly under pressure.

Every player must find their own routine – one that suits their personality. Often it is best to have a smooth and efficient one, rather than a slow deliberate set of preliminaries, which might build tension and mental doubt. Keeping things as simple as possible will for the majority of players prove the most effective. It is always easier to repeat something simple rather than complex.

Drills and Practice Aids

Fortunately the idea of using drills to help a golfer develop and maintain good swing movements is now a popular part of everyday coaching and practice. A drill is an action that is repetitious and relatively disciplined so that a movement can be memorized and replaced with an alternative improved one. It is, in effect, a physical rehearsal of the swing movement a player wishes to incorporate. A drill must be understood and applied correctly by the player, otherwise it might encourage an incorrect action and cause more disruption to the swing rather than enhancing it.

Top players not only use drills on the range, but can also often be seen repeating them on the course during their practice swing routines. These act as a reminder of positive swing movements and the feel required for repeating these actions when actually hitting the ball. They can be used to overcome poor swing positions or actions, or are also useful in helping a golfer develop a greater range of physical motion. A drill is most valuable when it is applicable or specific to the player's needs. Not all drills suit every player with the same swing fault so there may need to be some personal adaptations, but if a player is in any doubt the advice of a professional coach should be sought.

There are endless numbers of good drills for golfers – finding one or two that are particularly

beneficial is an important asset. An appropriate one will increase the golfer's effectiveness through regular swing discipline, and offer greater potential to use practice routines more constructively with the opportunity of helping to minimize poor play through the use of this regular form of swing reminder.

To summarize, drills serve an important purpose – they enhance learning and make swing changes more enjoyable and effective. Many coaches choose to use drills as a major part of their coaching structure. A drill will enhance both verbal and visual learning and help to develop more quickly a player's response by virtue of its high level of feel (kinesthetic) factor. A coach can use this in a highly constructive way both during lessons and also by giving a player a stipulated drill, which can be done during personal practice sessions. Once explained and understood the coach and player can feel more confident in the knowledge that the player has a positive reminder of the new action required.

Practice aids further enhance, and can often be used to replace the concept of drills. Verbal and visual communications cannot translate the same message as a practice aid, which can deliver a message through kinesthetic learning with the golfer being given a regular, correct reminder of how a particular movement or position should feel.

Teaching professionals sometimes use practice aids as training devices during coaching sessions, but are more likely to recommend their use and benefit when a player is not under their coaching supervision. It is not always easy to identify which piece of equipment will be most useful in helping a player develop a position, movement or feel as some can turn out to be more ineffective than effective. A golfer should either seek professional advice or confirm in advance that the product actually does what it is supposed to do, that it is easy enough to use, is likely to be effective on a personal basis, is cost-effective, offers advice on the frequency of use and is durable enough to stand up to regular use. Obviously simplicity is a key point but also ultimately does the aid help to produce effective results?

Skills Tests

In more recent years several amateur golf associations around the world have seen a need to be able to measure a player's level of competency and the

POWERFLYTE NATIONAL SKILLS TEST

Event:-... Sign Player A:-...

Date:-................................. Sign Player B:-..

LONG GAME

PLAYER A   PLAYER B

(.............)   (............)

WEDGE 3 METRE TARGET AT 70 m

9 IRON 5 METRE TARGET AT 100m

5 IRON 10 METRE TARGET AT 150m

DRIVER 20 METRE TARGET AT 200m

SHORT GAME:-

CHIP 7-9 iron

PITCH Wedge or Sand iron

BUNKER Sand Iron

PUTT 1 METRE DISTANCE

PUTT 2 METRE DISTANCE

PUTT 10 METRE SPEED

Skills Test Total =

Player A:-	driver	5 iron	9 iron	wedge	putt 1m	putt 2m	putt 10m	chip	pitch	bunker
Skills test score:-										
Player B:-	driver	5 iron	9 iron	wedge	putt 1m	putt 2m	putt 10m	chip	pitch	bunker
Skills Test score:-										

Fig 109 The Powerflyte Skills Test.

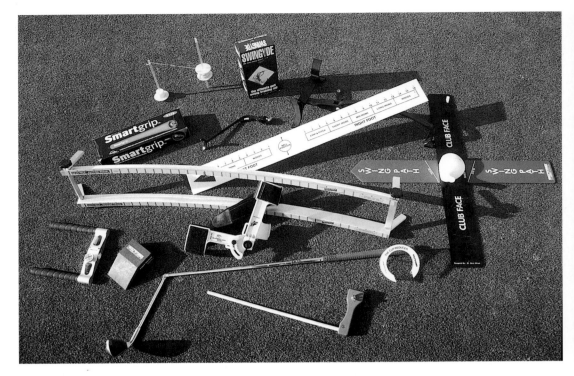

Fig 110 Just a selection of training and teaching aids.

ability to improve that level under test conditions. Consequently, there has evolved a fairly extensive array of potential criteria for measuring a player's capabilities ranging from the ability to hole a given number of 3ft putts, to hitting a driver between two posts set up at a stipulated distance apart.

It is doubtful that any one system is far in advance of the others, but it is obviously important that each offers the player a relatively honest measure of his ability to hit the ball to a target from a given distance. The formula must involve tests of accuracy and length control to include tee shots, mid- irons, short irons, chipping, pitching, bunker play and putting. The statistics can be logged or monitored as a player 're-sits' the test as and when required. Comparisons of improvement or decline can be registered, averages taken for comparison with others, and perhaps, more importantly, a player can identify through the test which departments of his game need some attention or practice. The greater the pressure factor imposed by the test the nearer the performance can be measured to competitive situations. The

information can also be linked or compared to on-course statistics to verify their accuracy.

The Powerflyte National Skills Test, originating from Australia offers a high level test with a database which allows some useful and meaningful comparisons with many other categories of the golfer (Fig 109).

The Value of Information

So far we have looked at the elements that include an appreciation of one's own capabilities and the scope to develop them. Also how to identify and practise correctly on a regular and pre-round basis. Prior to dealing with what can be a relatively straightforward art of course management, it is important to identify some further aspects of game control, and how we measure its value. Without this understanding, the player will lack the knowledge needed to appreciate that success at golf is influenced greatly by what the player does before he actually steps onto the golf course itself.

Often players fail to respond or even recognize the value of worthwhile information, but in this section lies much of the groundwork and answers to a player's inability to make the most of their own golfing potential.

The professional circuits throughout the world have long been correlating statistics to help provide useful information about player performance. This information covers aspects such as driving distances, fairways hit in regulation, greens in regulation, bunker saves, the number of putts per round, stroke averages per round, per year, the number of birdies, eagles and bogeys per round, per tournament, per year and stroke averages of individual holes on each tournament golf course. These are just some of the statistics put together to help analyse almost all relevant aspects of professional golf.

The average player may not see the value in recording this information for his own personal game, yet keeping simple records and using them correctly will help identify areas of weakness within a player's game, and lead to more profitable practice and greater rewards on the golf course.

It is relatively simple to record the number of fairways and greens hit and the number of putts per round taken, but this information alone can prove misleading if not used in the right context. Let us take putting as a useful example – nearly every golfer in the world will leave the eighteenth green and immediately condemn the holable putts that on this occasion did not go in the hole.

The golfer will complain that he missed two maybe three tap in putts, ran over the edge of the hole with a couple of 15-footers and 'horse-shoed out' with the odd long one. No mention is actually made of the ones that went in or were possibly fortunate to go in despite the player misreading or mishitting the actual putt. In most cases it is a balance out situation overall, with good fortune and bad luck generally equalizing for most players over a number of rounds. There is a factual variation of putting averages dependent upon the overall ability of the player – the professional scratch/amateur averages about 31 putts per round, with the best putting averages working out at just under 28 for every round played.

A middle handicap golfer may average out at approximately 34 putts per round, but obviously the more proficient putters might have averages below 30. The poorer ones perhaps near to 40. A high handicap golfer is more likely to average around 38 putts per round with the proficient lowering this to around 32 or 33 and the highest well above 40 per round. If we give approximate totals of 72 for the professional, 84 for the middle handicapper and 96 for the high handicap player we can see that the number of putts as an approximate percentage of each player's total score is 43 per cent for the professional, 41 per cent for the middle handicapper and 40 per cent for the average high handicapper – in percentage terms not too different overall and a pattern that reflects consistently when looking at the chart (see Fig 111).

PROFESSIONAL			MIDDLE HANDICAPPER			HIGH HANDICAPPER		
Score	Total putts	%	Score	Total putts	%	Score	Total putts	%
69	27	39	80	30	38	90	34	38
69	31	45	80	34	43	90	38	42
69	35	51	80	38	48	90	42	47
72	27	38	84	30	36	96	34	35
72	31	43	84	34	41	96	38	40
72	35	49	84	38	45	96	42	44
74	27	37	88	30	34	100	34	34
74	31	42	88	34	39	100	38	38
74	35	47	88	38	43	100	42	42
76	27	35	92	30	33	104	34	33
76	31	41	92	34	37	104	38	36
76	35	46	92	38	41	104	42	40

Fig 111 A comparison of putting totals as a percentage of the total score. All figures are approximate

There are a few slight anomalies in the chart – for example it is unlikely that a professional will take 35 putts when scoring a 69 on a par 72 course, unless his tee to green game was outstandingly good, that is, 34 shots in total. Also the high handicapper would have to have played exceedingly badly to shoot 104 with only 34 putts, that is, 70 shots from tee to green. Analysis can give a few simple pieces of information for each category of player. The professional or scratch amateur can least afford a poor putting average as in percentage terms it constitutes a significantly high amount of the overall score.

An obvious step would be to practise putting far more to improve the number of putts holed per round and lower those averages. This concept would obviously work fine as long as a player is hitting the ball close enough to give himself what would be termed a makeable distance putt on a regular basis – statistics prove that a distance 11ft from the cup is the optimum one-putt zone. If the player is hitting the ball outside of 11ft with his approach shot, it is fairly unlikely he is giving himself a fair chance of making the putts anyway. In other words and although it may seem obvious, players must endeavour to hit the ball as close as possible to the flagstick if they wish to hole a high number of putts. This will not only lower putting averages, but obviously the overall round scores.

By getting the ball nearer to the hole in the first place players would not only benefit by improving their single putt potential, but also by minimizing the risk of three or more putts from longer distances. The higher the putting average the less single putts are holed, and the more three putts are taken. Most average to high handicap players should seek to develop the consistency of their putting as a way of lowering their overall averages.

An interesting point to note is that if the professional or scratch amateur were to putt on the greens from the actual positions and distances that the middle or high-handicapped players do, it is unlikely that they would be able to reduce the overall score for that round by much more than 4 or 5 shots. It would actually be a case of making less unnecessary mistakes on the green rather than one of holing an increased number of sensational one putts.

There could be endless discussions on the relevance and importance of putting, but a good rule of thumb is to be aggressive on short putts where

A Comparison of Putting Statistics for Male and Female Golfers				
	Male		Female	
Handicap	(Scratch) 0	18	(Scratch) 0	36
Length of Putt				
3ft	81%	71%	79%	64%
7ft	50%	33%	45%	29%
14ft	10%	5%	9%	4%

The figures above summarize the percentage of putts holed in each category from 3, 7 and 14ft.

All figures approximate

the risk of unnecessary errors is fairly limited, and very positive but sensible on longer ones bearing in mind the importance of ensuring two putts. Remembering the 11ft rule is quite useful in helping players appreciate that anything below that distance offers them the ideal opportunity to single putt and reduce putting averages, whereas anything over that distance will tend to make one-putting more unlikely and increase overall averages.

So to enhance our putting chances and the potential number of single putts per round all golfers should be aware of the importance of improving approach play and short game shots. Obviously approach shots are made easier if they are played from on the fairway, so the relevance of accurate tee shots should not be ignored. Average ability players would benefit by noting which clubs they most use to play approach shots, how well they strike the ball with these clubs, and what position, that is, to the right or to the left, they tend to finish after the shot. A poor result is not only likely to add one extra shot to the score, it may also contribute to adding yet another if the recovery shot is not played well enough. It is a well-known comment but one worth reiterating – 'Don't follow a bad shot with a bad decision', look for the common-sense shot from poor positions and put the next shot into the most safe and effective position possible.

There tends to be a distance at which most golfers will realistically expect to hit the green. Unfortunately, not all players are realistic! For high handicappers this is well under 100yd, for middle handicappers under 125 yd and for lower handicappers under 175yd. This is realistic rather than optimistic. Inside these sorts of distances a player can be positive and aggressive, over them positive but sensible and able to plan the strategy to limit unnecessary errors. It is not negative for any level of golfer to look at a spot where the target may be best missed – for high handicappers the safest position, for middle handicappers avoiding trouble, for low handicappers the widest part of the green or apron. It is always best to play with your own natural ball flight, that is, fade, slice, draw, hook, and to fit each shot around that personal shape. If this is not possible then a player should proceed with caution and adopt an attitude of safety first. It is always an error with any shot to aim at trouble and hope a slice or hook will move the ball safely away from the danger. Ironically, it is on these occasions that a golfer usually hits one of his rarer dead straight shots into the trouble. Capable players should aim away from trouble and shape the ball towards it if necessary. Lesser players should always play to a safe spot and better still one that allows the simplest of following shots. Aiming for the opening of the green is a good percentage attitude and a positive course-management skill – the putter is always the easiest club to use! A good rule of thumb is to become more positive and aggressive the nearer the ball gets to the hole – tee shots can be played within oneself for accuracy and position on the fairway; longer approach shots for position, shorter ones attack the flagstick. The nearer to the green the ball is positioned the easier the game becomes.

The average player will definitely benefit by improving full swing consistency and accuracy with the irons. Hitting greens in regulation is a big bonus for all levels of player – it has a major effect on players' scoring ability and their overall competitiveness. Average players should only dedicate a high percentage of their time to putting practice if they are hitting a reasonable number of greens in regulation – somewhere between four to six per round. Otherwise they should develop their approach play and ability to chip the ball to inside 3ft from the hole as this not only improves the putting averages, but also lowers scores and increases confidence.

All players should accept that it is not possible to play consistently to the same standard each day. A player has to use what they have on the day in the most effective way possible. Every golfer has a selection of different clubs and should learn to use them in as many constructive ways as is possible. The more familiar a player becomes with their own style of play and learns to adapt around their strengths and weaknesses the more effective they can become. Some days the game feels easy and so aggression and confidence flow, on others nothing feels right and it becomes more of a battle and one of hard work, survival, good thinking and course management.

Making Comparisons

Statistics can offer some interesting overall comparisons between standards of players. The scratch golfer playing to par is likely to hit about 12 greens in regulation, hit 8 out of 10 fairways in regulation, take around 29 putts per round and make about 3 birdies. A middle handicap player scoring approximately 85 will hit about 5 greens in regulation, hit 5 fairways out of 10, take around 34 putts and might make 1 birdie. A high handicap player scoring 95 or worse, will rarely hit a green in regulation, hit an average of 4 or less fairways per round, take a minimum of 37 putts and rarely have a birdie during a round of golf.

It is relatively obvious that to shoot a par round a player must hit sufficient fairways and greens in regulation figures to give themselves the necessary opportunities to achieve low scores. The more greens missed in regulation the greater the need for sound chipping and putting. If the scratch handicapper misses 6 greens during a round, chips and putts all greens to make par and holes one putt per birdie, he takes 29 putts and shoots a one under par round. Good recovery skills are a key element.

Knowing Your Yardages

Almost all golfers now play a high percentage of their course shots with a prior knowledge of the distance the actual shot measures. This helps them to make as accurate a club selection as possible once they have accounted for the lie and climatic conditions. Accomplished players could hardly play without this information as it is now part of their pre-shot requirements and a vital aspect in allowing them to stand over a shot feeling comfortable and confident knowing that all necessary decisions have been accounted for. Lesser players believe it is vital for them also. Perhaps it is in

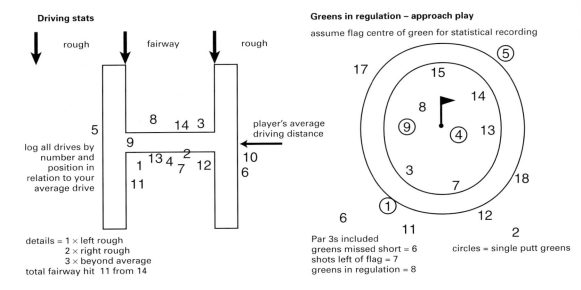

Driving stats

rough   fairway   rough

5

8   14 3

9

1 13 4 2 12   player's average
      7   driving distance

11

10
6

log all drives by
number and
position in
relation to your
average drive

details = 1 × left rough
         2 × right rough
         3 × beyond average
total fairway hit 11 from 14

Greens in regulation – approach play

assume flag centre of green for statistical recording

⑤

17   15

14

8

⑨   ④   13

3

7   18

6

11   12

2

Par 3s included
greens missed short = 6   circles = single putt greens
shots left of flag = 7
greens in regulation = 8

Fig 112 H + O statistics.

How to Learn How Far You Hit with Each Club

This really is a simple exercise, but one that all golfers who play on a regular and competitive basis should carry out before each season commences or if they change their clubs.

Select ten balls of similar quality to those that are played with on a regular basis. On a flat piece of practice area or some open ground hit a selection of irons and woods completing ten shots with each club in turn. Ignoring the two shorter shots and the two longest ones pace or measure the distance from the hitting point to the centre of the other six balls. This gives an accurate average distance for each club, assuming that a player is able to accurately pace or measure the distance.

It should not be necessary to hit every club in the set, but perhaps a selection such as 4, 6, 8, and Pitching Wedge plus No 1 and 5 Woods will be sufficient. It may also prove extremely useful to know how far it is possible to hit a full sand iron or lob wedge, as this could prove useful on long pitch shots or when stopping the ball quickly is a major requirement.

Most golfers will be a little disappointed with the actual distance that they hit their shots, but if we appreciate that almost all players leave 90 per cent of their shots to the flagstick well short, it further proves the need to be realistic as well as an intelligent player particularly as not all of these shots can be construed as mishits or mistimed ones. Also, what is extremely relevant is that so many mishits are the fault of underclubbing in the first place. A shot should be played within the player's capability not to the limit of it.

---

many cases, but there is usually one major difference between the two types of player – the accomplished ones actually know how far they hit each club, whereas lesser players *think* they know how far they hit their clubs. To use distance information effectively a player must establish a satisfactory knowledge of their own capability with each club.

Observing top players particularly when they are discussing club selection with their caddies illustrates the detailed knowledge they possess for their own distance control. Too many club golfers

overestimate their own capabilities in hitting the ball a given distance with a particular club. Often it is the case of wishful thinking, as they choose the club they would like to hit to the target rather than the one that can do the job correctly whilst allowing them to maintain control and balance. Unlike a disciplined player who has the strength of character to make their own personal decision based on their prior knowledge and course study, some are easily influenced by their fellow playing partners, and all too often make a club selection based on what they have seen or heard a moment or so earlier. An obvious example is on a par 3 hole where the first player often chooses a long iron rather than a wood and fails to reach the green. The player following rather than recognizing this fact and admitting, mainly to themselves, that a wooden club is required to hit the ball the necessary distance will often allow ego rather than their head to rule. An iron is chosen, an unnecessarily aggressive swing is made, the player knowing instinctively that the club will not have enough power, and a generally erratic impact with the ball often leaves the shot short of the green and also increases the inaccuracy as well. Good club selection is a necessity for all golfers and being prepared to select a stronger lofted one to help maintain ball control and increase accuracy is an important asset all golfers must learn to integrate into their intelligent style of play and course management.

An Example of Simple Club Distance and Measurement

When making use of these measurements on the course a player must take into account the following factors:

His natural ball flight high or low.

Ground conditions if hard the ball will roll possibly 5yd with a wedge, but up to 40yd with a driver. If soft there will be little roll from any club. **The wind** into the wind will decrease carry distance and roll, downwind the ball will carry longer and increase the roll even with a more lofted club. A side wind will increase or decrease distance dependent upon whether a player's natural shape of shot is from left to right or right to left – a fade or slice will lose considerable distance in a strong right to left wind. A draw or hook in a similar wind will gain distance both through the air and along the ground.

Elevation The elevation of the ground is important – shots uphill will travel less distance than those downhill. Side hill slopes can cause the ball to roll more on landing particularly in a sideways direction.

How to Pace Distance

It is preferential, but not always possible, to step a pace of exactly one yard or a metre. With a little practice it is amazing how accurate a golfer can become. Should a player not have a pace of a yard or a metre, then it may be beneficial to walk a pre-given distance such as ten yards counting the number of paces taken to cover that distance. In

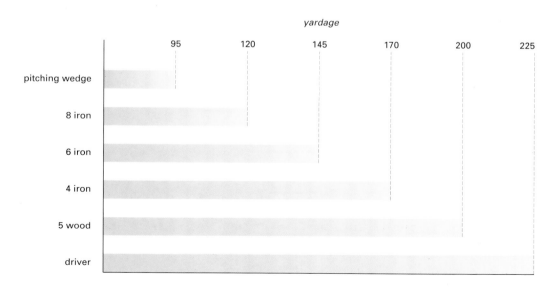

Fig 113 Player's average distance for each club.

this way when pacing a golf course a player will at least be able to have a mathematical equation that allows for a correct measurement of the given distance for each shot in yardage terms.

Course Management

Enhancing personal skills and ability during a round of golf will usually come down to a player's strategy and course management. This is in itself a skill, much of which is relatively instinctive, but a large percentage of what is not natural can and should be learnt and cultivated by all competitive golfers.

There is a large amount of personal preference in a player's style of course management, much of which is influenced at the point in time just prior to the actual execution of the shot. It is at this point that the player should be totally focused on what he or she is about to try to achieve, and in no way should be influenced by any mechanical swing thoughts whatsoever – they must now trust what has been practised and trained previously.

The basis of a solid round of golf begins with a good game plan. On a golfer's own course this game plan is fairly predetermined by virtue of the regularity of their play. The golfer benefits considerably through a high level of local knowledge learned through many rounds of golf – the natural contours of the course, the aiming points from the tee, the hidden bunkers or hazards, the odd bunker with little sand, or the quicker greens on the course, the prevailing or most difficult wind direction, the landing

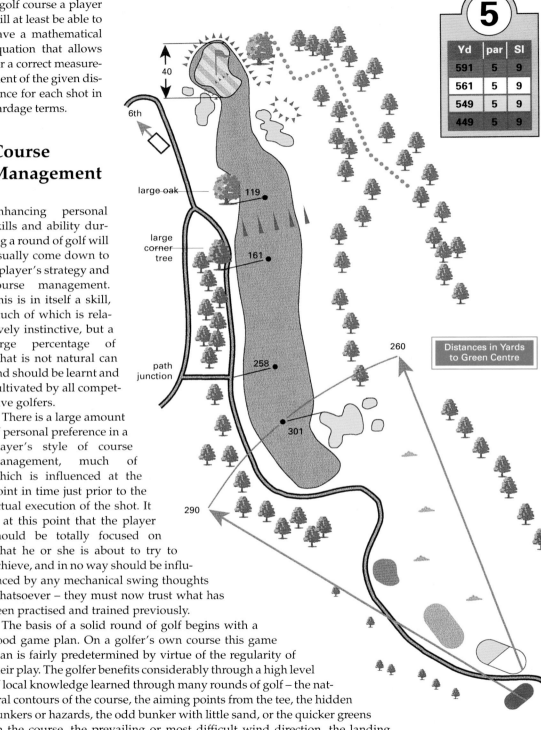

Fig 114 An example of a course/hole planner.

	5	
Yd	par	SI
591	5	9
561	5	9
549	5	9
449	5	9

Distances in Yards to Green Centre

areas for approach shots to the flagstick, and which holes might offer the best opportunities for a birdie or those that will demand more effort from the player. This experience is a great asset and one that is often wasted by many players even on their own golf course. Away from home a golfer must think more clearly and use their more limited local knowledge to greater effect. Accomplished players will in most cases have prepared themselves adequately prior to playing a match or tournament at a strange course. Few enjoy playing a course 'blind'. Practise rounds are extremely helpful and provide the player with a vital source of information. If a player uses yardages then a course planner or chart is an absolute must. Even if a player prefers to play by judging the distance personally, then a planner will help fill in the pieces of information that are not obvious when looking at the course. A typical example would be playing a hole with out of bounds or trouble behind an elevated green, which may not be visible to the naked eye, but this information would be supplied by that planner.

Some players prefer to make their own plan of the course, believing that they will gain more understanding of each hole and how they intend to plan their play. It is often a good idea just to walk around the course to enhance the game plan. Often it can be more effective to appreciate the subtleties of a hole by looking back from the green towards the tee. It can be easier to plot the ideal route, noting which part of the green is best to putt on, where to land the ball on the green, from which side of the fairway it is best to play to the green, and from the tee what to avoid and where to drive to be in the ideal position.

Details a That a Player Should Know for Each Hole

1. The total distance of each hole from the appropriate tee.
2. The distance from the tee to any hazards, bunkers, trees, corner of doglegs.
3. The distance from the tee to carry any hazard, bunker or tree.
4. Aiming points from the tee or for second shots.
5. The distance to the green from likely driving positions.
6. The position of all hazards, bunkers and course boundaries.

7. Lay-up distances for safety or recovery shots.
8. The shape and length of the green and notable features such as slopes or tiers.
9. Any particularly dangerous feature, for example, deep bunker, thick rough.
10. Slopes or elevations of fairways or greens.
11. Wind direction.
12. Green speeds – some may be slower or quicker than others.
13. The safest landing areas for positional play.
14. Local rules.
15. It may help to make a note of details from previous playing of that particular hole, for example, 12 hole, 'long elevated green, trouble short so play extra club to back for safety!'

Jack Nicklaus once said, 'There is an ideal route for every golf hole ever built – the more precisely you can identify it, the greater your chances of success.'

During a practice round it may be advantageous to hit an extra tee shot with a different club if there is a chance that safety rather than attack is an alternative in certain circumstances. A few extra chips or putts from different positions will all help to provide useful information. Please note that in some tournaments extra practice shots are not allowed. It can also be useful to keep a hole by hole score for the practice round as it helps evaluate your scoring potential for the tournament.

Competitive Play

Preparation is one of the main sources of successful competitive golf. Whether it be mental or physical factors, checking your golf equipment, making notes of all course details or playing practice rounds, they all combine to help a player perform that much better or at least offer the potential to perform to a higher level. It is always advisable to practise on the range the type of shots that are demanded on the course itself – a short course may require accurate tee shots and plenty of approaches with the wedges; a heavily bunkered course may need some extra bunker work; large greens might dictate some beneficial pace or long putting practice. Even a player's equipment might need some changes to suit the course – 3 wedges, pitching, sand and lob if lots of pitching will be required; a lofted wood if the course is long with narrow fairways and the

165

Tournament/Competitive Play Pointers
1.   Arrive with plenty of time before the round is due to commence – enough time to have a snack if necessary, to practise both long and short game and to save a little time to get the mind correctly focused.
2.   Do not concern yourself with other players – concentrate on your own game. Use your preparation correctly and enjoy the experience!
3.   If the general scoring is low, look forward to matching or beating it. If the scores are high, accept that it is likely to be a challenging round ahead and be determined to 'grind it out' to get a score.
4.   Gain positive information from your playing partners. Learn to recognize what is useful or what can have a negative effect. 'Tune In' to the positive aspects, for example, another player's good rhythm.
5.   Play within your own 'space'. Do not be influenced by the actions of others, for example, club throwing, loose comments about the course and so on.

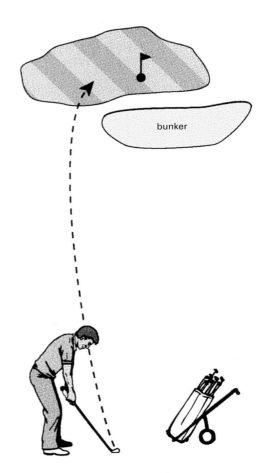

Fig 115 When the pin is positioned close to a bunker, it may be better to play a percentage shot to the centre of the green.

rough fluffy and long enough to make long irons difficult to hit reliably. It is very much about being adaptable as a golfer.

Few players go to a tournament with all parts of their game to the standard they would wish. It is a matter of accepting that perfect golf is not only impossible, it is highly unlikely even for the very top players. Golf is about how many a player scores not how he accomplishes it. The ability to be able to put together a good score even though certain elements of a player's game are not functioning particularly well is a mark of a successful player.

All rounds of golf should be played with some sort of predetermined plan; a player must be flexible though – if the wind changes direction it may be advisable to adjust the club selection to suit; if the course becomes wet and plays longer, selecting a more powerful club may be a necessity. If the drives are not going well from the tee, a 3 wood may be a sensible alternative choice. It is important to think well and play intelligently should things not go as desired. Aggression will more than likely make matters worse, affecting a player's potential to keep a clear thinking process and to stick to their predetermined game plan.

The first few holes must not be allowed to affect the player's game, and neither must one or two less than desirable shots or putts work detrimentally for the rest of the round. Developing the round is part of the challenge. The preparation, game plan and pre-shot routine disciplines all combine to keep the player's game together. All golfers will be confronted with certain difficulties throughout the round; mistakes will be made and must be overcome if success or winning is to be achieved. It is often very little that separates the winners from the losers – attitude and technical ability are the obvious advantages. Practice, preparation, game control and course management are all measurable and achievable by most golfers. It is a matter of commitment, planning and good discipline that helps build a solid golfing structure!

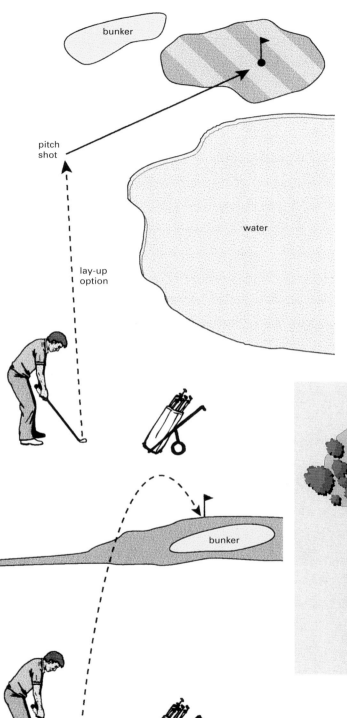

Fig 116 Evaluate the risks of playing longer shots to the green. Be realistic about your ability and either ensure the club chosen is sufficient to carry the water easily, even if the ball finishes at the back of the green, or play a strategic shot to take the water out of play.

Fig 117 A lofted wood or long iron off the tee will leave the ball short of the trees and keep the water out of play (below).

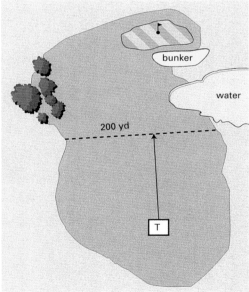

Fig 118 When playing to elevated greens a player should always make sure the ball carries comfortably up onto the green (left).

167

12
PSYCHOLOGY AND PHYSIOLOGY

Fig 119 Colin Montgomerie, a man who always gives 100 per cent.

It is not the intention of this book to take a detailed look into the fuller aspects of both psychology and physiology with regard to golf. Rather it is intended to offer some sound advice and examples of how important the role of each one is in the context of the game itself.

Good technique is definitely required if a golfer wishes to compete successfully. Fitness and strength are valuable assets also needed, as are of course a good short game, course-management skills and the correct equipment. Yet, above all, golf relies on the quality of the player's mental approach. Golf is a slow game played with a ball that lies motionless. The pressures involved are compounded by these two factors. Ultimately it becomes a matter of fear – fear of missing the shot, fear of failure! Everything a player does when playing a round of golf is centred around the ability to control the nervous system and to allow the natural and trained ability of that player to perform effectively.

Psychology: Key Strengths

There are many ways of highlighting what mental qualities are required to succeed as a competitive golfer, but it is doubtful that a simple answer is available – patience, perseverance, attitude, control, concentration, confidence, commitment, focus, fortitude, toughness, guts, determination, heart, desire, aggression and probably a host of others just as descriptive. In highlighting a few of these we can begin to see the qualities needed to succeed.

Patience

No game has ever required the character trait of patience more than golf. A patient golfer is one that never gives up. Patience is a virtue required by all consistent performers. It allows players to reach their potential; it allows them to be winners. It is not something a golfer can cultivate overnight. For some it is a natural asset, for most, one to be envied in others. Clear goals and a true belief in one's own ability allow a player to work patiently towards their targets. No one poor shot or hole can seriously affect the patient golfer as the ability to appreciate such mishaps only serves to help maintain greater focus.

Control

This probably sums up the ultimate criterion for successful golf – control of the physical aspects, control of the mental ones. In summarizing the latter we much appreciate that controlling the mind is perhaps the hardest aspect of golf. Rarely can a player maintain control at all times. There are those who appear calm, collected and in control, even when round disasters have occurred, but somewhere deep inside there is likely to be a personal volcano waiting to explode. Learning self-control and using it to positive effect is a vital part of developing a game that bears the hallmarks of consistency and a winning ability. It cannot be developed too highly.

Desire

Desire and/or motivation are much as one. Talent, skill, flair, character and even hard work are never going to be effective unless a golfer has the desire to work to bring about improvement and success. It is desire that drives a player to practise harder, learn new and better skills, learn from others, have realistic goals and to appreciate how to set about achieving them. This desire overcomes almost all obstacles and makes the ultimate dream possible.

Attitude

Attitude is everything – without it there can only be limited achievement! It is attitude that makes a golfer a complete player – with the correct one there is no limit to a player's potential for achievement. Gary Player, a senior golfer, provides the living proof of this. He was not the most gifted golfer to play professional golf, but his positive attitude prevented him from finding obstacles to limit his progress, and instead has given him the motivation to strive to be the best.

A player may not always be able to replicate the golf swing, but it is possible to control one's attitude toward the next shot. It diminishes negative thoughts and allows a player to appreciate and enjoy all endeavours experienced. For those who do not appreciate its relevance, observe Seve Ballesteros's short game or Phil Mickelson's when putting – it is not just skill that these players display, it is their attitude that makes them great.

Confidence

A golfer with a high level of confidence will believe that he is capable of achieving anything within reason, one without it will believe that very little is possible or achievable. Self-confidence helps people to be positive and to believe in themselves. They are prepared to try anything to improve their skills and to raise the level of their ability.

Concentration

Concentration is about being able to focus one's attention on the next shot or action required however small, such as club selection or identifying a correct rule of golf. Being able to concentrate effectively for the right amount of time, and make the correct decisions is all-important to the golfer. Concentration throughout a whole round is not possible, and so it is necessary to appreciate when to 'tune in' or 'turn off'. Tuning in is needed just after reaching the ball and the player is beginning to evaluate all relevant information. As the moment to play the shot gets nearer the concentration becomes more strongly focused. Turn off, but not until after the ball has completed its journey and come to a complete standstill, as this encourages a better evaluation of both the flight of the ball and how the shot was played. It is an error not to watch the ball until it stops.

The Mental Edge

It would be ridiculous to believe that a golfer could eliminate his body from the game. The same is true of the brain. The golfer cannot disengage it in the belief that without it no mishaps can occur. Just like learning the technical aspects of the game, the golfer must learn to think effectively when swinging a club.

Often one key thought is about as simple as it can get and this helps a golfer to stay totally focused throughout the pre-shot and swing executions. Focusing on one thought allows other distractions to be blocked out. The one key thought could be anything that concentrates the player's attention in a consistent, reliable and regular way. It might be any one of the following – the target itself, the flight of the ball, the speed of the swing, balance throughout the movement, focusing on impact, or simply imitating a star player. Whichever is the player's preference it is important to keep making the effort throughout the round and to maintain these key thoughts regularly during all rounds played, as repetition is a major source in gaining the benefits.

Without sufficient competitive golf it is not likely that a strong mental attitude can be developed successfully. Players must always try to maintain the quality of their efforts throughout a competitive round no matter what they are scoring. The more this is practised the better and easier it becomes.

Of course learning or improving these skills does not happen immediately – when we are learning the physical movements we accept errors and the need to develop feel and repetition to gain some form of improvement and consistency. Development of all mental aspects is no different – a player must be receptive to learning these new skills.

Personalities vary from player to player with consequent differences in behaviour and habit. To some winning is everything – it is the only thing that matters; to others, whatever the result, competing is what it is all about; some may be more intense and dominated by planning and analysis; and there are always those of a more relaxed nature, who go with the flow and enjoy the experience whether it be a success or a failure. There is room for all – although appreciating where personal weak links can be strengthened is important for all types.

Most players never reach their full potential even at professional level where there is no lack of ability to strike the ball. Accepting good days and bad days, learning to handle pressure, avoiding distractions, maintaining confidence and focus are all clearly visible in the best players. Often, to an observer, a player's concentration is perceived to be their greatest asset. This is partly true – good concentration allows a player to focus on the present, not what might happen, and to eliminate harmful distractions, but it is the completeness of a top player's armoury that is really on show. Understanding the make-up of this overall package allows golfers to appreciate, copy and develop their own mental skills.

Young players in particular rarely show concern or fear whilst playing golf. They play confident, aggressive golf. Unfortunately as time passes and players' proficiency increases, making mistakes becomes more costly in scoring and winning terms.

Most golfers find themselves questioning the reasons for missing a particular shot, especially for example a shortish putt and, as this cross-examination becomes a more regular pattern of self-analysis, so a player can lose out through a decline of confidence and self-belief. It is often said that a 4ft putt is not a problem until it means something and a player has to hole it. Pressure is a state of mind – it is self-inflicted. Unfortunately most golfers cannot come to terms with this truth. At important moments during a round, particularly on a difficult shot, a player will often feel that the eyes of the world are watching him. It is not unusual for a golfer to criticize what he/she feels was an unnecessarily unfair bounce, poor lie, poor tee shot or any such incident that affects their game. Golfers like to stay inside their comfort zone, and once they feel that a shot or situation pushes them outside this zone, they begin to get a little unsure of themselves, and doubts begin to develop and pressure increases.

The conscious mind should perhaps be the easiest to control as it tends to allow us to think more logically and remain in some sort of state of control. Yet this is not the case. The conscious mind is the one filling a player with confusion, doubt and fear, attributes that always appear ready to inflict themselves on a player just at the precise moment they least wish them to. It is clearly visible in golfers under competitive pressure, and even the very best players in the world suffer the same fate – often in front of the spectating sporting world through the eyes of the television.

Ironically, it is the subconscious mind that allows a golfer to function at his best. This is when the extinctive mode takes over, allowing a player to perform more naturally and successfully. On these occasions players find the game far easier to play – they experience fewer negative thoughts, play more freely and in a more focused fashion.

Top players refer to these moments as being in a 'bubble' or 'cocoon' of concentration. Thoughts and actions are far clearer and more effective. Everything appears to happen with less effort, but with more intensified results.

It would be unrealistic to believe that negative influences can be ignored, they are there in all golfers, it is just that some are able to block them out better than others. Learning to acknowledge their existence and developing techniques that improve the control of these resistant aspects, is an important step for any successful golfer. Of course there are those who enjoy pressure more than others, and appear to savour the heat of battle, but ultimately everyone has their own personal limit.

Emotional Control

Most golfers dream about great rounds or competing in major tournament events, but deep down most would probably be too scared to take the opportunity if it was actually available to them. How many times has a golfer started a round of golf playing way above his expectations, then said to himself 'This won't last!' It certainly won't with those thoughts dominating the mind. Player's expectations are often very low for themselves. Yet ironically, if they were asked to imagine a fellow golfer shooting a career best round they would be able to see or visualize this happening. It is this type of mental attitude that leads to golfers failing to reach their potential. These expectations are often so low because fear plays such a significant role. Fear of success, as well as fear of failure. The fear of success is one of stepping into the unknown and of the potential changes it might bring about – the pressures of playing better and reaching a higher level are often harder to come to terms with than the pressures experienced by the safe, but erratic and going-nowhere type. Golfers may fantasize about success only to bail out if the opportunity arises, allowing themselves to accept a standard of mediocrity that keeps them in their own comfort zone. If players want success they have to recognize it when it is there to be had. They must really want it, be prepared to raise their personal expectations, visualize what it is like to be there, and be prepared to take the opportunities when they arise.

When a golfer plays well it is often the case afterwards that he believes it may never happen again. This is not true – it is not just as a result of luck that the player has shown himself to be capable of such competence, but as a result of the correct mental and physical application, and a brief indication of what his true potential could be. Golfers rarely trust what they have worked hard to develop. When they lose the feel of application for good play, they believe that they will never be able to get back the heightened qualities they experienced during this successful period. This is a fallacy – we do not lose what we have previously learned – it may just be difficult to get back to it again as and when required. It is there! Belief and confidence help draw it out. Having a clear vision of what is achievable, and a focused attitude towards achieving it, helps players to draw more out of themselves, to consistently higher levels and on a more regular basis. These types of players enjoy dwelling on good shots and are able to relive them fully to help draw on the positive feelings they create.

So what are the emotional aspects that cause the game of golf to be such a challenge, and what methods can be employed to deal with these challenges?

Stress, Anxiety, Fear, Anger and Excitement

It is doubtful that any golfer has not experienced the ill-effects of some form of stress or anxiety during each and every round of golf they have ever played. These feelings are related to almost any situation on the golf course which causes a player to alter his emotional state, increasing the heart rate and creating a demand for adrenaline. It is a player's reaction when they are in what they see as a stressful situation that is the most critical factor. Some react positively to the situation and enjoy the exhilaration of taking on the challenge – a Seve Ballesteros approach. They have great confidence, a cool head and can maintain concentration whatever the situation. Others react in a more negative way and doubt their ability to handle the situation or shot in hand. They will have less confidence, feel confused, less focused and have difficulty with maintaining concentration.

In reacting in a more positive way to stressful situations a player has to be aware of the effects that an increased flow of adrenaline may have on him. It speeds up his reactions, increasing the likelihood of everything being carried out too quickly – walking to the ball, deciding which shot to play, selecting the correct club, and perhaps, most importantly, the pre-shot routine and swing action. The extra adrenaline can also effect the player by increasing the potential to hit the ball further – to perform above their normal level. This can be an exhilarating experience, but requires certain disciplines to help maintain control. Top players experience it more than most because of their competitive lifestyles – their drives may gain an extra 20 yards, which can be of benefit, but approaches to the green require extreme care, as on many an occasion a player has hit the ball further than normal with a particular club, and has flown the ball well over the green due to his emotional state.

Negative reaction is the most common emotion, and is where players exhibit more of the anxiety and fear characteristics. Performance will be at a lower level when faced with certain situations with which a player feels uncomfortable or incapable of coping. Fear causes a player to freeze up, their thoughts become less clear, decision-making is slower and less decisive, the ability to think in a positive way severely diminished – the first tee shot is a major challenge, the out of bounds, water hazards, rough, wind, noises – all appear of greater importance. Once again a player will quicken the final stages of the shot-making routine – both during the pre-shot and swing stages. Invariably the swing will be faster and shorter than normal, co-ordination will suffer and the potential for an acceptable result will be limited. Fear and anxiety are the most powerful elements in limiting a player's ability to compete and ones which must be overcome if competition success is to be enjoyed. If the mind can only contemplate the fear of hitting a ball into water or out of bounds, it is hardly surprising that the body responds to these thoughts.

Anger usually affects golfers when something has gone wrong. It is difficult to control this emotion, particularly if a player feels a mistake has been made through unnecessary complacency or plain stupidity. Unfortunately, genuine or acceptable errors also often get categorized this way by the players as they generally set themselves unrealistically high expectations or demands. Anger will often be hard to get rid of and will flow through into shots that follow, making the chances of success fairly remote. Anything can set off the emotion or compound it – the slightest noise, a poor bounce. Throwing clubs, kicking golf bags or clubs, berating a caddy – are the actions of golfers out of control through anger. Anger does nothing to help a golfer play good golf – it is detrimental and is an emotion that needs close control.

Perhaps the lesser of these negative types of emotion is that of excitement. This overenthusiasm

before an event or a particular shot will once again have detrimental effects by causing the player to act without discipline or control. Although perhaps a happier state of mind, it will soon have adverse effects and the poor shots that result can lead to some of the other emotions already discussed becoming factors also.

Mental Skills

One way of describing a golfer with effective mental skills is 'one who is able to carry out the swing action automatically under any circumstances'. All players have a natural ability to let the golf swing take care of itself, combining practised physical movements with a confident and unrestricted mental attitude. It is evident on the practice range and in social golf course play. Competition golf brings out the doubt element, so that the same automatic pilot controlling a golfer's swing under normal circumstances appears to be replaced by a less co-ordinated, questioning one that makes the game more difficult than it really needs to be.

A golfer has to accept that mental skills are needed and those who wish to learn or improve what they already have must be prepared to put some form of time and practice into developing them. As with the golf swing, change is not always easy and the benefits do not always come immediately. The often quoted statement 'practice may not make perfect, but it does make permanent' is as relevant in this instance as it is for physical training. The more effort made to introduce and to adhere to well-proven mental skills will invariably lead to a golfer achieving greater consistency and success from the game. It is these mental practice routines that can lead to far greater rewards than long sessions spent on the range hitting balls in a meaningless way.

Visualization or Imagery

By using our minds to imagine or visualize a shot in advance of playing it we are able to go through a stage of mental rehearsal that offers a golfer the opportunity to play effectively a form of practice shot. As there are few other opportunities to play physical practice shots on the course, it is a benefit that all players should give themselves. Not all players possess the ability or need to use visualization or imagery skills. Some prefer to focus directly at the ball and then the target and just to make a positive swing action to send the ball to that target. Most, however, do or would benefit by using these skills. When watching top players concentrating prior to the execution of a shot, it is not always obvious that they are going through this mental rehearsal process. However, close observation reveals how focused they are, by watching their facial mannerisms and eye movement as they build up information from this shot visualization. These skills will help improve concentration and positive thinking – visualizing a successful shot gives a player a clear image of the task he is about to perform and what he will expect from the outcome.

At no time must negative thoughts such as a poor result be visualized. Thinking out a shot prior to playing it activates the automatic actions every player has practised to perfect. Poor thoughts generally lead to poor actions – the body responds to the mind.

Tips for Visualization
1. Stand behind the ball and focus on the target.
2. Mentally rehearse your set-up routine and see yourself aiming correctly.
3. Observe and feel the swing action.
4. See the ball's flight, its landing on the green and its coming to rest by the flag.
5. Feel your own satisfaction with the outcome.
6. Commence the real routine.

Fig 120 Lee Janzen.

Fig 121

For Putting
1. See the line to the hole.
2. Visualize the ball burning a line or mark in the ground as it rolls towards and into the hole.
3. Hear 'the sound' of the ball falling into the hole.

Imagery can be taken a step further by using these visualization skills prior to playing an event. This might be a week, a night or even one hour before actually teeing off. A player can use two types of imagery, one where they observe themselves from a spectator's viewpoint, or the other where they visualize their own actual play, shot by shot, sensing their pre-shot preparation and swing feelings, hearing the sound of the impact on the ball, watching the flight of the ball and the result of the shot. By taking this a stage further and imagining winning the event, perhaps signing the card for a record-making round, receiving the trophy, accepting the applause of the crowd, a player can further strengthen these positive thoughts, enhance a strong competitive attitude and provide further motivation to do well. Both methods have positive mental benefits and so a player should try either or both in their quest for better golf.

Reliving quality shots or rounds from the past also helps to build strong emotional confidence. Remembering a particularly successful 4 iron on a difficult hole will not only provide a positive thought, but also allow the player to feel the sensations and pleasure of the shot over again.

When used correctly visualization and imagery help provide positive thoughts and raise levels of confidence. Anxiety, fear, stresses – all the negative elements can be kept under control. Good mental skills also enhance technical proficiency and increase the effectiveness of the player's physical skills.

The Pre-shot Routine

Although this has been dealt with in detail under a previous section, what must be appreciated is the importance that the pre-shot routine plays in allowing a player to block out distractions and negative thoughts prior to the swing movement. Good concentration and focus leading into a regular practised physical and mental pre-shot routine carries the player positively through the execution of each shot.

Improving target focus can enhance the pre-shot routine. Not only must a player look at the target itself; he must pick out the exact point on that target to focus on both visually and mentally. This exact definition of the target point creates powerful positive thoughts that once again block out negative ones and other distractions. A typical example is when a player focuses his attention on hitting a drive onto the fairway. If he picks no particular target except the whole fairway he will, in all probability, miss it as often as he hits it. Alternatively, if he focuses on a target point – a tree in the near distance, but also aims for a particular branch of that tree, then his total focus invariably leads to a far more accurate shot. Even a slightly off-line one is still likely to hit the fairway itself.

The target has to be precise, the mental rehearsal positive and consistent, the pre-shot routine smooth and repetitive.

Staying in the Present

This is a far harder mental task to achieve than it first appears, but its relevance is something all golfers will have experienced knowingly or unknowingly at some time or another. Playing or scoring well early in a round often leads to a player doubting his ability to keep going at this high standard. Knowing that finishing with a few solid pars will potentially win an event, or thinking about the difficulty of the next hole or a possible 3-putt situation, are all examples of a player failing to stay in the present. Often the mind is focusing on the score for the hole or round rather than the shot in hand at that precise moment in time. Fear and indecision begin to take over. The thought of spoiling a potential good score or finishing off a well-played hole with poor putting are all negative thoughts that can disrupt or destroy a round of golf.

It is imperative to learn to stay in the present by playing one shot at a time rather than trying to make a particular score on a hole. Concentrate on what you are doing rather than how you are doing it. The more a golfer focuses on how the score is progressing, the more likely he/she is to lose the flow of the round. Getting on with what needs to be done next will put thoughts of scoring and maintaining a current score out of the player's mind. If preparing for a putt is the next priority, concentrate on the slope of the green, the length of the putt, the feel of the stroke and the roll of the ball. Evaluating a hole or a score has to be carried out after the round is completed, not during it. This also applies to letting the mind wander forward towards the end of a round. Thinking what to say in your speech, the prize-giving, is not a practical mental thought, but one of distraction. Worry about such things after the final putt drops and your name is on the top of the winners' list.

Self-talk

Many golfers convince themselves that they cannot play a particular shot or, in more extreme moments, even the game itself. With this type of self-belief it's unlikely that they will carry out the necessary actions successfully. Players have to persuade themselves that they can perform successfully – the doubts have to be driven out. Positive words or statements can provide the golfer with enhanced self-confidence and improved performance, by triggering a series of positive thoughts. Negative thoughts should be turned into positive ones. Typically golfers berate the weather prior to and during play, using it as an excuse for their poor play, rather than taking a more positive attitude by accepting the conditions and convincing themselves that a dedicated and determined performance, despite all the difficulties will bring about a successful result. This attitude is also common when golfers believe that golf course conditions are less than favourable – ironically there are always players who putt well on poor greens, or score well on 'unfair' courses. It is doubtful that these players have seen any problems at all with the golf course.

Relaxation

Relaxation would appear an easy exercise to do and not one that would need practice to achieve, yet this is often not the case, and effort must be put into practising relaxation techniques. With a peaceful mind, a relaxed physical state allows the recovery of thoughts, emotions and energy levels. Stress can be kept under control, concentration and mental focus can be more beneficial, swing actions both in practice and competition more effective. The mind and body need to be relaxed so that the swing is able to function in the automatic mode. Understanding the need for relaxation and how to relax are important if this skill is to be used correctly.

The relationship between mental and physical relaxation is closely related. The mind will rarely relax if the body is tense. Therefore, techniques to release this tension are important, but need

regular practice – perhaps daily – for the feelings of relaxation to be understood and appreciated.

Tips for Relaxation

1. Breathing – Take a deep breath through the nose. Let the air flow into the lungs, allowing the stomach to expand naturally. Hold for about three seconds. Slowly release the air out through the mouth, allowing the muscles of the shoulders, chest, stomach and arms to relax. Repeat until a relaxed sensation is experienced.
2. Muscles – Breathe in gently, tighten your muscles, for example, across the shoulders. Slowly breathe out, relaxing the muscles and allowing any tension to flow out of your body. Repeat ten times.
3. Mind and body – Find a quiet place, make yourself comfortable by either lying or sitting down. Takes some deep breaths and close your eyes. Continue the breathing exercise and count backwards from twenty to number one and, whilst doing so, focus on individual parts of your body moving deeper and deeper into a relaxed state. It is beneficial to start at either the head and work downwards, or the toes and work upwards so that by the time you have reached the number one, the whole of the body is in a state of total relaxation. Whilst in this state your mind is receptive to your positive thoughts and goals. Remind yourself of them, repeating them as many times as is necessary. After a short period of time allow yourself to return to normal by slowly counting from one back to twenty. Open your eyes, feel relaxed and positive.

A good state of relaxation improves a person's receptiveness and, therefore, the potential for learning. It helps stress to be avoided rather than the need for it to be cured. It releases the pre-event tensions that many golfers experience, particularly the night before an important tournament. The breathing and muscle relaxation exercises can be very effective during play, by improving mental focus and enhancing a player's ability to concentrate on the shot in hand.

Routines

Following a routine helps set a more regular and acceptable lifestyle for most golfers. Preparing equipment, arriving at the course on time, warm-up and practice sessions and pre-shot routines are all part of a behaviour pattern that each player should adhere to on a regular basis. Good routines are a key factor in helping any player establish a pattern or style of play that operates on a basis of trust and consistency. This structure helps prepare the player, and once again limits unnecessary distractions and interference prior to, and whilst playing golf. All players must have certain and well-established routines.

There are many aspects that combine in the makeup of a successful golfer, none more so than that of courage, determination, guts, heart and an 'always give it my best shot' attitude. Self-motivation, self-control, self-confidence, a realistic outlook, strong focus, energy, enthusiasm and desire all help formulate a golfer's strengths and subsequent success. The correct mental attitude takes into account that golf is a game of mistakes – it is a player's response to these mistakes that matters. In most situations being positive and decisive is more important than being correct.

Golfers must have an uninhibited swing if they wish to follow a path of success. Mental training helps players sustain commitment and maintain emotional control. Enjoyment and pleasure from the game will certainly enhance performance.

Setting Goals

All golfers should acknowledge their ambitions realistically and set themselves a series of goals that are achievable given that they follow a relatively disciplined pre-planned route. It is important to repeat – these goals must be *realistic*, and *achievable* and, as such, requires some serious and sensible thoughts from the individual. It is advisable to have short-, medium- and longer-term goals. Generally the longer-term goal dictates the level set for the shorter-term ones, so for example, a sixteen-year-old student with a handicap of six might set the following goals.

- Short term: to have a handicap of three by the end of the summer season.
- Medium term: to play for the County Junior Team this or next season.
- Long term: to be selected for the National Junior Squad within two years.

These are realistic and achievable if the student has sufficient desire and ability to develop an increased amount of skill and experience to raise the level of his performances. He may need to seek coaching advice, have an organized practice structure, manage his itinerary for competitive events correctly and keep his goals clearly in mind to help motivate him at all times.

A recognized term for goal setting is called 'SMARTER goals'.

S – *Specific* – to help a player focus attention and planning.
M – *Measurable* – assessed against standard levels.
A – *Accepted /agreed* – by the player and the coach.
R – *Realistic* – achievable and realistic.
T – *Timed* – short-, medium- and long-term definitions.
E – *Exciting* – challenging and inspiring.
R – *Recorded* – for evaluation and feedback.

However these goals are set, the player must truly believe in them and be dedicated to achieving their outcome. This belief will keep a player who is suffering from poor performance determined to play on through the difficult times, and help maintain the confidence of the on-form player as he takes positive steps towards his next goal. If short-term goals have been set that are too easy or even too hard to achieve they may need to be reset or revised, to help motivate a player; for example it may be that a short-term goal of finishing in the top five of the next tournament is a sufficient enough target to aim for, so that a player can focus on this and step forwards towards the higher reward of achieving the next goal.

The Qualities of Determined Players

In pressurized situations or when the chips are down we clearly see the type of qualities that determined competitors display. This strength of character comes from within themselves and allows them not only to handle the pressure of that moment or occasion, but also to raise their performance over and above normal expectations.

At such times, these players will exhibit a clear control of their emotions, quelling any fear, frustration or anger. They will excude an air of confidence, calmness and control of the situation. They appear to be totally in their element, energetic, positive, realistic and mentally focused. It is as if they are enjoying the experience and find increased stimulation and determination as the situation develops.

These types of players are highly self-motivated, and have superb attitude and direction with regard to their goals and performance. They take full responsibility for their actions and show no signs of intimidation in any situation. Above all, they are winners!

Coaching Psychology

Coaches not only work at physical aspects of technique, but also provide encouragement and help to develop motivation, confidence and belief for a player. Some players develop better skills by working with their own golf coach whilst others may need to separate these psychological areas from the physical part of learning and perhaps use specialist mental training coaches to help them develop this part of their game.

There is quite a variation in mental training concepts, and the style of coaching them. Sports psychologists have become a more integral part of the game of golf over the last few years, with top players in particular seeking to explore every avenue that can help improve what they already have, and to develop that extra something that may help give them more of an edge. The amateur game has also seen involvement from these mental training experts, particularly if a player is at national or representative levels. The role of these experts varies from player to player depending upon personal requirements, but in basic terms it is fair to say that they help a player to understand and make more use of their own capabilities, increase the capacity for learning, and develop skills for controlling pressure and improving relaxation.

Age, sex, background and mental attitudes all have a strong bearing on a golfer's emotional state. Coaches have to understand the differing personalities or moods of players and to appreciate how the levels of pressures differ for each individual – what is pressure for one is quite acceptable to another. Advising players how to control their emotions so that they are able to keep their play at an optimum level is crucial when helping players to compete successfully. It is also vital if they are to use their technical abilities to a proficient level. The coach must work with the player to help capitalize on the positive aspects of these emotions and to minimize the negative ones. It is also important that players are not pushed beyond their personal boundaries.

Coaches help players to focus their attention on the tasks in hand. They have to spot when someone lacks enthusiasm and motivation, and guide them towards the all-important positive and progressive attitude required. Learning mental skills will nearly always benefit from a one-to-one learning environment, and not all techniques suit all players. A golfer is an individual performer who with the right help and guidance can learn how to enhance his capabilities with enjoyable and beneficial mental training.

The use of a sports psychologist should not be seen as a sign of weakness, but just another opportunity to increase knowledge, skill and performance levels. Look at some of the top players who have both swing and mental training coaches.

Basic Fitness

It has for too long been thought that golfers did not need to be fit to play golf. There is some merit in believing that walking, on occasions, quite quickly, for up to five miles and four hours around a golf course would be a beneficial programme in itself. Yet looking at the high standards of current players, and following the examples of the world's best, it is fairly obvious that more specific exercise is required. Today's tour stars are very strong and athletic. They recognize the importance of physical conditioning and now have access to mobile fitness centres at every tournament. Not only do they have personal fitness programmes, they are fully aware of the dangers of sports injuries, and of how poor movement can compound such problems. A good fitness programme is not just about improving a player's physical condition; it is to help prevent injuries and to enable a player to maintain higher standards for a longer period of time. Training programmes have to be tailor-made to suit a player's individuals needs, and many factors have to be taken into account – a person's current level of fitness, the level of fitness required, injuries, general and golfing lifestyles, mental attitude to the game, age, sex and swing technique. It stands to reason that women with good flexibility but with poor strength will not have the same requirements as those of a senior golfer with good strength and low levels of mobility. If a swing lacks power, poor balance and co-ordination and has limited movement in terms of rotation, it is not likely to be one of great efficiency or consistency. Increasing age or loss of acceptable levels of fitness reduce strength and flexibility, and will cause noticeable deterioration in a player's ability to play successful golf.

In learning the game, all golfers formulate swing actions that emphasize their better physical qualities and steer away from their weaker ones. Hence a player with strong hands will rely heavily on them to generate the power and control the club face requires. A weak-wristed player may well compensate by an overemphasis of the body action, or possibly a tendency to fold the left arm at the top of the golf swing. Scenarios are relatively endless, although generally fall into a pattern of hand, legs or body-dominated swing actions. Unfortunately when a player's standard of golf deteriorates noticeably they will tend to integrate errors into their technique to compensate for rather than improve their physical limitations or deficiencies. There is no doubt that a person's physical condition has a significant effect on their ability to perform. Every player can benefit from the correct type of strength and conditioning programme.

There are five key elements in this process:

• Strength
• Endurance
• Flexibility/Mobility
• Balance/Co-ordination
• Nutrition

Strength

Muscles provide the power in the golf swing and so it is important to have sufficient muscular strength to generate the required clubhead speed at impact. This strength also provides a golfer with much of the control required in swinging the clubhead.

To increase strength, programmes involve muscles being loaded with high-repetition, low-resis-

tance exercises. It is important to build strength in both sides of the body, particularly if one side is more naturally favoured than the other. An increase of strength in the relevant muscle groups provides the source of more power. Modern golfers tend to get most of their strength from the muscles around the abdominal and upper leg regions.

Endurance

Both cardiovascular and muscular endurance are important to the accomplished golfer who is practising and competing on a regular basis, particularly if a high amount of travel or climatic changes are experienced. An average golfer playing a round a week may not need to concern himself with improving endurance to any great extent, although it would obviously be of benefit both to his golf and self-esteem. Improved endurance increases a golfer's capacity for work without feeling the effects of tiredness. The improved efficiency of the heart and lungs in supplying oxygen to the blood will cause less exertion to the player.

Two of the best exercises for endurance are walking on a treadmill, particularly uphill or riding an exercise bike.

Flexibility/Mobility

Strength and flexibility work side by side. Being able to create a powerful rotation of the body whilst maintaining control illustrates this relationship. A player must be able to reach certain positions during the swing action. Any lack of mobility will limit this necessity.

Although it is a proven fact that a good range of movement reduces injury and muscle stiffness, improves co-ordination and offers the potential for longer hitting, golfers generally choose to ignore this one important factor. Few make the effort to warm up and stretch their muscles prior to play, and even when they do manage to get to the practice range they choose to hit full shots immediately, usually with their driver – the longest club in the bag and the one requiring the most physical effort.

Fig 122 Colin Montgomerie. Heat and dehydration can have a very debilitating effect on any player.

Balance and Co-ordination

It is doubtful that there has yet been a successful golfer who did not have a plentiful supply of both good balance and co-ordination. These are two of the most important assets that any golfer possesses. All sport requires good balance. Some golfers possess it naturally, whilst others exhibit very little prowess at being able to stand solidly on both feet at the end of their swings.

Balance is not just about being able to stand upright during the swing action. It is about good posture both at address and impact; it is about being able to maximize the correct weight distribution during the swing action; it is essential in helping keep the body in a co-ordinated position throughout the whole swing. Swing co-ordination pulls together most of all the other attributes – balance, strength, flexibility, and is a major contributor to the timing and subsequent clubhead speed factors for a player.

The player with good balance and co-ordination can hit the ball long and straight without a high level of all the other physical attributes. Without these two facets no amount of strength, endurance and flexibility can pull together the swing action in a consistently successful way.

Nutrition

A healthy diet is one that supplies the right amount of essential nutrients and energy to allow a person to remain in good health and help maximize a physical performance. It will vary from individual to individual, but will include a balance of the following:

1. *Carbohydrates* – which enable the muscle cells to function correctly. They provide energy for the muscles and all golfers need to be stocked with carbohydrates prior to training and play. They include: rice, beans, potatoes, cereals, nuts, fruit, porridge.
2. *Fats* – although they are an essential component of a balanced diet, vegetable fats are preferable to animal ones. Avoid fats whenever possible. They include – red meats, bacon, burgers, crisps, cakes, cheese, and chocolate.
3. *Protein* – protein protects and repairs muscles. When activities are physical protein provides the essential component. They include – meat, beans, potatoes, bread, milk, and eggs.
4. *Vitamins and Minerals* – most vitamins are normally supplied in normal foodstuffs and there is no evidence to suggest that extra supplies will necessarily improve levels of performance. Calcium and iron are sometimes lacking in young sports persons, and women, particularly if they adhere to a vegetarian diet. They include: fruit, meat, fish, vegetables, dairy products, bread, cereals, potatoes.
5. *Water/Fluids* – it is very important that golfers maintain their levels of hydration – the intake of water or fluids. A lack of these will lead to a player becoming dehydrated, which in turn will lead to a decline in performance, particularly in warm temperatures when a player will perspire a lot. It is important to drink regularly during a round of golf, perhaps every two or three holes. It is too late to drink water when you are thirsty. This indicates that you are already dehydrated. Alcohol acts like a poison to the body, and should be avoided before or during competitive play.

The necessity of maintaining acceptable levels of physical condition are fairly clear when appreciating the dynamic nature of the modern golf swing. Power is generated from the ground upwards, and transferred up through the body down the arms and through the club shaft to the clubhead. The process begins by a winding up of the body through a co-ordinated rotational movement. This coiling action allows the arms to swing the club on a wide arc to the top of the swing. The unloading of this coil or spring effect generates tremendous force and power back through to the clubhead. Skilled players expend less energy and effort than lesser golfers, but generate more speed due to the bio-mechanical efficiency of their swings.

Golfers are prone to injury particularly in the back, shoulders, elbows and knees. It is obvious that all players should be aware of golf's physical requirements as well as his own personal limitations. Rest and relaxation are also required, and must be an accepted part of any fitness programme. Good eyesight is another important requirement and not one to be ignored.

Both the psychological and physiological areas of the game are now more appreciated and understood. They both play a vital and integral part in the search for success of any player.

Fig 123 Simple exercises and stretch routines.

Trunk Rotation
(a) Sit on a chair or stool with a club positioned across the back of your shoulders.

(b) Rotate from the abdominal area as far as possible. Hold this position for 3–5 seconds. Return to the original position and relax. Repeat 10 times.

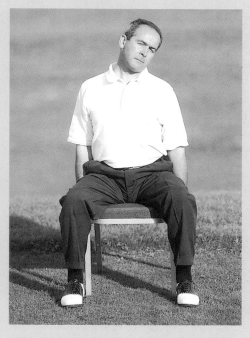

Lateral Neck Stretch
(a) From a vertical position, lower your head as far as possible towards your right shoulder. Hold for 3–5 seconds. Return to vertical position and relax. Repeat 10 times.

(b) As before, but lower your head towards the left shoulder.

Fig 123 Simple exercises and stretch routines *(continued)*.

Back Arch and Stretch
(a) Kneel on the ground with your back straight and your head up so your eyes look forward *(left)*.

(b) Lower your head and arch your back upwards at the same time *(below)*. Hold for 3–5 seconds. Return to the original position and relax. Repeat 10 times.

Wrist Rotation
(a) Using a No 5 iron, stand upright with the clubhead vertically in the right or left hand. *(Not illustrated)*
Rotate wrists to the right until the shaft is horizontal. Hold for 3–5 seconds. Rotate the wrist 180 degrees in the opposite direction, once again hold for 3–5 seconds. Repeat 10 times *(below)*.

(b) Repeat the exercise with your other hand.

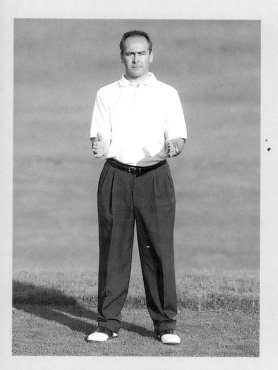

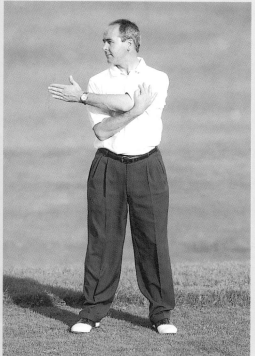

Rotator Stretch
(a) Stand upright with your elbows into your sides and forearms, and hand outstretched and horizontal.

(b) Whilst holding your upper arms and elbows into your body, rotate your forearms outward as far as possible. Hold for 3–5 seconds. Return to the original position and repeat 10 times.

Shoulder Stretch (*left*)
Stand upright and whilst keeping your shoulders as square as possible, grasp your elbow with your opposite hand and gently pull it across your body. Hold for 3–5 seconds, relax and repeat 10 times. Now repeat with the opposite arm.

With all these exercises remember to breathe correctly. Try inhaling through your nose as you commence the exercise and breathing out through the mouth as you go into the relaxation stage.

13
COACHING

Coaching plays so much more a relevant part of the modern game than it used to in past times when hitting a few balls on the practice area in front of a coach and then being offered some corrective tips was the norm. Players now demand higher personal standards to satisfy their golfing goals, and in addition the general standard and knowledge of coaches is that much more advanced; the availability and use of up-to-date facilities and equipment has transformed the coaching environment.

Golfers now seek to enhance their skills and consequently deserve greater satisfaction and pleasure from their game so today's coaching is geared towards this desire, and is built to accommodate the needs of every type of golfer.

There are many objectives to be delivered through the coaching format, but ultimately the outcome is to improve a player's performance through both physical and mental learning. Coaching cannot just be set out to teach the game of golf; it must be structured as a positive learning experience. Without this learning process, progress is slow or even non-existent and the reasons for being coached become meaningless.

The development of a player's game can often be sporadic with regular highs and lows being experienced between intermittent spells of consistency

Fig 124 Juniors progress quicker when the coach uses simple demonstration and sets interesting tasks.

and reliability. Every golfer will experience at least one plateau of development when their game levels off, making progress feel difficult, if not impossible to achieve. Often, players feel as if they are actually going backwards, so a need to embark on some form of new approach frequently leads them in the obvious direction of coaching. This can follow either a quick fix approach or perhaps a more ongoing longer-term development programme.

Coaching needs to incorporate a whole variety of criteria into its format that both the player and coach between them set out and follow. These will include, planning and organization for the coaching; a structure and clear set of objectives that offer motivation and direction and are instructional and meaningful. There must be the potential to offer variety and breadth to the content, which might include other disciplines such as fitness and mental training, and above all the coach and player must develop the use of feedback to enhance the quality and content of the coaching programme. There has to be something for everyone within the structure, for example there are clear differences in coaching with regard to adults and youngsters; whereas adults prefer to feel in control, need some form of critical analysis and enjoy the experience and satisfaction of learning, youngsters tend to need to be coach-directed at all times, and react in a negative sense to critical or non-positive information and feedback.

Whichever pattern or direction the coaching format follows, the coach must recognize a player's needs, and the player in turn must trust and commit himself or herself to the coaching programme.

The Rôle of the Coach

So many times it has been said, 'Golf is the only sport where there are more teachers than players'. As the game has evolved over the decades the desire to play to a higher standard has led to the development of the rôle of the golf coach or teacher. Understanding basic technical skills is now no longer sufficient to satisfy an ambitious golfer. Aspects such as equipment specification, course-management skills, rules of golf, mental training and physiological requirements now form just part of the basic foundation of a coach's expertise. The coach has to be knowledgeable in all aspects of the game as there is a requirement to identify each individual golfer's needs, quickly coming to terms with their short- or mid-term limitations, and setting about organizing a suitable, effective development programme, or a shorter corrective cure if required.

Whether the coach chooses to favour a method or system style of coaching, or perhaps a combination of both, he will have to come to terms with the positive and negative qualities of his coaching, fully understand his communication skills and look to develop his knowledge and experience.

Philosophy of the Coach

Although it may appear there are great diversities in coaching philosophies, the nature of the game and method of swinging the club invariably condense many concepts into a similar pattern. The coach may have a wide range of knowledge and interpretation, which will be applied through daily coaching programmes, but in almost all cases these will condense down to a central or core element. Most coaches work around this central theme, whether it is in relation to the swing technique or a style of play itself.

A coach will invariably build a philosophy over a period of time, and this will be refined or even changed as a career is developed, and knowledge and experience are increased. Many factors influence a coach's philosophy, but the success of technical advice, the importance of mental stimulation for players, the capacity to help players successfully take their skills onto the course and the personal enjoyment and satisfaction of the coach for his art, are all very dominant aspects.

Golfers' expectations vary depending upon personal characteristics and a coach must be aware of the responsibility of helping players of all levels to enjoy the game, as success for some is not always measured by the capacity to actually win. Creating a learning environment whereby a player has the desire and interest to progress to higher levels of enjoyment and success will invariably play a large part in the coach's philosophy. Ultimately, it is the player's proficiency at a particular level, and the satisfaction and pleasure created by this personal achievement that stimulates the golfer, broadens golfing goals and confirms the fact that the coaching he or she is receiving has a valuable and fulfilling rôle within his or her golfing lifestyle.

A coach's success and gratification upon seeing the positive results of a coaching philosophy, work in unison with regard to fulfilling his own personal rôle and in creating a desire to enhance current skills and increase knowledge for future benefit. It would be impossible to set out strict guidelines as to a pre-formulated programme that culminated with the end product of a successful coach. Many youngsters have a goal to become a professional golfer and to emulate the achievements of their heroes. All but a few will fail as players. Fortunately, it is not necessary to be a good player to become a successful coach, many are content to follow the route of a PGA Club Professional fulfilling a limited rôle as a player, but concentrating on a commercial and/or coaching status. The PGA training scheme is currently completed after three years apprenticeship, whereupon with a good level of theoretical swing knowledge and a varying degree of practical experience the incumbent coach steps forward to begin the potential journey of their lifetime. Further playing experiences at a number of levels, plus coaching golfers of a wide variety of standards, will enhance and develop the coach's experience and philosophy. Some have a particular natural flare in communicating their learning aspects, and will possibly have an ambition to become well-known as a coach concentrating on working with the most accomplished players, whilst others are more content to aim less high and to help the average golfer. Whichever path one follows, to be successful, the coach will always need to maintain the desire to improve and progress his skills.

There are instances whereby certain aspects of coaching success have been achieved without an individual obtaining the status of a professional coach or having an extensive knowledge of the swing technique itself. The Golf Foundation Scheme has long been successful throughout schools, colleges and at club junior level, enhanced by enthusiastic school or college teachers, whose good practical knowledge and common sense in golfing terms has helped the development of opportunities for younger golfers. The same is true at club junior level, where dedicated junior organizers, very often inspired by fellow officers, country coaching schemes, or previous club successes, have sought to offer junior members the type of coaching opportunities that help individuals progress to higher levels. Most of these enthusiastic officers and those at country or national level

play a major part in the infrastructure that makes up the successful development of a coaching scheme. In fact it is very likely that the top coaches of today have at some time in the past been part of one of the previously mentioned groups or schemes. A lack of in-depth technical knowledge can in many instances be temporarily substituted by showing young players additional ways to enhance their skills or by offering encouragement and sound advice in the periphery skills that work so closely with the technical ones. For instance, throughout the collegiate system in use in the USA, many of the golf coaches are not golf professionals, but have coaching qualifications that supplement the technical emphasis, and highlight player management and self-knowledge through regular practice disciplines, analysing course play statistics such as greens hit in regulation and developing the physical and mental aspects. Physiological and psychological coaching can have dramatic effects on players' performance without involving swing technique whatsoever.

An Effective Coach

It is important to clarify the basic distinctions between teaching or coaching a subject. In teaching we set out to communicate information to the pupil, how to appreciate its importance or relevance and how to set about learning the information so that it can be utilized, hopefully with success from that point onwards. In other words the pupil is being directly taught new information, understanding and particular skills.

Coaching has a more subtle application and in essence is a combination of understanding a person's knowledge, ability and experience, and then showing them how to use these more proficiently whether it be by utilizing their strengths, developing their weaknesses or building an improved playing programme around their overall skills. A second element of teaching new skills to the player as an enhancement of the qualities they already possess may well be integrated into this coaching process.

I mentioned earlier that coaching meant understanding a player's knowledge and ability, thus allowing the coach to identify and meet the needs of the player or team. The coach must set out a structure incorporating a development programme that allows both competitive and overall performance to be measurable and progressive, plus the coach must create an environment in which players are motivated to improve their standards and performance levels. There must be a structured set of objectives worked out for each individual player based on personal requirements or needs.

It is fairly obvious that the likelihood of any one player having a full supply of all the key elements together is very rare – a player like Tiger Woods comes close – so the coach is always working with the supply of 'imperfect material'. As such the coach must identify the priorities and work with the player to formulate how the intended training programme can best suit that player and how reaching their goals can be best achieved.

In identifying and setting out a programme the coach has to:

1. Prioritize relevant aspects for the individual.
2. Plan the amount of technical work and practice required by the player.
3. Emphasize the percentage of time dedicated to the short game and putting departments.
4. Suggest routines to the player, help develop effective ones and encourage the player to practise them often.
5. Help co-ordinate an overall balance to the structure including course practice and competitive play.

The routines will invariably change as competitive events draw closer. It is also important that both player and coach are able to assess the developments and improvements that will affect the player's game as the programme begins to take effect. It is vital that the coach analyses how and where changes to the programme might be introduced if the desired results are not forthcoming. Setting appropriate workloads and helping to programme realistic timescales for practice, skill enhancement and competition success all rely on the coach's expertise. The coach must also recognize that there is a wide variation of individual talent and receptiveness, and so a balanced view is one that must always be a priority.

All this planning will offer the potential for success, but ultimately it will be the player's response that dictates the final results. The coach must utilize his knowledge, experience and communication skills to maximum effect.

Coaching Styles

There is not just one style of coaching, but an indefinite number depending upon a coach's interpretation and knowledge of the fundamentals of golf and how these are adapted into coaching sessions. On a wider basis it may be preferential to view things more as an interpretation of coaching forms for which there can only be two main ones, that of corrective coaching and the other of a more creative style.

Corrective coaching is possibly still the most popular form of coaching particularly for the average or less ambitious player. In effect, corrective coaching means that a player has a problem and a coach fixes it. No complications, a relatively immediate remedy is applied, and one that involves little frustration, pain or dedication to put right. In most cases this corrective coaching is fairly short term, and once the player has lost the feel or even overexaggerated the cure, then they must return to the coach for another 'fix'. It will not suit the more ambitious player who may wish to strive to develop a potentially more regular and reliable style or method of play.

In more recent times there has been a move for coaching to take a more creative and progressive direction. This might just not involve swing technique, but mental physiological and strategic aspects also. Nick Faldo sought the advice of one of these new progressive types of coach, this being David Leadbetter, who has studied widely the golf techniques of top players throughout the twentieth century, and by using this information and knowledge, formulated a style of coaching that was more or less unheard of until then.

In creative coaching, both player and coach look a little more laterally at what is possible. The player may have strong desires and goals for his game, but might not be able to clearly channel this ambition without the help and direction of the appropriate coach. A technical coach will invariably view the swing movement as one of a more pure and aesthetic style, and will look to impart their more progressive thoughts to the player. The coach will look for the potential in all receptive players, and having an enthusiasm to impart the possible benefits for the future, will play an important part in the overall philosophy of this creative element. This will generally involve a mid- to longer-term development of the player's technical capabilities.

Clear understanding, vision, determination and commitment are some of the vital elements. The pursuit of technical excellence will be a high priority, giving the player reassurance that under extreme pressure, even with the most difficult of shots to play, the swing movement will have the greatest chance of repetitive success, producing the required high-quality results, or at the very least a minimum of destructive elements. This is a high ideal indeed, and one that all technical enthusiasts will strive for and be stimulated by. Creative coaching helps provide a stimulus for a golfer's desire to improve, succeed and to win, or even just to satisfy their determination to play with an acceptable level of consistency.

Whichever way we look at it, creative coaching is now a popular way forward. The golf swing fundamentals may not change, most have been studied to a near ultimate analytical point, but it is the interpretation and possible creative use of them that drives the coach and player forward to find out what potential success is possible.

Developing mental training philosophies and new routines work in a creative and effective way for many, stimulating players who may not appreciate the benefits of purely technical dedication. Improving physiological capacity through the development of strength, fitness and greater flexibility can also provide a stimulus for some players to alter their regular routines. For some, to discuss and develop a more imaginative and adaptable attitude to course-management strategy provides the answer. Having an open mind, looking at all possibilities and showing a willingness to work to develop something new and beneficial are all part of the creative thinking process that a coach can utilize in helping a player to progress.

The Challenge of Coaching

The demands required of the coach mean that he must identify and meet the needs of the player, and create an effective learning environment, which stimulates the player to make progressive improvement.

Whilst analysing qualities for coaching we need to look at distinguishing characteristics and attributes that encompass what is best in achieving regular and consistent success within the coaching rôle. There will be common denominators that are

proven to be effective – the coach's philosophy itself, the ability to communicate, technical understanding, strategy, the environment, organization and coaching procedures. Within these fundamental areas there are many other related aspects, and it is within the combination and relationship of these that the successful challenge of coaching is achieved.

The philosophy of the individual coach puts into perspective the style and ideals that the individual prefers to work with. The coach will create a structured environment for learning and will establish key fundamentals that work successfully within that structure. The environment will not only be keyed up around the mental philosophy of the coach, but will have facilities and equipment that enhance the potential to develop the required skills and lead to greater potential for player success. Although facilities themselves are dealt with in more detail a little later in this chapter, it is important to appreciate that in certain circumstances the coach is not always able to control the overall philosophy of the coaching environment, and will therefore have to work within given limitations or parameters, and also possibly with non-specific equipment for the ideal purpose.

A coaching environment itself has to offer the maximum opportunity for progress and development. If the golfing surroundings do not contain the right learning facilities then the coach's rôle of identifying and setting out areas of improvement for the individual will be more limited and less effective. In basic terms if the golfer is a poor bunker player, there must be an adequate bunker facility within the environment to allow the coach and player to improve that weakness, and to build it up to an acceptable standard.

In identifying the qualities and responsibilities of the coach we highlight the importance of sufficient knowledge and in-depth skills. The players, under whatever profile they might be categorized, have their own playing attributes and personalities. Their desire is to play golf to the highest possible standard and to achieve their full potential or even perhaps to find out what that true potential really is. The coaching system available to them must hopefully be one that helps them to move successfully towards their individual goals. This is of great importance not only to them, but also to the development of the sport as a whole. The nature of golf is such that an individual player is faced with a relatively large barrage of information and possibilities from the day they begin to play the game. If no professional instruction is sought initially, golf still requires a great deal of mental thought and stimulation. We cannot play the game without understanding its idiosyncratic nature and, as such, the players themselves are affected by this and develop their own idiosyncratic thoughts and movements.

When faced with a decision on whether to seek professional advice, how to go about finding it, choosing an appropriate environment based on location, cost and structure, booking a lesson and finally arriving at the venue, golfers have had to commit themselves in a fairly demanding way. All this before experiencing the challenge of what the coaching session may require of them in sheer physical and mental golfing terms.

So this coaching process relies heavily on creating an effective and friendly atmosphere where the player–coach relationship is made up of mutual stimulation, good communication and understanding, and a desire from both parties to see the effective improvement of the player.

Communication is possibly the most important single fundamental when it comes to analysing success in coaching. Without efficient communication the whole coaching procedure will break down, and any effectiveness will be lost early on. Communication can be broken down into three basic headings – visual, verbal and kinesthetic.

Visual We use illustration and demonstration to impart the information.
Verbal We use words to tell the player the necessary information.
Kinesthetic We use movement to create the physical feelings we wish the player to understand.

Before developing these topics further it is important that the coach not only has the skill to use all three forms of communication, but is also able to identify which of them is best suited to the individual player. It can often be the case that the coach changes to an alternative form, finding that the player responds to certain pieces of information better when it is channelled in a different way.

Visual Communication

The best illustration of first-class visual communication is to watch young golfers after they have

Fig 125 By using visual communications the coach is able to demonstrate the movements he requires the player to make.

observed an informative swing demonstration. They imitate the movements relatively correctly within a short period of time. It is always stimulating to observe a young golfer who is influenced by his or her idol. The young player becomes a 'carbon copy' of their hero, from the pre-shot waggles to the flourishing follow-through, and even some of the individual facial expressions that we have all associated with the star golfers.

The visual aspect of teaching golf is a vital element; from learning the fundamentals such as a correct hold of the club, to the relevance of balance throughout the whole swing movement, the golfer is able to appreciate the importance of the correct technique. For the coach to be able to communicate to the individual the importance of allowing the clubhead to enter the sand behind the ball when playing a bunker shot, or how to read the slope or borrow on the putting green, or even how to play a controlled slice spinning shot around a tree on a golf course, then the visual aspect of learning and coaching can not be underestimated. Ball flight, ball control, swing speed, judging the correct distance on the golf course, illustrating the correct application of the

Rules of Golf, all demand a high percentage of visual work.

The coach must be sure to use illustrative vocabulary with words such as 'see', 'look', 'watch', and 'observe'. The comparison of swing movement with another player, the use of photography and video are all useful in aiding the player and coach to achieve success through efficient visual communication. In many cases the simple and beneficial aspects of visual communication get somewhat forgotten. Golf can be a complicated and intense sport to learn and in which to develop one's skills, so a coach in particular should always be aware of using the easiest of teaching forms whenever possible. Visual communication also works in an alternative way as it allows the coach the opportunity to see instantaneously if the player has understood what is required, and has the capacity to translate the information into a physical swing movement.

Verbal Communication

In its most simplistic understanding verbal communication allows the coach to give out and receive information, and therein lies a potential danger –

Fig 126 Good explanation helps the player to understand any swing changes.

the amount of information supplied. A coach must be sure of the clarity and content of what is being said. The use of words and phrases such as 'listen to', 'hear this', 'tell me', 'let me explain', etc. are important. Listening to what the player has to say is vital, as this is one of the most common areas of information. A coach should never devalue a player's opinions and in offering advice, must be clear and precise in what needs to be communicated. Above all verbal comments should be of a positive nature. Pointing out negative aspects to a player to aid the clarity of the explanation is not incorrect, but it must be used in a way that enhances the positive aspects of all discussion.

Through verbal communication a coach can convey important aspects such as direct commands used in certain technical fundamentals. He can explain how or why something is relevant to the player, and can enhance visual and demonstrative communication. It plays a major rôle in conveying the relevance of good course management, the correct use of equipment and facilities, and is a factor in how to motivate and encourage a player throughout a coaching relationship.

Players are relatively notorious for not giving the coach a clear explanation of what they feel is wrong or for not correctly assessing the areas that truly do need addressing, and for not clearly explaining how they have reacted to certain playing situations. In asking a player questions and making the player aware of certain analysis from the communication, the coach can increase the value of what they are seeking to achieve. This *feedback* is vital.

The coach is not setting out to dictate the swing movements and style of play of their pupil, but is obliged to describe the benefits derived from the concepts they are working to develop. The player has to be in control, and progress has to be at a pace that they can handle without too much physical or mental conflict. The coach is able to communicate simple application of the method and to encourage the correct amount of planning by the player.

Verbal communication is possibly the most potent of the three forms, but at the same time it has the potential to be the most dangerous. Simplicity should be maintained whenever and wherever possible. Knowing what to say and when to say it is an important rule for all coaches!

Kinesthetic Communication

How can we describe 'feel' to a golfer? It is not an easy subject and yet it is a word that is synonymous with golf and within the concept of coaching the game. The coach will regularly use words and phrases such as 'touch', 'feel', 'hold onto', 'relax', 'move your …', etc. In other words the game is based on correct and repetitive feelings. When we remember a successful shot or even a poor one we will invariably remember the feeling it created in the physical as well as the mental sense. In fact when observing beginners hitting their very first shots, it is interesting to watch how they relate everything at that stage to the feel of the club and the contact they make with the ball. They are blissfully unaware of any other more complicated fundamentals that many more accomplished and invariably more frustrated golfers relate to. The coach needs to use these kinesthetic skills to describe and demonstrate rhythm and balance. They need the player to experience these factors themselves. It may be necessary to use a more physical method of coaching whereby the coach personally moves the player into swing positions so that a feel of what is required enhances and accelerates the learning process. This latter form of coaching is now more popular, particularly with creative coaches, who appreciate that a player may not respond efficiently if the visual and verbal aspects of teaching are the only dominant ones. It is a major feature in motivating players to use drills and exercises to develop good-quality repetitive movements. It is also vital to encourage players to personally experience and feel the correct swing positions, so that their own practice and on-course play is more controllable and productive.

Kinesthetic communication is undoubtedly the most interactive of the three possibilities. It requires the coach and player to work in close relationship with one another, and is one of the more important aspects in establishing a successful working relationship between the two. It is certainly clear when watching the best players in the world, working with their coaches, that this interactive relationship plays a major part in their daily training routine.

So we see the importance and vital ingredient that communication plays within the challenge of coaching. It is the one factor that brings all fundamentals together above all others, and it allows

Fig 127 By helping a player move into correct positions the coach is able to relate the feel of the new action.

the coach and player to work towards improving performance.

Before looking further into the challenge of coaching, it might be appropriate to mention the great diversity of human resource that makes up the game itself. It is a game that is open to all age groups, in some senses it is quite a phenomenon when comparing it with some other sports. It can be played with limited fitness, strength or mobility, and so from the age of six to ninety there is scope for player participation. It would be correct to say that as long as a person can walk or get around a course, they can play a round of golf. There are many physically disabled people enjoying successful golfing experiences. Some need buggies to transport them around the course due to having suffered from heart attacks or strokes, others have lost limbs, have partial or no eyesight or hearing and there is even potential for wheelchair-bound persons to at least experience some of the golfing aspects that make up the game. Due to the physical nature of golf courses themselves there are obviously certain limitations for some people, but with the advent of

modern driving ranges, chip and putt courses, putting greens and dedicated practice facilities, the scope for potential golfers to try out the game has increased immensely.

It is also worth noting the overall decline in male domination of the game. Although male golfers still easily outnumber female ones, there is a steady trend towards greater female participation. It has never appeared to be a sport with a strong appeal for young teenage girls, perhaps due to its individual characteristics, yet in recent years more and more are taking up the game, perhaps influenced by their mothers or the greater publicity created by the success of the ladies' professional tours, and certain individual players such as Laura Davies or Alison Nicholas. Many women take up the game not only to enjoy the healthy environment, but in an effort to join their husbands in a sport that can be shared socially and played on an equal basis due to the competitive structure and handicap system employed within the game. It would be fair to say that women have some excellent natural advantages over men. They rely less on their physical prowess and generally have a better mental attitude towards the game.

Youngsters tend to be rather more adventurous, less disciplined and perhaps a little less emotionally controlled, but are often able to use their more youthful physical capacities to greater effect.

Responsibilities of Coaching

The coach carries quite an influence with regard to the individual golfer and as such must understand and accept these responsibilities. The coach should respect all players and treat all those who seek advice on an equal basis. The coach should clarify as early as possible with the player what the player/coach expectations are likely to be, the potential commitments required to achieve these, the financial and time implications involved, and the type of working relationship that might be expected based on mutual trust and respect.

The coach must be capable of recognizing the capability of the player based on their age, maturity, experience and desire, and should set high standards of behaviour, etiquette and appearance both for themselves and the player. This is particularly important with regard to junior golfers in competitive situations where winning or losing and success or failure must be conducted in a dignified manner. The player should be encouraged to take responsibility for their actions and performances as part of the development of their golfing skills.

The coach will on numerous occasions be required to work alongside other coaches or specialists and should always seek to co-operate fully to the best interest of the player. Confidentiality should be maintained whenever and wherever necessary. Support and encouragement for the player and possibly the player's family is important, particular when poor results are experienced.

Finally, but very importantly, a coach should seek to develop his own skills and knowledge in aiding the potential development of his pupils.

Organization for Coaching

When a coach is setting up a coaching structure or is involved in an organized scheme there are certain responsibilities that may well require quite a

high degree of commitment whether it be due to research and development, training, writing reports, attending meetings or being available to offer advice to the relevant interested individuals, groups or organizations.

For coaches involved with associations or bodies who are responsible for training schemes the commitment is far more far-reaching, and invariably envelops a wide number of other personnel and institutions. The process of putting together a structured training module and the relevant points that it should encompass are worthy of note.

Training is the process of bringing a person or team to an agreed standard of proficiency by practice or instruction. The rôle of any organization must be to put together a system that fulfils the criteria needed to develop a successful scheme. It can be broken down into several key areas:

- The qualities that a successful training scheme embodies.
- The personnel involved.
- The content of the scheme.
- The facilities and equipment used.
- The participants/players involved.

What are the qualifications for a successful training scheme? One that works, obviously! But what components make up that potentially successful element:

- Constructive in nature – the whole scheme needs foresight and vision to ensure that it is built around sound fundamentals.
- Structured – the scheme must be structured and cohesive in all areas.
- Balanced in content – the fundamentals must contain breadth and variety offering participants plenty of scope for learning and development.
- Well-organized – good content still requires an organized, unified and co-ordinated itinerary.
- Adaptable – there must be room to be flexible within the structure, and the potential for further adaptability should it be necessary.
- Progressive in outlook – the development of the scheme must always be of a high priority. Each component must be set up so that expansion in some areas and refinement in others is a natural and progressive situation.
- Well-funded – not always a popular topic, but under-financed schemes will always struggle to achieve their goals.

There are many other aspects that must also be considered such as ensuring that the scheme is meaningful, motivating and skill enhancing for the participants. Quality information must be readily available and interesting. Players will make improved progress within well targeted schemes, which must be directed at both the individual in one-to-one situations, and for group work. It is rare that any scheme can achieve instant success as insight and experience help so much.

All schemes are reliant upon the personnel involved, without whom its effectiveness would undoubtedly be diluted and might, in certain cases, have a detrimental effect on players. The qualities of a successful coach have been covered earlier, but in team training will require the additional ability to communicate well in group situations and to work efficiently and progressively with others from allied professions.

With physiological and psychological aspects now becoming so relevant within the golfing field, the correct industry personnel can play an important rôle within the scheme, and these experts must receive the co-operation and support of all others within the structure.

The content of training schemes developed enormously throughout the 1980s and 1990s, particularly in some European countries, and in New Zealand and Australia, where some very innovative ideas have been brought to fruition. It is important to keep up with these ever developing advances and to learn from, adapt and integrate the benefits into any ongoing scheme.

It is important to be aware of the potential game improvement aspects, whether it be swing technique, short game, putting, course management, time management, planning, Rules of Golf, fitness, nutrition or mental training – plus many others. One area that is currently developing in a positive way is the Skills Test Programme – a system that encompasses the measurement and analysis of all departments of the game under a controlled, pressurized situation (*see* Managing Your Game).

Modern golfing facilities continue to develop at a rapid rate, and without this improvement the expansion of a training scheme and the development of the individuals will be limited to some extent. All schemes should seek to use the best facilities and equipment available. Progress continually makes even the most extensive and high-tech advances of the current time look rather inadequate within a few years.

How about the benefactors of these developments in training – the participants? The individuality of golfers is appreciated, yet for all this individuality there are always common denominators in helping develop skill levels. Individual weaknesses – technical, physical or mental – can all be identified and improved through common programmes.

At times many young players risk the danger of being overcoached or overloaded with an excess of information. As schemes develop locally, regionally and nationally, administrators, parents, coaches and players must be aware of this potential overload.

Participants need to understand the opportunity that training schemes offer them, and must be encouraged to work constructively to enhance their own personal capabilities, to develop their levels of tolerance and to build their competitive skills by working with experts and alongside their peers.

Training schemes are not there to take away or to be a substitute for natural talent, but to provide constructive information and guided direction.

Systems and Methods

Although it is subject to opinion and/or personal preference, it may be worthwhile identifying the differences between coaching a method as opposed to using a system. They have many common principles, but one or two defining points. Basically, a method style encapsulates a set technical or mental requirement from the pupil during a lesson, whereas a system structures the coaching with a set content, but adapted for each individual golfer's needs.

Method coaching generally relies on certain key swing aspects which have a high degree of relevance in terms of the pupil developing their swing movement and, as such, it will be necessary for the player to adapt and change their own swing towards the style they are being coached. Once a swing movement or position is established the player is then able to move onto the next stage. This continues until hopefully the player has adopted most of the relevant method points. It is fair to say that even in method coaching there has to be a reasonable amount of flexibility towards the player, particularly with regards to the coach's acceptance of what is and is not physically possible. Method coaching does have many pluses, in that players understand the set fundamentals and will always be able to relate to these in practice and play. Also should a player have been taught by one coach who is not available for any particular reason, there is often a structured team of method coaches available who will not only provide an alternative, but will guarantee to 'talk the same language' so to speak. In more recent times there have been a number of high-profile coaches who have worked with top professional players using a method style, and subsequently this extends into their daily programmes for all players. This has been further developed by some into national and international operations with coaches from all regions coaching the method formulated by the parent coach. It is always systematically structured, but method-orientated in application.

What is worth pointing out is that although some method coaches have received a certain amount of poor press at times, to my knowledge all successful individual coaches teach a method, it just depends on how adaptable or flexible it or they are.

A system style of teaching is really one that can be adapted to almost any standard of player. It is the content or itinerary of the lesson that remains constant rather than the swing action itself. There can be no one system as there is no one method. There may be a large number of systems available, but they will all have one proviso – the system will work to a pre-set plan. Each lesson will have been incorporated into a programme that keeps the structure of the lesson or series of lessons on a specific track with regard to the teaching information. In other words the content is laid out in advance, rather than the way it is applied during the lesson. All players and the coaches will adhere to this pre-set lesson content. The pupil will be able to come to terms with how the system helps inform and coach them within a given structure. There is little risk of missing something out or getting too far ahead of oneself. So the content is pre-set, but the way it is put over is not. There are few disadvantages within system coaching except a player may wish for a more personal style, and one that works along at their own pace and development rather than at one that has been pre-set. It might not appeal to lower handicap players who may look for a more direct style of coaching.

Most locations that use system coaching will have extensive facilities, a sufficient supply of coaches and a relatively large throughput of pupils. There will be a fairly large amount of local and regional advertising, and the facility will look to build an extensive reputation to help develop the support required to finance this larger concept of coaching golf. System coaching might well appeal more to the higher handicap player or beginner, who will benefit from the structured system of the lessons, whereas method coaching particularly a proven successful method, will attract more accomplished lower handicapped players who will thrive off the potential success achieved by the method coaching and the system.

Examples of System Coaching

Example 1

Beginner	A course of six lessons.
Lesson 1	Grip and set-up.
Lesson 2	Aim and ball position.
Lesson 3	Half-swing fundamentals.
Lesson 4	Full-swing fundamentals. (short irons)
Lesson 5	Full-swing fundamentals (mid-irons/wood).
Lesson 6	Review/Video lesson.

Example 2

High Handicapper	A course of six lessons.
Lesson 1	Full-swing review.
Lesson 2	Long irons/wood play.
Lesson 3	Short game review.
Lesson 4	Sloping lies/trouble shots.
Lesson 5	Bunker play/putting.
Lesson 6	Video lesson.

Notes: Video lessons, personal coaching tapes, lesson binder, record sheets, rules and etiquette, on-course coaching, might also form part of the schedules. Certificates of proficiency will add credibility for both player and the scheme.

Example 3

Mid-handicap player	A course of 6 lessons.
Lesson 1	Full-swing lesson.
Lesson 2	Trouble shots.
Lesson 3	Golf course coaching.

Lesson 4	Course management/
	competitive play.
Lesson 5	Short game and putting.
Lesson 6	Video lesson review.

Example 4

Single Handicap A course of 6 lessons.

Lesson 1	Video analysis of swing
	technique.
Lesson 2	Short game review.
Lesson 3	Rules of Golf and Course
	Management Techniques.
Lesson 4	Golf course coaching.
Lesson 5	Fitness and mental aspects.
Lesson 6	Video lesson review.

An Example of Method Coaching

Lesson 1	Correct set-up position and posture.
Lesson 2	Wrist-set and angles of shaft during backswing consistent to set method.
Lesson 3	Body, hand and arm positions in acceptable relationship throughout swing movement.
Lesson 4	Clubhead and body release factors.

Player–Coach Relationships

There have been many famous sporting partnerships between players and their coaches. In golf a few have become quite renowned over the years – Jack Nicklaus and Jack Grout; Nick Faldo and David Leadbetter; Tiger Woods and Butch Harmon. To a lesser extent there has to be a working relationship between all players and coaches when the former is wishing to work on a regular basis with the latter. There has to be mutual respect between both parties which allows the coach to enjoy and be stimulated to help develop the player's capabilities, and for the player to be motivated by, and strive for the potential improvement that the coaching programme sets out to achieve. Without 100 per cent commitment from both parties there can only be a shortfall in the overall success of the working relationship. The coach must maximize his skills to the full potential, seeking to use both his experience and knowledge to find the simplest and most effective way forward for the player. The player must be committed to the coach's recommendations, truly believing in the information offered, whilst endeavouring to adhere to the pre-determined coaching format, and must appreciate the amount and style of practice required if a positive and long-lasting outcome is to be achieved.

It is fair to say that these principles still apply to the players who prefer a 'quick fix' or corrective one-off type of lesson, but obviously the needs of the player are more immediate, and so the discipline of a more ongoing routine may not appeal.

The coach must work to develop the feel and swing action that the player can relate to and achieve successfully, whilst always seeking to encourage and praise the player, recognizing the commitment and effort that ultimately should bring about success, or at least rewarding experiences.

The Skill Factors

All people are born with ability, but obviously some have more than others. The opportunities to use this ability or talent are not a guaranteed factor. In many instances talent goes to waste either through lack of knowledge, direction or opportunity to enhance it. One of the main rôles of the coach is to help the golfer improve so that they can gain pleasure and success from the game. Developing a player's skill is a major contribution towards improvement and one that must always remain an important priority.

The coach can help analyse technique, but must bear in mind that this is only the vehicle by which to execute the swing. Skill concerns the when and why of this execution and qualifies the ability to perform whilst on the golf course. A player is seeking to develop a game that is consistent and effective so the coach must respond to these needs by helping guide the player through an efficient learning programme.

At first players are required to understand the need for certain technical requirements and the necessity to learn the basic art of making the relevant movements. Once this is established they then need to learn how to develop these aspects further and how to recognize basic errors or faults in their own game. This will involve developing a feel for the correct swing movements and working with a coach helps continuity and development. Eventually a player is able to perform the correct actions and follow the necessities required by the game in a natural, automatic

Fig 128 Tiger Woods works with coach Butch Harmon at the US Masters.

manner. The more proficient they are the greater the opportunity for success. Practice is a key rôle in helping the progress of any golfer as it is during practice that the player can develop and learn new skills as well as offering the opportunity to ensure that these benefits become relatively positive and permanent.

The coach can put together a structured programme for a pupil so that technique and skill can be most enhanced and must identify the most constructive and effective programme for the individual, whether it incorporates a variety of disciplines in one session or the need to repeat a certain movement or shot until it is of established benefit to that player. Feedback is also important for a coach and player. It can come from the player himself when swinging the club or striking the ball – this forms an intrinsic learning pattern, or from the coach or fellow player supplying the

information in a verbal or visual capacity (with video) – this form of learning is extrinsic. The qualities of a player's performance and results will supply further feedback. By highlighting the key features in a player's swing action the coach is able to enhance a player's skill level through varied practice drills and routines. This increased knowledge and understanding of how to perform more skilful technical aspects of the swing allows players to learn and develop improved ball-striking, ball-control and shot-making aspects.

The coach must be able to select the appropriate learning information and experiences to suit each player. It is often the case of restricting the player to only a limited amount of information and technical movement at certain times so that as the player makes positive and successful progress, further input can be added. The inclusion of varied and challenging practice helps

197

increase a player's skill level as does the necessity at times to demonstrate the correct features of an action. This can be carried out by the coach himself or by using more skilful players with correct techniques.

Identifying a player's potential and the enhancement of skilful technique to develop this potential are important criteria for a coach. Players must be encouraged to use this skill on the course and, more importantly, in competitive situations, where they are able to demonstrate their prowess by skilful execution of shots in a variety of ways or styles.

Motivation and Performance

Motivation is one of the key elements in golf. Without the desire to successfully achieve a personal goal or reach a required standard, players will be unable to dedicate the appropriate level of commitment towards their game. Motivation is not just about getting psyched up for a tournament or just one shot, it is part of what makes a player strive to learn and develop greater skills, drives forward the need to train and improve technical aspects, and allows players to achieve their goal when the opportunity arises. It is because personal motives affect a player's performance in a significant way, that a coach must strive to understand these factors on an individual or personal level. Often younger players have little understanding of what they are trying to achieve. Players must be motivated to an optimum level to enhance their overall performance and results.

Understanding a player's motives means that the coach must establish close communication and trust with the player, so that targets and challenges can be set and monitored correctly. Players must be encouraged to be open about their ambitions and what motivates them personally. Some may wish to gain self-satisfaction from successful performance, whilst others might measure it more by their ability to win competitions or prizes. For most it is a combination of the two. Observing players in a competitive or training environment allows a coach to appreciate their qualities still further. Motivation can be further enhanced as a player achieves success and enjoyment from the game. Setting up quality practice environments and structures helps motivate players more effectively. Encouraging them to enhance and take responsibility for their

Fig 129 Ernie Els wins the 1997 US Open.

own development helps their involvement in the overall plan or programme. Helping players set personal goals is one of the most important aspects of coaching. It is part of the motivation factor that drives them forward to learn new techniques and increase their skills. The more successful a player is in reaching a goal the more motivated, confident and focused they become. Goal setting is dealt with in more detail under the physiological section in Support Systems.

Each player has different motives for wishing to achieve a goal, often dependent upon their backgrounds, opportunities and experiences. Those with a high level of desire to achieve success for personal satisfaction generally have strong motivation and are not always driven by the rewards success may bring, such as a winner's trophy or prize. These more extrinsic rewards are often just the bonus that competent performance brings, but they can help motivate some players to achieve success when they know that winning is rewarded with a worthwhile extrinsic reward. These players often need the same sort of stimulation during practice or social play – for example the shot nearest to this hole wins fifty pence. The potential ill-effect of this type of motivation is that when the reward no longer stimulates the player, the drive and desire is considerably reduced and

198

is often replaced by complacency and lethargy. A more intrinsic attitude with a high level of personal satisfaction and pride as the reward is likely to have the stronger influence, be more effective, and last far longer. Coaches need to recognize these factors, then to stimulate and nurture the desire in a way that satisfies the player and yet develops the most effective form of motivation for each individual. The more intrinsic these motivating factors the greater the potential for longer-term success, particularly if the player plays a major part in accepting responsibility for their own levels of behaviour and performance.

Coaches need to be innovative in technical coaching and in the way they encourage successful practice sessions. Continual repetition can be frustrating and de-motivating after a while, and so interesting and effective advice must be used to stimulate players. The greater the variety of practice suggestions, the more likely this is to strike the right note at some point. Communicating with players in a simple and effective style provides a strong vehicle to help motivation. The coach must be a good listener and able to provide clear, simple and concise information and advice. Using instinct to identify a player's state of mind and emotional feelings is a strong asset – often a player fails to, or lacks the ability to communicate these aspects. Players will respect a coach's knowledge and understanding of the sport if appropriate terms and references are used; particularly one who maintains a positive, confident attitude and approach. It is important, however, for a coach to have a variety of styles within their repertoire, so that a different approach can be used should a particular style not prove successful with a particular player, or in a particular situation. In communicating feedback to a player, the coach must balance out the virtues of both positive and negative aspects. Negative feedback will deal with the discussion about poor performance, lack of results or technical or mental errors. Positive feedback, by far the most effective of the two, deals with what the player is doing well, and should be used whenever possible. This positive approach can be used when a negative aspect has to be discussed, by emphasizing what the player did successfully, followed by constructively emphasizing how a negative aspect diluted the effect, but then once again reconfirming the positive points in conclusion.

All players go through periods of success and failure – the highs and the lows. The highs are relatively simple to deal with and generally only require the player to keep maintaining a realistic attitude and approach. The lows are far more complex and involve both the physical and mental state of the player. The coach must be able to recognize these fluctuations within a player and be able to react to them in a way that helps the player to maintain as high a level of motivation as possible. An effective coach is also able to spot the potential loss of form earlier, react appropriately and help reduce the drop in form, that is, to make the highs and lows more compatible, with the lows having less of a bottoming-out effect. If practice routines are stimulating and constructive, a player can use these to re-establish their form and move out of a low spell or slump more quickly and effectively. Competitive golf is the ultimate test of a player's ability both physically and mentally. Coaches need to work closely with a player to help prepare for a competition or a series of events that may run over a certain period of time, limiting a player's time to practise to any great extent. It is important to ensure the player is correctly prepared and well-motivated with a clear understanding of what their goal is from the event or series of events. A player must be prepared in a technical, tactical, course management, physical and mental sense. The more a coach can help a player to become familiar and comfortable with the competitive situation, the more confident and focused they will be. It is at this time that competitors must believe that they can achieve their goals, otherwise they will be far less likely to respond in a positive way. Some will believe in de Coubertin's ideal that they fulfil themselves by just taking part, others have a desire to win and to be winners.

In competition the coach's rôle is relatively one of being in the background. The player must focus on performance – when concentrating solely on winning or the rewards for winning, there is a danger that a regular lack of success will eventually lead to a decline of confidence and motivation. Golf is a game in which most players lose about ninety-nine percent of the time, so winning needs to be put in the correct context. Playing well and gaining results that fall within the scope of goal achievement, enhance motivation and player experience. Failures will always have a detrimental effect, and so coach and player should be fully aware of the varying levels of competition and standards. Sometimes competitive goals have to be reassessed to help maintain the correct level of motivation – a poor result might require an achievable goal to be set in the next event, a good one might require the goal to be one that includes the possibility of winning at the next tournament.

Team Spirit

Because of the individual nature of golf, the relationship of players in a team environment adds to the complexities of providing the necessary levels of motivation. Individuals need to be able to maintain confidence and belief, so that the pressure of supporting the team, club, county or country do not interfere with their ability to draw the best from themselves.

Within all team environments there is a settling-in period where players strive to find their place within the group both in a mental and physical sense. Settled or team selection gives players time to adjust and feel comfortable, whereas regular changing around of team members causes disruption and limits the settled feeling that a player needs to have to perform most effectively.

A strong team spirit must be achieved, with all players being aware of the goals of the team itself, for example, winning the national league. If players respect one another there will be a greater degree of co-operation and support within the team, leading to higher levels of motivation. A good captain, a respected coach and the opportunity for open discussion and communication all help build a solid team foundation. Past success through both team and individual performances help promote pride and respect. Wearing a team shirt, sweater or blazer and tie are often major factors in team motivation. A coach will often have to work with the team captain to develop team practice sessions and discuss appropriate ways of getting the most out of the individual players. When an individual player's goals run parallel to the team ones, then a harmonious, successful environment is created.

Certain players will be natural leaders and looked up to by other members of the team. This influence and example plays an important part in the overall team attitude and ultimate performance. Team training should not function as separate individual sessions, but must incorporate a wide variety of practice sessions and routines that offer each of the individuals what they want from their team participation. It is during these times that players can become more familiar and comfortable with each other's technical and playing styles. The coach should ensure that each player

Fig 130 Moments of team excitement during the Ryder Cup.

is comfortable in a team environment, and that every player also feels comfortable about discussing or disclosing their thoughts with the team coach who is often unlikely to be the player's own personal coach.

Finally, however the team performs, it is important that all members strive for success as one unit, and that no one player suffers the ignominy of individual defeat as a reason or excuse for team failure. This can only lead to a retrograde spirit and one that causes resentment and conflict within the team itself.

Summary

Looking at the subject of motivation as far as the coach's rôle is concerned there are a number of significant issues. Patience, understanding, sense of humour, knowledge, credibility and the right level of competitiveness are all-important attributes. Good organization and natural ability to encourage players are also needed to enhance a player–coach relationship driven by the correct levels of motivation.

Facilities and Equipment

Advances in equipment and facilities in golf continue at a competitive rate. Golfers now look particularly favourably upon the modern golfing complexes that offer many up-to-date and user-friendly advantages. Apart from well-designed full-length 18- or 36-hole layouts, academy courses offer the beginner or novice an exciting opportunity to venture onto a golf course without too much previous experience or a golfing handicap. These courses tend to be built with 3- to 9-hole layouts, the holes varying in length and design depending on the topography of the land used, and the level of difficulty the facility wishes to achieve for the golfer it services.

Driving ranges are now being designed to a more sophisticated standard, with target greens, water hazards and bunkers replacing the regular flagstick and distance markers. Even the tee mats used for hitting the ball from are of an ever improving standard and achieve an almost similar sensation to striking the ball off natural turf. Range balls feel more like those that are used on the golf course itself.

Short game practice and teaching areas are now purpose designed and built. Pitching and chipping greens have several tiers, and around their perimeters mounds, hollows, swales, humps, rough, semi-rough and bunkers have all been added to reflect the on course experience in enhancing effective practice. Sand traps now offer all possible variations from small seaside pot bunkers to the large, shallow American style ones.

Practice putting greens provide every opportunity to work at the golfer's weakest distances, from the long lag putt distance to the tricky downhill short ones. Feature putting greens have been built by some golf complexes, some incorporating narrow 'fairways' and even water hazards.

Every conceivable on-course shot can now be practised in a learning environment, from a lofted wood shot in a fairway bunker, to a delicate high flop shot with a lob wedge.

Indoors the golfer can experience some of the world's most famous golf courses on computerized course simulators. Every normal shot is possible, from the drive to the final putt, with the computer working out the exact distance and direction of each shot played by the golfer, even to the point of landing in a water hazard, lakes, bunkers and possibly even a hole in one! There are many other indoor centres that have abridged versions of what players can experience outdoors – driving ranges, bunkers, chip and putt courses and putting greens.

The evolution of all these facilities has meant that an important development has been possible in the sector of golf coaching. A player can now be coached in a practice environment specifically with regards to a shot that they might have had difficulty in playing on the golf course itself, yet in almost identical circumstances to the course. Problem shots can not only be clarified for a player, but constructive practice can be made by the player on a regular basis and until the problem is minimized or solved altogether. Golfers no longer need to experience a lesson as just a straightforward technical analysis. Pinpointing the weaker departments of shots, leads to quicker and more effective improvement in a guided coaching and practice environment.

Indoor coaching rooms, some with roll-open electronic doors to allow the golfer to watch the ball flight, have been impressively furnished with high-tech equipment giving detailed and accurate

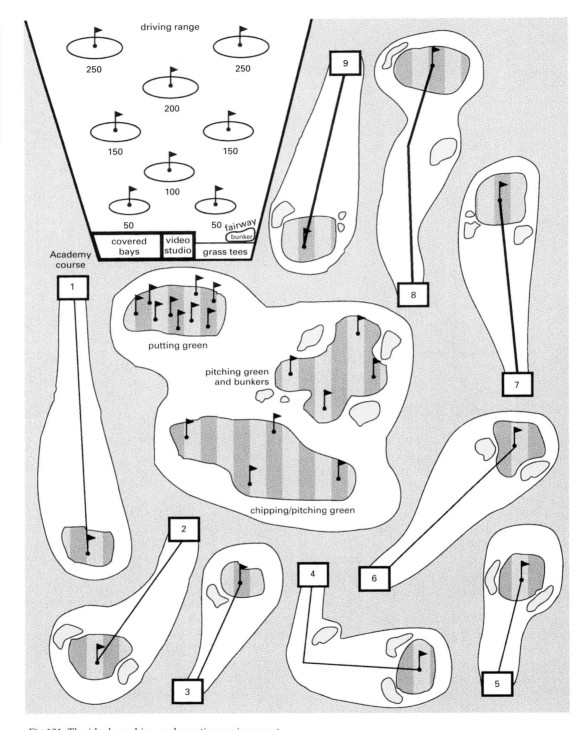

Fig 131 The ideal coaching and practice environment.

Fig 132 An ideal indoor coaching environment.

playback. Video equipment, in itself a perfect medium for coaching purposes has now been upgraded, if not superseded by computer-linked or computer-driven equipment. Swing playback in slow motion and still facility help communicate swing movement, but computers have further enhanced the information available, and have improved the coach's potential for visual communication with the player, by allowing the coach to illustrate points more clearly using drawing graphics and overlays. Golfer swings can now be stored on record forever if necessary. Software programmes have been written to enhance the use of the computers in coaching with an individual now being able to compare themselves with the world's best players, or to be shown how their movements differ from what the computer assesses is the perfect swing motion for someone of their build and physical attributes through biomechanical swing systems.

High-tech equipment has certainly changed the face of basic coaching and so for the foreseeable future coaching procedures will continue to change and adapt as this development of improved technology helps the coach to use improved visual, verbal and kinesthetic communication techniques.

Summary

There are so many factors that complete the make-up of a successful golfer – technical, mental, physical and management. No one player will have the perfect mix of each factor, or the ideal amount of one or two, but not the others. It is a combination of all components that completes the final individual mix or makeup. The world is full of competent golfers and although in each generation there has been a number of top players who have dominated the game to a certain degree, it is has never been to the same extent as with some other sports.

Coaches also have a vital rôle to play. A good instructor has to be one who gets successful results in the most efficient manner. One who passes on knowledge, information, skill, understanding and above all a sense of enjoyment to the player.

203

14
GLOSSARY OF GOLFING TERMS

Ace A hole in one.

Address The position of the club and the player in relation to the ball when preparing to play a shot.

Air Shot A stroke which fails to make contact with the ball.

Albatross A score on one hole of 3 under par – a 2 on a par 5 or a hole in 1 on a par 4.

Alignment The aim of a player's body and club face in relation to the target.

Amateur Golfer who plays the game with no income benefit.

Approach Shot played towards to the green.

Apron The grass area around the green that is cut shorter than the fairway, but not as short as the green itself.

Arc The path of the clubhead during the golf swing.

Back 9 Holes numbered 10 to 18 on an eighteen-hole golf course.

Back Spin The backward rotation of a golf ball which causes it to fly high and grip when landing onto the ground.

Ball Mark The indentation that a ball makes when landing on the green's soft surface.

Birdie A score of 1 under par for the hole.

Bogie A score of 1 over par for the hole.

Borrow In putting the amount of compensation made by a player to allow for any side slopes, gravity or grain on the green's surfaces.

Boundary The perimeter of a golf course. Outside this perimeter is called 'Out of Bounds'.

Break The amount of curvature a ball takes when struck towards the hole on the green.

Bunker A hollow or depression in the ground generally filled with sand.

Caddy A person who carries a golfer's clubs.

Carry A distance the ball travels through the air from where it is played originally to where it lands.

Casual Water Temporary accumulation of water that is not part of the normal hazards of the golf course.

Chip A low-flighted mainly running shot around the green.

Choke Down To grip lower down the club for greater control.

Closed Clubface The toe of the club is turned inward making the club face aim left of the target.

Closed Address When a player's body and feet aim to the right of the target.

Cup Into which ultimately all golfers are trying to get the ball.

Dimples The indentations on a ball's cover which help control ball-flight characteristics.

Divot The small piece of turf removed when playing a golf shot.

Dogleg A hole which bends either to the right or to the left.

Drop The action a player takes in returning a ball into play having taken relief or a penalty.

Duff A term used for a very badly struck shot.

Eagle A score on one hole of 2 under par – 3 on a par 5 or a hole in 1 on a par 3.

Etiquette The good behaviour and conduct expected of all golfers.

Explosion Shot The shot made from a buried lie in a bunker in which the club digs down and displaces a considerable amount of sand.

Fairway A closely mowed part of a hole between the tee and the green.

Fat A term used to describe a shot where the club makes contact with the ground before the ball.

Flex The bend of the golf shaft during the swing.

Flier When a ball flies quicker than expected and with less control, usually from a semi-rough or a grassy lie.

Flight The path or trajectory of the golf ball through the air.

Fore The traditional shout to warn golfers that the ball is travelling in their direction.

Grain The direction in which grass grows or lies on the putting surface.

Green Fee The fee charged made by a golf club to a visiting golfer.

Grip Either the handle of a golf club or the way the hands are positioned onto that handle.

Groove To be able to continually repeat an action or the action of the golf swing.

Grooves The straight lines cut into the face of every club.

Ground Used when referring to the placement of the club behind the ball.

GUR Ground Under Repair. Any part of a golf course stipulated as unfit for play.

Half A drawn hole or match.

Hazard Any bunker, ditch, pond, stream or lake as defined by a golf club.

Hole in One When a tee shot goes directly into the hole.

Honour Privilege of playing first from the tee.

Hosel The part of the clubhead to which the shaft is fitted. Sometimes referred to as the neck.

Impact The moment in time that the club face contacts the ball.

Lateral Water Hazard When water lies parallel to the line of play rather than across it. It is a lateral water hazard.

Lie Position of the ball in relation to the ground.

Line The direction a shot or putt should be taken in relation to the hole.

Lip The edge of the hole.

Lob A high soft-flighted shot similar to a pitch.

Local Knowledge A benefit gained by a player when playing his own golf course.

Local Rules Those rules that appertain to the individual club itself.

Loft The amount of angle built into the club face to help elevate the ball.

Lost Ball When a ball cannot be found within five minutes of searching for it, it is deemed lost.

Marker Usually a small coin or disc used to mark the position of the ball on the green. Also a fellow competitor or scorer who records the players' scores.

Nap Another term for the horizontal growth of grass. Also referred to as a Grain.

Nineteenth When a match is drawn after eighteen holes it may be necessary to play an extra hole or even more. The next hole played after the eighteenth is referred to as the nineteenth.

Out This refers to the first nine holes played, that is, 1–9.

Out of Bounds When a ball goes beyond the boundaries of the golf course.

Par The assessed standard score for a hole based on length and difficulty.

Penalty Stroke A stroke or strokes added to a score because of the breach of the rules of golf.

Pitch A relatively high shot played when approaching the green or from around the green's edge.

Pitch and Run Similar to pitch but with a lower trajectory and usually played when nearer to the green.

Pitch Mark Another term for the indentation made when the ball lands on the green.

Pivot The turning movement of the body around a fixed axis during the backswing.

Plane or Swing Plane The angle of the swing based upon the player's height, posture and the club in use.

Plugged Ball A ball that retains its own depression on landing.

Practice Swing Usually made by a player before the execution of the shot to gain extra feel and act as a rehearsal.

Professional A golfer who makes a living by either playing, teaching, retailing or business administration from the game of golf.

PGA The Professional Golfers Association.

Recovery A shot that returns the ball to play from a difficult position.

Rough The longer grass area bordering the fairways.

R & A The Royal and Ancient Golf Club of St Andrews.

Run or Roll The distance a ball travels along the ground once it has landed.

Semi-Rough A lie of grass between the fairway and longer rough.

Shank A ball that is struck from the socket or neck of an iron club and travels to the right.

Sole The bottom of the clubhead.
Splash The usual term for playing a normal sand bunker shot.
Square When the club face is at right angles to the target line.
Stance The position of the feet when the player addresses the ball.

Takeaway The first few inches of the backswing movement.
Tee or Teeing Ground The area of freshly mowed grass where each hole commences.
Tee Peg The small implement used on which to place the ball when commencing a hole.
Thin A shot that is struck from the bottom edge of the golf club.
Through the Green All parts of a hole except the hazards, the teeing ground or the green.
Timing Sequence of movements of the body and club to achieve an effective swing action.
Torsion The twist of the golf shaft. Not to be confused with flex.

Trajectory The flight and path of the golf ball through the air.
Trap Another term for bunker.

Up and Down A term referring to the ability to get the ball into the hole from off the edge of the green. One short shot plus one putt.
USGA The United States Golf Association.

Winter Rules Played throughout the winter to allow players to clean and place their ball due to adverse ground conditions.

Yardage Charts Course Planners. The layout and design of golf holes with lengths measured from important features on each hole to help the players judge which club they need to play.
Yips Caused by a lack of confidence or a physiological problem and making a player have little physical control of the putter when playing a shot.

INDEX